Private Companies

For other titles in the Wiley Finance series
please see www.wiley.com/finance

Private Companies

*Calculating Value and Estimating Discounts
in the New Market Environment*

Dr. Kerstin Dodel, CFA

This edition first published 2014
© 2014 John Wiley & Sons, Ltd

Registered office
John Wiley & Sons Ltd, The Atrium, Southern Gate, Chichester, West Sussex, PO19 8SQ, United Kingdom

For details of our global editorial offices, for customer services and for information about how to apply for permission to reuse the copyright material in this book please see our website at www.wiley.com.

Library of Congress Cataloging-in-Publication Data – to follow

Print (pbk) 9781119978787
Epub 9781119960492   Epdf 9781119960485

A catalogue record for this book is available from the British Library.

Cover design/image: Jim Wilkie

Set in 10/12pt Times by Aptara Inc., New Delhi, India
Printed in Great Britain by CPI Group (UK) Ltd, Croydon, CR0 4YY

Contents

List of Exhibits

Preface

The book looks at private company valuation in the context of M&A transactions. It addresses some of the issues in the area of private company M&A:

- Understanding the mechanics of M&A involving private targets.
- Understanding influence factors on acquisition prices paid for private firms.
- Estimating the size of the Private Company Discount (PCD) and providing explanations for its application.

When selling or buying a company, M&A professionals, decision makers and other parties involved have to overcome two hurdles. On the one hand they have to develop a more or less exact asking price – they have to value the target – and on the other they have to execute the transaction process.

Looking at the transaction process, research shows that transactions between private and public firms differ not only because of the private status but also because of unique private firm characteristics and psychological aspects which play an important role for the owner who is selling. These aspects are often ignored because they are difficult to evaluate and to measure. Although there is a huge amount of research on M&A and it covers a whole range of aspects, from company valuation, game theory, liquidity of stakes, psychological interactions to the family firm's characteristics, the research is not able to show, besides anecdotal evidence, how the characteristics of private firms influence the transaction and its outcome and how the transaction process itself impacts the price finally agreed.

Developing a valuation for private companies is challenging; most approaches result in an indication of value which presupposes liquidity. Therefore, the concept of a discount for the lack of liquidity constitutes a crucial aspect in the valuation of privately-held companies. A discussion is ongoing that on the one hand challenges the situations to which a discount is reasonably applicable, and on the other hand, the size of discounts to be applied. People discuss whether majority shares of privately held companies need to be discounted for the lack of liquidity at all and what the factors which influence such a discount are: these discussions allow people to speak not about the Discount for Lack of Liquidity (DLL) in the context of private firm valuation but rather about the broad term PCD.

Given the discussion around the PCD and specialties of private firm transactions, Chapter 2 addresses the M&A process by taking a detailed look at the transaction process and how the process and company characteristics influence the outcome (the purchase price agreed) of the process. This analysis takes a look at the process from the preparation of the long list to the signing of the sales & purchase agreement (SPA) and uses measurable statistics to capture the influence of factors like competition, trust and other private firm characteristics. To address uncertainty with respect to the Private Company Discount, further analysis presented in Chapter 3 of the book offers new empirical evidence on the PCD and its influence factors for the different markets. In particular the market and companies in Germany are considered, but the book also includes detailed evidence for North America, Western Europe, and the UK.

In reading this book, you should gain a better up-to-date understanding about the appropriate PCD applied to private companies. The analysis of different markets addresses a problem that many valuation specialists in Europe and Germany face: that the majority of PCD studies are done in the US and the results are not applicable to the market situation and company structures over here. The inclusion of the North American and other markets provides actual data for the PCD for international valuations and valuation specialists and helps to pin down the broad range of discounts used to date. To look up a PCD quickly, the reader may choose the respective region and focus on the empirical results he/she is interested in.

Furthermore, the book shows that approaches which are considered when valuing minority interests are difficult to apply to control situations. As comprehensive studies supporting the liquidity discount for controlling interest are missing, the book uses the acquisition approach as an independent assessment of the potential PCD for private companies.

Because of the different problems that are examined in Chapter 2 and Chapter 3, the analyses presented in these chapters are conducted with two different data sets. The chapters are connected insofar as both examine specialties of private firms; Chapter 3 in relation to valuation (application of the PCD) and Chapter 2 in relation to the M&A process. Whereas the results of Chapter 3 apply to all private firms, Chapter 2 adds a special focus on independent private firms. The analysis in Chapter 3 uses global data, Chapter 2 only uses transactions with German target companies, but those firms can be seen as representatives of any other private firm. International readers should not be put off by the German term "Mittelstand" that appears in Chapter 2 and Chapter 3. This term is used in Germany only to refer to independent private companies. As in all other countries it describes a class of privately-held companies with no direct access to public equity markets which are legally and economically independent and with a strong linkage between the owner and the enterprise.[1]

The book aims to be a practical guide that would allow a reader, who already had a strong foundation in financial valuation, to apply those skills effectively to the valuation of private companies.

Taking into account the increased importance of private firms, it is crucial for everybody involved in situations that trigger a company valuation to obtain a real understanding of the key characteristics and associated problems in the context of private firms. As quantitative studies on the M&A process and the PCD are rare, this book can help to improve the readers' understanding of the M&A process and the PCD.

INTENDED AUDIENCE FOR THE BOOK

The book is relevant for professionals dealing with private company valuation and M&A professionals: analysts/associates in investment banks working in M&A and corporate finance, analysts in smaller banks (equity research), professionals in corporate finance houses, private equity fund associates, analysts/ consultants in accounting and consultancy firms, corporate

---

[1] A detailed description of independent private firms is given in Section 1.1.2.

lawyers as well as CEOs and CFOs of private companies. While the part about the M&A process is most interesting to M&A professionals and those corporate officers faced with M&A, the empirical analysis in Section 3.4 and following are mostly focused on valuation professionals. These two categories of reader should gain different benefits. While M&A professionals should be able to optimize the process and therefore the result of negotiations, valuation professionals should gain a credible source for quantifiable discount data and a thorough understanding of their application.

1

Introduction

Private firms are the most dominant form of entrepreneurship in the world; 99.8% of all enterprises worldwide are not publicly traded. The majority of private firms are in the hands of families, around 55% of all businesses are family firms. They are truly important to the national economies as they employ around 50% of the current workforce and earn 50% of the Gross National Product globally.

Over the last decade, the global market environment has seen a constant stream of mergers and acquisitions (M&A) below the mega merger size involving privately-held companies. In the course of the subprime crisis, with declining M&A volumes worldwide, the importance of private companies has increased further. The importance of private firms for the M&A market is expected to increase with impulses coming from difficult public M&A markets and continuing succession problems within the family firm class. For example, in Germany, 55% of family owners are expected to retire within the next 10 years, the figure in other countries is lower, but it is fair to say that a double-digit percentage of private companies within the small and medium size categories will be confronted with the transfer of ownership and/or management within 10 years.

It is therefore rather strange that there is a comprehensive amount of literature available on M&A issues of large enterprises, while acquisitions involving private firms, especially with family ownership is still a neglected issue although the valuation of private firms and their M&A transactions are different:

- In addition to the difficult application of fundamental valuation methods like Discounted Cash Flow (DCF) models due to lack of data, valuation professionals generally agree that some downward adjustment is justified to account for a lack of ability to convert an investment into cash in terms of timing and costs. But the magnitude and the correct application of that adjustment is often a contentious subject. Former court decisions especially in the US rejected the application of a standard discount and required a solid and reasonable argument for the discounts in valuation reports.
- Empirical research shows that transactions between private and public firms differ with respect to the transaction prices paid and control premiums achieved and provides various explanations for the differences. In addition to the most prominent factors – liquidity or lack of it – and quantifiable differences concerning financial performance and deal size, there are other factors that might drive the transaction outcome when private targets are involved compared to public ones. Ignoring the influence of ownership structure and the family perspective can jeopardize a thriving M&A transaction (Gisser and Gonzalez, 1993; Mickelson and Worley, 2003). According to these authors, family issues need to be addressed to increase the likelihood of successful acquisitions. This holds true when a private owner or a family wants to sell its company and for potential acquirers of these firms.

The book therefore presents two different analyses; the first one shown in Chapter 2 describes features related to M&A with private firms and contains a detailed analysis of factors which influence the result of a successful M&A process, meaning the transaction price. These factors include competition, motives and those factors that relate especially to family firms as described in Section 1.1.

The second analysis in Chapter 3 contains a comprehensive analysis of the PCD to provide an understanding of various studies available on the DLL and PCD and how they relate to the particular entity being valued. In addition, the analysis shows whether the applied liquidity discount is reasonable for the situation in question, i.e. is it below, equal to or above the discounts suggested by DLL studies. The acquisition approach is presented in a study that attempts to explore the magnitude of discounts in Germany, the US, and other countries and investigates additional factors which have turned out to have an influence on the value of private companies.

1.1 PRIVATE FIRMS – SETTING OUT THEIR STALL

The obvious characteristics of private firms are the lack of quotation and their independence from stock markets (if positively expressed) or the lack of access to share capital (if negatively expressed). Further classification of private firms is done according two dimensions: size (usually measured by turnover and number of employees) and the relationship between company and ownership. These factors are often correlated, but there is no 100% overlap. To understand, to value and to sell or buy private companies, the ownership dimension in particular needs to be understood by appraisers and other investors, particularly the relationship of certain owners (private persons and families) to the "their" company. Depending on the ownership, private companies can be roughly distinguished into independent (of which mostly family firms) and dependent (non-family) firms.

Independent private firms are firms which are legally and economically independent, whereas dependent private firms are subsidiaries of corporations (whether public or private) or other institutional owners like private equity investors. In these companies there is no personal identification between the owner(s) and the company and the management is often performed by outside managers. According to the size dimension, private firms can be classified as small and medium-sized enterprises (SMEs) and large enterprises. The problem is that there is neither a universally valid definition for SMEs nor is there one for family firms, so the challenge faced by all researchers involved is to find acceptable and useful definitions.

1.1.1 Introduction to SMEs in Different Countries

Governments of many countries and many of the multinational organizations are targeting SMEs for their political agenda and special financial business support, and therefore provide their own definitions and criteria.

According to the European Commission, a small enterprise has a headcount of less than 50, and a turnover or balance sheet total of not more than EUR 10 million. A medium-sized enterprise has a headcount of less than 250 and a turnover of not more than EUR 50 million or a balance sheet total of not more than EUR 43 million. The Commission has a third category called micro enterprises. A micro enterprise has a headcount of less than 10, and a turnover or balance sheet total of not more than EUR 2 million. The Commission considers application of this definition by Member States, the European Investment Bank and the European Investment Fund to be an aid to improving consistency and effectiveness of policies targeting SMEs.

In the US, there is no universally accepted definition of an SME, even within the US government. Furthermore, unlike the European Union, size standards differ for firms in the manufacturing, agricultural, and service sectors to reflect the relative nature of the "small" and "medium" size classifications.

The definition used for SMEs by the Small Business Administration's Office of Advocacy (SBA Advocacy) is the most straightforward, as it includes all enterprises with fewer than 500 employees for all three sectors. In addition, the SBA uses different annual revenue parameters to classify SMEs in various service subsectors. The vast majority of SME service subsectors fall in the USD 7 million category; for some (computer services) a USD 25 million category is used. For agricultural firms, the US Department of Agriculture (USDA) also uses annual revenue to differentiate farms by size, but it does not use a "medium" category; it defines as "small" only those farms that earn less than USD 250,000 in annual revenue, and considers all others "large". In an attempt to partially harmonize these definitions the United States International Trade Commission uses for their annual statistics the SBA Advocacy's "fewer than 500 employees" definition of SMEs across all sectors, as that accounts for the vast majority (approximately 99%) of firms.

In Germany, the Institut für Mittelstandsforschung (IFM) classifies SMEs according to annual turnover, balance sheet value and number of employees, based on the recommendation of the European Commission. According to the IFM definition, small companies are companies with an annual turnover below EUR 1 million, and a workforce up to 9 employees. Medium-sized companies are companies with an annual turnover of EUR 1 million to EUR 50 million, and a workforce of between 10 and 499 employees.

In the UK, sections 382 and 465 of the Companies Act 2006 define a small company as one that has a turnover of not more than £6.5 million, a balance sheet total of not more than £3.26 million and not more than 50 employees. A medium-sized company has a turnover of not more than £25.9 million, a balance sheet total of not more than £12.9 million, and not more than 250 employees. It is worth noting that even within the UK this definition is not universally applied.

A summary of definitions is provided in Exhibit 1.1.

1.1.2 Introduction to Family Firms in Different Countries

It has been difficult to formulate an unambiguous and transparent definition of family businesses because a family is an interrelated system which influences a firm's structure, strategy, conduct, and success. As financial programmes and support by governments and organizations are aligned to size classes, there is no official definition for a family business nationally or internationally but definitions stem from different academics and scholars who are interested in family firm research.

The definitions of a family business all have a common direction. A family business is a company which experiences a degree of "familyness". Astrachan and Shanker (2003) describe three different levels of how to perceive a family influence from family participation and control of strategic direction (base level) over the second level, which sharpens the definition and adds founder/descendant management and the intent to keep the business in the family as criteria. The last level considers the true family business, as the firm must include multiple generations and more than one member of the family must hold a managerial responsibility. It is important to understand that the business has to be influenced by a family or by a family relationship, and that this influence leads to an identity of ownership and management, to a strong emotional investment by owners and staff and to an emphasis on family and business continuity.

When/at which level of family member influence the identity of ownership and management is reached, depends on the provider of the definition. Some scholars define a family business

Exhibit 1.1 Quantitative definitions of SMEs

| | EU | | | US | | Germany | | | UK | | |
	Small	Medium	Large	Small & Medium	Large	Small	Medium	Large	Small	Medium	Large
Annual sales	≤€10m	≤€50m	>€50m	<$7m*		<1m	<€50m	≥€50m	≤£6.5m	≤£25.9m	>£25.9m
Balance sheet	≤€10m	≤€43m	>€43m						≤£3.26m	≤£12.9m	>£12.9m
Employees	<50	<250	≥250	<500**	≥500	<10	<500	≥500	≤ 50	≤250	>250

*only for the service sector
**varies depending on industry classification

as an organization having at least three family members active within the company or as an organization where at least two generations have had control over the company or where the next generation is prepared to enter the company. Others define family businesses as businesses where, inter alia, the shares are held by several family members or several branches of the family or businesses where, within a single branch, several generations are involved in various roles in the company. Sometimes, more elaborate combinations of criteria are used, e.g. a family businesses is a firm where the name of a director is part of the name of the company, at least two directors have the same name or at least two directors (who do not have the same name) live at the same address.

Overall, the most important criterion for family firms is the interaction between the company (business sphere) and the private /family sphere. This interaction influences how the firm works and leads to unique characteristics of family firms that need to be addressed in business valuation and transactions. The identity of ownership and management does not necessarily mean that the owner needs to be in active management as CEO or CFO but that he/they have control over important business decisions as members of the supervisory board or with a veto power of the controlling shareholder.

Therefore one can ask if all independent private firms are family firms: in some firms, there is a strong linkage between the owner and the company but the owners are not necessarily a family or part of a family. For example, with a Management-Buy-Out (MBO), the existing management acquires the company from former owners and one can say that the link between owner and companies is strong and the interaction between ownership and management exists as in a true family firm. From this viewpoint all independent private firms are family firms and in the later chapters of the book, the term "independent private firms" is used to describe private companies with no direct access to public equity markets and a strong linkage between company and owner irrespective of whether the owners are relatives or not. In contrast to that, the term "dependent private companies" refers to legally and economically dependent companies with no direct access to public equity markets and with no special linkage between management and ownership. Whereas in family firms there is an overlap between the private system (the family system) and the company (the company system), in non-family firms both systems work independently.

1.2   THE RELATION BETWEEN THE TWO DIMENSIONS OF PRIVATE FIRMS

The relation between the classification criteria for firms and the respective definitions can be seen in Exhibit 1.2 using the example of Germany. Most private firms belong to the SME class. Of those, the overwhelming majority are family owned. Some SMEs may be public companies, and some big family firms are listed. But in the size and family classification scheme, listed companies should usually be found in the upper left rectangle.

1.3   A NOTE ON GERMANY AND THE GERMAN MITTELSTAND

In Germany, a class of companies exists that is called the "Mittelstand". It is difficult to give an exact definition of the term because the word "Mittelstand" (directly translated) refers to the "middle class" and dates back to the Middle Ages when the German word "Stand" described an individual's socio-economic status. Clergy, nobility and stand (including the bourgeoisie and the farmers) were three levels of status to be distinguished. The bourgeoisie

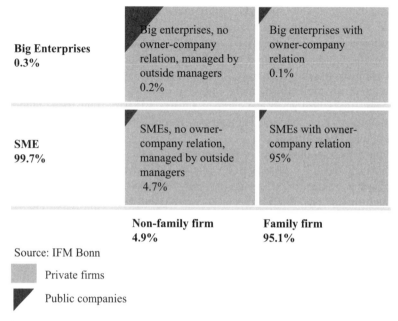

	Big enterprises, no owner-company relation, managed by outside managers 0.2%	Big enterprises with owner-company relation 0.1%
Big Enterprises **0.3%**		
SME **99.7%**	SMEs, no owner-company relation, managed by outside managers 4.7%	SMEs with owner-company relation 95%
	Non-family firm **4.9%**	**Family firm** **95.1%**

Source: IFM Bonn

Private firms

Public companies

Exhibit 1.2   SME, family business and listing

were called Mittelstand to differentiate them from the farmers. Nowadays, the "Mittelstand" term comprises not only a definition of a class of companies, but it is also a description of a social class which has great economic and political influence. The term Mittelstand is often associated with the German "Wirtschaftswunder" (Germany's post-war economic success) and the success of the German economy in general and in contrast to other European countries and the US, this term is much more widely used in politics and the media in Germany than the term "SME". For example in Germany the terms "Mittelstandspolitik" and "Mittelstandförderung" comprise a central point on the agenda of major political parties. The question to ask is what constitutes the typical Mittelstand firm and how does the Mittelstand firm fit into the "independent/family firm" and "SME" categories?

The official definition of the IFM uses company size and qualitative criteria to classify the Mittelstand. According to the IFM, Mittelstand firms are SMEs. However, the focus only on firm size as the defining characteristic falls short of an adequate description of the typical Mittelstand firm, therefore the IFM adds qualitative criteria and defines Mittelstand companies as privately-held companies with no direct access to public equity markets; they are legally and economically independent, and there is a strong linkage between the owner and the enterprise, meaning that these companies are controlled and managed by the founder(s) or the family/(ies) of the founder(s).

1.3.1   Mittelstand vs. Family Firm

According to the IFM, family business, SME and Mittelstand are practically identical. Looking at the IFM statistics, 95.1% of firms are family firms and 99.7% are SMEs, so from the numbers, the two IFM criteria for Mittelstand companies are fulfilled for the majority of firms.

Section 1.1.2 argues that in emphasizing the linkage between ownership and company all independent companies are family firms, and with this emphasis so are Mittelstand companies. As outlined before, the relation between ownership and company plays a pivotal role in the definition of the Mittelstand. According to theory, a family business is a company which is controlled and/or managed by a family.

The whole group of Mittelstand firms is not necessarily in the hands of or managed by families. They can be founded by an MBO or sold to other outside (private) investors by the founder or the founder's family. In the context of the book the qualitative aspects of the Mittelstand definition are important, especially the strong linkage between the owners (not necessary family) and their enterprises, meaning the identity of ownership and personal responsibility for the enterprise's activities and success, a personal relationship between employer and employees, and the identity of ownership and personal liability for the entrepreneur's and enterprise's financial situation. This emphasis makes the definition of the Mittelstand identical to the definition of a family business with owners not necessarily being relatives.

1.3.2   Mittelstand vs. SME

As the qualitative dimensions of the Mittelstand definition are most important, meaning the relation between ownership and company and the resulting special attitude and behaviour as previously described, the size constraints in terms of turnover and employees are disregarded for the definition of the Mittelstand. Therefore, Mittelstand can be SMEs but are not necessarily so. For the empirical analysis in Chapter 3, only companies with positive turnover are included to as to avoid useless data sets.

2

The M&A Transaction with Private
Firms – A Process Analysis

This chapter analyzes the mechanics of the M&A process and shows that the transaction process itself and factors beyond pure target characteristics influence the purchase price at the end of the transaction process. This chapter tries to quantify some of these influence factors and focuses especially on those that are important when an independent private firm (those firms with strong linkage between company and owner) is acquired. The chapter does not show how to incorporate these factors in a standard valuation model for better price estimation nor does it discuss any of those models. Furthermore, the results of this chapter cannot be used to estimate an absolute price for a company or to value a company. Instead the reader may use the results of the chapter for a better understanding of the dynamics of M&A, a better transaction preparation, and for negotiation purposes. Although the analysis presented uses transactions involving German target firms (with an international buyer set), the results can be generalized for international usage because private German firms can be seen as representatives of any private firms. Furthermore, the focus of the analysis is on soft factors influencing the transaction process and outcome and the mechanics of M&A are somewhat comparable everywhere.

Differences between private and public firm transaction are striking and several authors have already evaluated them. Examples are:

- The control premium studies of Ang and Kohers (2001). They compare the book value of equity to acquisition price paid and link explanatory variables to the differences. Ang and Kohers analyzed around 30,000 acquisitions (of which more than 22,000 with private companies as targets) between 1984 and 1996 and found that privately-held companies whose M&A activities are not monitored by the investment community achieve on average higher prices as they break out of an unfruitful M&A process without incurring high prestige costs that lower the likelihood of hubris-motivated acquisitions or hasty disposals.
- Studies on the effects of cash payments on transaction prices. Cash payment has proven to be important for private targets because of their desire for liquidity. Owners of privately-held firms who have a desire for liquidity are willing to accept lower premiums from liquid bidders (e.g. trading on the New York Stock Exchange (NYSE)) compared to bidders trading Over-The-Counter (OTC). Fishman (1989) and Gilson (1986) show that cash payment increases the courtesy of the target management and cash payment enables more rapid deal completion. In the context of the second analysis of the book, Section 3.11.3 discusses the importance of the cash payment in the context of the PCD in more detail and shows that transaction multiples of private targets are influenced by the payment method.

All studies indicate already that the outcome of the M&A transaction not only depends on pure (financial) target characteristics and other measurable items like potential synergies that can be realized, but on structural differences between private and public firms which influence prices in the transaction. In addition, the transaction itself, as a process where different participants are acting within the context of a (competitive) M&A process, influences the transaction price paid. Especially when family firms are involved, the linkage between owner and company influences the outcome of the transaction process.

The analysis presented later aims to measure variables that capture the influence of the linkage between owner and company, as well as the influence of other factors that are not related to the target's financial characteristics. These variables are linked to the prices offered in the transaction process and we examine how they influence the outcome. The main questions to be answered are:

1. What are those factors which influence the M&A process and the price paid?
2. Which factors may play an additional role when the target is an independent private firm?
3. How can possible factors be analyzed?

Question 1 will be answered in Section 2.2, question 2 in Section 2.3 and the measurement of factors including study set-up is discussed in Section 2.4. Before embarking on the questions, Section 2.1 gives a short summary of the transaction process for audiences not specialized in M&A transactions and therefore not familiar with the terms used.

2.1   THE M&A TRANSACTION – THE PROCESS AND IMPORTANT ELEMENTS

M&A processes can be distinguished depending on the number of participating bidders. In a bilateral auction ("rifle shot"), only one or two selected bidders are approached. Therefore, this process is less complex and easy to execute. On the other hand, due to the limited number of offers, the comparability is low and bargaining is more difficult. Hence, most sellers prefer a controlled auction process where different offers can be compared as this gives the seller an improved bargaining position. These auctions comprise medium bidding competition and, at the same time, have a higher level of confidentiality than open auctions. Open auctions are characterized through a high number of bidders in the process. They give the seller a good bargaining position, but the auction process is more complex and the level of confidentiality is lower. The controlled auction process can be executed by only involving strategic investors (in a strategic auction), or by including additional financial sponsors. Exhibit 2.1 shows the different transaction types and their main characteristics.

The further description of the M&A process is given from the perspective of the seller respectively his advising investment bank because the selling banker's perspective is taken in the empirical analysis which begins Section 2.4. Therefore, the process does not start with the decision-making process at the seller's company. These preliminary steps have already been conducted.[1]

Because they are from the seller's perspective, the following paragraphs should not be regarded as an exhaustive overview of M&A transactions. The M&A process itself can be divided into different phases, which cannot be completely separated but overlap (see Exhibit 2.2).

---

[1] These steps start with the decision to conduct an M&A transaction and putting together the necessary resources to proceed with the transaction including the set-up of an internal M&A team and the appointment of an external M&A advisor (usually investment bank/boutique). The seller identifies team members, including a senior executive with time to devote to the process, assign responsibilities, and educate the team on their responsibilities, if required. Some companies are able to develop and retain an internal M&A staff. However, this is not the case for all companies. Firms (also those with internal M&A capabilities) normally use external consultants that organize the process, support valuation, and help to anticipate issues.

Exhibit 2.1 Different auction types

	Bilateral auction	Controlled auction	Open auction
Addressees	1–2 potential investors	Limited number	Wide selection
Confidentiality	High	Limited	Low
Competition among bidders	None	Medium	High
Advantages (from the seller's point of view)	– High degree of confidentiality – Quick closing possible – Action at later stage possible	– Possibility to compare offers – Confidentiality mostly granted – Bidder selection for best fit possible	– All potential investors approached – Excellent bargaining possibilities – Optimization of terms
Disadvantages (from the seller's point of view)	– No/limited comparison of offers – Difficult bargaining – High probability of transaction failure	– Process more time consuming – Risk of "leaks" – Higher publicity of internal documents	– High publicity of internal documents – Longer and more complex process – Process failure damages image – Later financing possibilities

The analyzed M&A processes consist of a series of steps that, on average, take six months to complete.

2.1.1 Preparation Phase

During the preparatory stage, the investment advisor kicks off and organizes the M&A process, which means that the internal deal team and the timeline are set up and additional advisors like lawyers and accountants are selected. During this stage, the investment banker will also prepare and qualify a long list of the most logical buyers according to predefined criteria. These will be reviewed and approved by a company's owner and usually its senior management to come up with a finalized shortlist comprised of the potential buyer universe the seller wants to approach in the first place (shortlist).

2.1.2 Marketing Phase

During the marketing phase, the investment advisor will begin soliciting interest from the shortlist, usually by sending out an anonymous teaser – a one pager encompassing the most important facts (including basic financials) of the target company. Often, investment banks call the potential bidders on the shortlist and convey basic facts about the target via phone. Interested buyers sign a confidentiality agreement. A confidentiality agreement (CA) is a legally binding document between the seller and a potential bidder that outlines the terms under which confidential information with respect to the target company will be provided to the bidder. It is a contract through which the bidder agrees not to disclose information covered by the agreement and, therefore, creates a confidential relationship between the parties to protect any type of confidential and proprietary information. After signing the CA, the potential

Exhibit 2.2   The M&A transaction process

	Preparation	Marketing	Due Diligence	Negotiations
General	– Project organisation – Preparation of information and time table	– Approach of potential acquirers – Reception of non-binding offers	– Further information exchange with selected bidders – Reception of binding offers	– Negotiation of contract with preferred bidder(s) – Signing and closing
Period	4–8 weeks	4–6 weeks	8–12 weeks	4 weeks
Key steps	– Define bank's project team – Select/propose further external advisors (e.g. lawyers) – Identify and assess potential acquirers – Company valuation – Prepare data room – Finalize information memorandum	– Approach potential acquirers – Sent out confidentiality agreement – Exchange confidential information between seller and bidders – Analysis of non-binding offers	– Organize and manage data room – Co-ordinate site visits and management presentations – Analyse and select binding offers	– Design SPA together with lawyers – Execute timely negotiations – Solicit antitrust approval
Key documents	– Short list	– Confidentiality agreement – Information memorandum	– LOI	– SPA
Key terms		– Indicative bids	– Due diligence – Data room – Management presentation – Revised offer – Exclusivity	– Negotiation – Signing – Closing

Overview of the sell-side process from the perspective of the seller's investment advisor.

buyers receive the information memorandum (IM). The information memorandum is a sales document providing important information for potential bidders. This includes items such as the financial statements, company history, industry and market information, management biographies, a detailed description of the products and services, as well as the key competitive advantages. After a review period of three to four weeks, potential bidders submit written indicative offers outlining the price range they would be willing to pay for the company and how they would address key issues such as due diligence, financing, management retention, and speed to close.

2.1.3 Due Diligence Phase

After the receipt of the indicative offers, the due diligence (DD) commences. DD is a term used for a number of concepts involving either the performance of an investigation of a business or person, or the performance of an act with a certain standard of care. It can be a legal obligation, but here the term will apply to voluntary investigations of the target company through the bidder(s). DD is a key element in the transaction process. Although the seller may be sensitive to disclosing all aspects of its business to the buyer before heads of agreement have been signed, from the bidder's perspective, a detailed and rigorous target screening yields a significant advantage in placing a successful bid and prevents the bidder from taking the deal too far through the process. The following areas are screened very carefully: (a) financials (analysis of historical balance sheets, historical profit and loss statements, historical cash flow statements and historical capital expenditure, analysis of the contribution margin, financial planning and budgeting and R&D-budget planning, and analysis of important line items), (b) legal (review of relevant contracts: customers, employees, management, service agreements, ongoing litigations), (c) tax (analysis of last tax audit, tax risks, assessment of level of exposure, discussion with tax advisors), (d) sales & distribution (analysis of sales organization, breakdown of sales by region, products and services, analysis of contract details, customer structure and market information) and (e) human recourses (key managers, remuneration, structure of staff, qualification of staff, pension obligations, development of personnel costs). During the DD phase, selected bidders are invited to the data room and have the chance to interview the management within a management presentation. Nowadays the data room is mostly virtual, so the term data room is actually a database that grants the bidders access to all information about the seller for the bidders' DD. In context of the study in Section 2.4, the data room is non-virtual, i.e. the data room is set up as a supervised, physical room in secure premises at the office of the seller or the seller's advisor with controlled access. Only one bidder team at a time is allowed to enter the room and there are strict controls for viewing, copying and printing. The data room enables interested parties to view material relating to the business in a controlled environment.

The management presentations during the DD phase generally take place over a two to three week period. The owner and management team, together with the investment banker, narrow the field to a handful of buyers, who will be invited to tour the facilities, hear a management presentation that highlights key information, and have an opportunity to query the management directly. The length of the total DD phase depends on the amount of bidders and their familiarity with the target company. On average, this process lasts six weeks. At the end of the DD phase, a limited number of buyers will submit a revised bid together with/as a part of a draft letter of intent (LOI). The LOI not only contains the price they are willing to pay, but should discuss acceptable financial terms, explain the details of the transaction structure, and possibly early operational integration considerations.

2.1.4 Negotiation Phase

The discussions on the LOI initiate the negotiation process. Although LOIs are usually not considered to be legally binding, except for those with very specific conditions attached, they certainly do set the direction for the SPA as the LOI captures the guidelines set by the respective parties and sets the framework for negotiations. The LOI will usually set forth conditions prohibiting the selling company from negotiating with other potential buyers while the SPA negotiations are underway, meaning exclusivity is granted. Granting exclusivity to a preferred bidder is a means of locking competition for a certain period of time after the DD, and is a sign of the seller's good faith. Within the exclusivity phase, the bidder has the opportunity to engage in exclusive negotiations and additional DD with the bidder. The SPA is developed by sending mark-ups back and forth between the seller and the buyer, and therefore represents a written understanding between the parties involved. It also ensures that both parties are working in the same direction and with the same overall intentions. Its creation forces the discussion of many important and specific items that might have been initially overlooked but would have ultimately been encountered later in the process. Negotiations can be time consuming, depending on the level of agreement in the LOI and additional DD findings. Once a SPA has been signed, the buyer will already have committed a great deal of management time and spent a lot of money on lawyers' and accountants' fees, and other general expenses. Therefore, warranties are included in the SPA to impose conditions under which the purchased price can be lowered, or if and how the seller has to reimburse the buyer for a breach of warranty. Conditions refer to significant changes (e.g. in the net working capital over a specified amount) until closing (the actual transfer of ownership) or beyond closing (e.g. "Earn out clauses")). Therefore, the value of the transaction, meaning the price ultimately agreed for the selling enterprise, changes between the signing and closing of the deal and beyond closing. However, it is common practice to include a host of limitations on the seller's liability and to provide a lengthy disclosure letter so that it is difficult to claim compensation in the event of a breach. The closing of a deal takes place in one day, which is the day the money is wired and the executed documents are delivered.

2.2 QUESTION 1: WHICH FACTORS INFLUENCE THE M&A PROCESS AND THE TRANSACTION PRICE PAID?

To look at the whole M&A transaction as a process means to take the "processed based view" of M&A: the ultimate price paid in an M&A transaction is not only a function of the target's descriptive characteristics, but also a function of the participants in the transaction process, their motives, their interactions and the competition among them. The process view emphasizes that instead of solely analyzing the environment, the motive and the strategic fit between the two firms, the M&A process itself has to be analyzed and considered since it is extremely important for value creation and prices negotiated. Therefore, the price paid in the end is not only determined by firm characteristics and potential synergies that can be realized, but also is a result of the competitive M&A process involving different parties pursuing various goals.

The most important ones are the buyer(s) and the seller with their opposite interests. Generally, the buyer wants to pay as little as possible, while the seller wants to receive as much money as possible. These differences can cause conflicts between a buyer and a seller which have to be managed within the M&A process. Owners of independent private companies must not even pursue financial goals in a transaction process, but they may be more concerned about their reputation or the loss of the company's identity after its disposal to a foreign investor. Furthermore, the transaction process itself and the interaction between the participants influence the price paid in the end. In this chapter those factors are presented that have proven their influence on the purchase price in other research (irrespective of whether the target is private or not): the motives of the seller and bidder, competition, transaction charges and trust. In addition, the focus is on those factors that especially relate to private family firms.

2.2.1 The Seller – Disposal Motives

Firms have a wide variety of reasons for divestitures and disposals. Divestitures are disposals of a part of the business initiated by the parent company's management. For example, a common reason is to increase a firm's focus on its core competences. Another reason for divestitures is to eliminate a low-performing division or business, which has been acquired as an unrelated division in the course of a conglomerate merger. This so-called "correction-of-a-mistake" hypothesis holds that managers who undertake poor acquisitions can redeem themselves, at least partially, by subsequently divesting the unwise acquisition (Allen et al., 1995).

A third reason for divestitures is to increase managerial efficiency. By spinning-off parts of the business, managers may be able to operate more efficiently alone in the spin-off firm than together in the parent firm. Spin-offs can create value by improving investment incentives and economic performance. A fourth reason is to achieve a specific organization by doing a spin-off or a carve-out. By splitting the firm into its component businesses, the market may be able to value the components more accurately than if they were combined. When firms are undervalued due to unobservable divisional cash flows, they may resort to divesting this division to raise capital.

Different reasons exist for a complete disposal of the company. The two main reasons are lifeline problems and (only in case of family firms) secession problems (discussed later in Section 2.3).

Lifeline (financial selling pressure): Lifeline is a situation in which the seller usually experiences financial difficulties due to a lack of capital or cash flow. Alternatively, it could just be that the company requires fresh external input to be able to operate further. In this scenario, a company may seek a suitor, or a suitor may see the potential and pursue the company. The position of the seller in such a situation is relatively weak, as the financial challenges the business is facing make competitive bargaining relatively difficult. Financial selling pressure is a prominent disposal motive, especially in countries where debt levels of independent private firms are high. For example in Germany, family companies are traditionally highly debt financed, mainly caused by the housebank concept that constitutes a strong relation between local bank and company and nearly all financing needs are transacted via debt from the local (house) bank. Furthermore, many family businesses and their owners want to maintain total control and to be as independent as possible, so they prefer to take on debt instead of equity capital in their balance sheet. With an equity investor, autonomy is no longer possible. Hence, owners of family companies only look for outside investors when some financial selling pressure exists.

Financial selling pressure can be a reason to initiate a process to dispose of part of the business (divestiture). In contrast to an independent company, the target itself does not need to be experiencing any financial difficulties. Financial disposal pressure can also exist at the parent company. The pressure can be exercised not only by banks, but also by shareholders of the mother company (market expectations) concerning returns or takeover threats through declining market capitalization.

The value of the targets, which is the marginal price at which the seller is willing to dispose of the company, varies depending on the motives for selling a company or a division. The disposal can obviously be attributable to weak financial data, but it also has something to do with the lack of ability to commit to future investments. As a consequence, the selling company is in an inferior position to market the company in the due diligence phase of the process.

In addition, financial pressure from banks influence the seller's bargaining position in the negotiating phase: starting from a low valuation, a potential acquirer can more easily negotiate additional discounts for a company with selling pressure than for a company with unfavourable prospects but without any explicit pressure to raise fresh equity capital. Altogether, financial selling pressure weakens the position of a seller in the due diligence and negotiating phase of the process.

2.2.2   The Bidder – Acquisition Motives

Several motives exist to acquire a business, such as synergies, hubris, diversification, tax considerations, management incentives, or purchase of assets below their replacement cost. In particular the synergy motive is discussed widely and regarded as the most important reason for strategic buyers to acquire a business because financial theory suggests that managers should take actions that increase firm value. The analysis of the sample set in Section 2.5 shows that around 25% of the bidders stated synergy motives as the main reason for the planned acquisition. Cost cutting, revenue enhancement and risk reduction are possible factors behind successful acquisitions. These factors refer to genuine synergies which can be achieved after a transaction by all potential bidders through restructuring or changes in the business model. Other synergies ("true synergies" or "individual synergies") can only be achieved by some acquirers as they depend on the nature of the acquirer.

The specific match between the target's and the acquirer's resources influences the assessment of the target's value. Therefore a target will have different Investment Values (as defined in Section 2.7) for heterogeneous buyers and single buyers can afford to pay a higher synergy control premium without given away shareholder value. Different studies show that the consideration of synergistic benefits leads to an increase in the price a bidder is willing to pay, and justify a premium to the target firm (Bradley, Desai and Kim, 1988; Mulherin and Boone, 2000; Feldman, 2005). Feldman (2005) measured the synergy control premium by the difference of the reported control premium and a pure control premium that has been estimated by option pricing theory. He shows for a sample of 86 firms between 1999 and 2001 that the synergy control premium is higher than the premium for pure control: only 26% of the total control premium is caused by pure control.

Synergy potentials are taken into account by the bidder not only before entering into an M&A process with a specified target and when submitting an indicative bid. It is also necessary for the acquirer to assess during the process how the acquisition turn will affect his strategic goals and organization. It is recommended to (re-)consider and analyze the strategic and organizational fit between the firm and the potential partner before entering into final negotiations.

It is reasonable to assume that the marginal price for an investor with synergy motives is higher than those for the others, and that this investor is more willing to negotiate a price upside with the seller. This assumption leads to two consequences in the transaction process: firstly, the indicative and the revised bid can be higher for an investor with synergy possibilities. Secondly, in the second stage of the process (due diligence phase), this bidder is more likely to be able to increase prices in the revised bid compared to the indicative. In addition, in the negotiating phase, this bidder has the possibility to negotiate an upside without sacrificing too much of the shareholders' or stakeholders' value.

2.2.3   Competition

Competition means the existence of rivalry or pressure that bidders are exposed to during the transaction due to the existence of other parties in the process with the same objective. The outcome of the negotiating process is naturally influenced by the number of bidders and the ability of the seller to generate competition among them. Competition can exert influence in different ways: competition is for example a good substitute for the missing bargaining skills of a seller, competition can create effort incentives for the bidders, and competition can make the auction process more disciplined (McAfee and McMillan, 1999). How exactly does competition exert its influence? Literature and practitioners commonly agree that competition between rival bidders through information asymmetry and outbidding positively influences the purchase price.

Information asymmetries: the existence of information asymmetry between rival bidders has a significant influence on competition for deals (Smit, van den Berg, and de Maeseneire, 2005). A bidder gathers information about the target's value and its assessment through his rivals. Each bidder's estimate of the target's value is subject to error, and assessing the competition is difficult in the first place. During the process, the bidder learns more about the target's value as more and more information is revealed. For example, not being invited to the data room after making an indicative offer is a signal for a bidder that his bid is too low and undervalues the target from the seller's perspective.

Outbidding: when the bidder learns that competitive bids are higher, he has to amend the bid and offer more to stay in the process. An accommodating bid from one bidder provides an accommodating signal to the second bidder. This bidder has to invest in due diligence and increase his bid so that an auction unfolds where bids become larger and larger until no one is willing to increase his bid (Smit, van den Berg and de Maeseneire, 2005). This setting is not directly applicable to the M&A process, but the seller and its advisor "play" competing bidders off against each other and communicate the valuation results of the competitors, thus increasing the price pressure on the bidders to offer a higher revised bid. So the seller and its advisor can always use bidder rivalry to increase bidding prices. The existing bidder rivalry leading to a competitive auction mostly takes place in the later stages (DD and negotiating) of the transaction process. In the first stage after the marketing phase, where only indicative bids from varying bidders are received, this aspect is not very important. At this stage the number of bidders strengthens the seller's position because the seller gathers information on its attractiveness and the market's awareness of it.

In an M&A process, a seller is a mixture of a passive bid taker and an active bargaining partner. At the beginning, a seller does its own valuation, which is needed in the bargaining stage with the remaining bidders (e.g. to argue with credibility for the price demanded), but it does not know the maximum price at which it can sell the company. The bidding process reveals more information on this price. In the first step, the received indicative bids reveal different valuations to the selling company. In addition, the seller's ability and knowledge with respect to valuation issues can be improved as they learn from the bids.[2] The selling company learns about its attractiveness and the market's awareness of it not only from the stated Enterprise Values (see Section 2.4.1) in the received bids, but also from the number of interested bidders. At the beginning of the process, the seller's position is improved to generate further competitive pressure in the ongoing process. Altogether, the existence of more than one bidder and the degree of competition to be generated between them impacts the complete transaction process. It influences the relative change from the initial bid to the revised bid. In addition, competitive pressure also exerts its influence in the negotiating phase as the threat of other bidders puts pressure on the participants to negotiate favourable terms for the seller.

---

[2] Competition reveals information and it is a good substitute for bargaining skills with the seller reaching higher than expected outcomes in a bidding contest. Prices reached are higher with at least two competing bidders than with direct negotiation with one bidder (McAfee and McMillan, 2005).

2.2.4 Transaction Charges

The whole M&A process requires costly resources, which are summarized under the term "transaction charges". Information gathering requires due diligence costs. These can consist of direct costs for financial advisors or opportunity costs in the form of committed management time. The due diligence investment of an interested bidder can be considered to be the purchase of a real option on the target's value (Smit, van den Berg, and de Maeseneire, 2005). The due diligence costs represent the option premium which potential buyers need to bear to reveal the target value (underlying value), and are thus a prerequisite before making a bid at the exercise price. A potentially interested bidder will only perform due diligence and incur the associated costs if this is justified by the real option value. The total consideration of a bidder encompasses the exercise price (purchase price of the target) and the option premium (transaction charges). If a bidder can reveal or confirm the underlying value of the target at a lower cost, he is in a position to revise his bid to a higher exercise price than other bidders, despite creating the same amount of expected shareholder value (comprised of the underlying value minus exercise price minus option premium). Therefore, the lower the transaction charges are, the higher the potential upside from the indicative to the revised bid.

It is reasonable to assume that the bidder has invested a significant amount of transaction charges by the later stages of the process and the pressure to sign off and close the deal is greatest at this stage of the process. Therefore, the higher the incurred transaction charges (already invested), the higher the closing pressure on a bidder in the negotiating phase of the process. This may enable the seller to negotiate on an upside compared to the revised bid.

Transaction costs are not only incurred by the bidder, but also by the seller. Besides the direct cost for an external advisor, especially for the seller, senior management is involved in the transaction process and therefore is disturbed in his daily business. The longer the process goes on, the more complex the whole transaction associated with higher transaction charges becomes. Therefore participants should act quickly, as an efficient and smooth process can be a prerequisite for a successful M&A transaction, and should be part of the participant's strategy from the beginning. In addition, the longer the process goes on, the harder it is to maintain confidentiality, and sellers in general want to close deals quickly. Transaction charges which have already been incurred are assumed to increase the pressure on the seller to sign off the deal in the negotiation phase of the process. This pressure may be so high that it leads the seller to forgo some purchase price upsides during negotiation to get the deal done.

2.2.5 Trust

The term trust is a little fuzzy. It is used in many sciences and is generally regarded as an integral part of social interaction that expresses a relationship of reliance (Misztal, 1996). In sociology, the degree to which one party trusts another is a measure of belief in the honesty, benevolence and competence of the other party. Therefore, trust prevailing in an M&A process may increase the outcome and efficiency of the M&A process and can also influence a bidder's estimate of the target's value. According to Misztal (1996) trust is a mental state, a *prediction* of reliance, which cannot be measured directly and is based on what a party knows about the other party. This knowledge can be based on direct contact or on some kind of perception, meaning what somebody thinks he knows about someone in cases where he does not have direct contact and this perception is strongly influenced by someone's reputation.

So, how can knowledge as a prerequisite of trust be narrowed down a little better? Parties involved in an M&A transaction can either know each other through a business relationship or a stakeholding before the transaction, or else one party has a well-known reputation.

Business relationship: the development of a business relationship requires investments associated with exchanges with the partner. Sometimes it is a long-term and costly process before the partners show the necessary willingness and ability to utilize the inherent benefits of the relationship. Andersson et al. (1997) show that business relationships are important assets and serve as a platform for future business and knowledge development. A former business relationship might even be an introduction to M&A activity. The continuous exchanges within a business relationship and the knowledge of a counterpart builds trust, and trust created in this pre-M&A relationship can serve as social capital, as a basis in the M&A process upon which people are willing to work towards the benefit of the new organization and are not interested in pursuing their own selfish interests.[3] Trust might be worthwhile from the bidder's perspective as performance-limitative obstacles are mitigated through former interaction. Trust influences the efficiency of the M&A process through lower transaction charges for the bidder because the bidder knows his counterpart.[4]

Initial stake: despite an existing business relationship, an initial stake of a bidder (toehold) in the target company might increase the knowledge of the respective parties and the trust the parties have in each other. An ownership interest can result in a financial and strategic advantage compared to others, especially when buying a private firm or a subsidiary rather than a public firm, and can be explained partially by limits to information availability, higher information costs for rival bidders and lower competition for the target (Bradley, Desai, and Kim, 1988). This means that, despite the higher purchase price, the same return on investment can be generated, as the additional costs are lower compared to other bidders and therefore the total consideration stays the same. With respect to the level of ownership interest, the study shows that even minority interests lead to competitive advantages for the respective bidder.

Reputation: in addition, another factor which might influence trust is the reputation of a party. A financial sponsor may be well known for its industry experience or ability to guide the management, which increases the competitive position of the target after a takeover. In addition, a strategic investor or the target may be known by all industry participants because of his leading market position. According to Burkhart and Panunzi (2003), company reputation is an asset that gives that company a competitive advantage because this kind of a company will be regarded as reliable, credible and trustworthy.

The reputation can also be attached to an individual who is known to be an expert, or is especially trustworthy. Nilsson, Isaksson, and Martikainen (2002) show that the relationships between customers and suppliers seem especially strong/good in companies with an owner-manager who is an experienced and well-known manager in the industry. From the bidder's perspective, a high reputation might increase his trust in the target and might thus raise the bidder's esteem. The resulting confidence positively influences the bidder's willingness to negotiate favourable terms for the seller.

How does the existence of trust exert its influence on the transaction process and outcome?

---

[3] Social capital can make people put organizational interests before their own. Collective goals and norms can make people feel it is worth doing things that are useful to the organization and its members. Furthermore, trust and associability may provide a context in which people decide whether it is worth putting individual interests aside or not.

[4] Due diligence costs should be lower since less information needs to be gathered in the data room and analyzed thereafter. In addition, the trust existing in a business relationship lowers direct transaction costs because less scrutiny is applied when analyzing data and requesting information.

Lower transaction charges, a financial and strategic advantage compared to other bidders and the confidence on the bidder's side about the target prospects and his confidence in the realization of potential M&A synergies influence the bidder's calculus. He is in a position to hand in higher bids and the seller is able to negotiate favourable (from the seller's perspective) terms without giving away too much of its stakeholder value. Therefore trust is assumed to exert its influence in the DD phase and in the negotiating phase of the process.

Trust does not only exist on the bidders' side but also on the seller's. The trust of a seller in a bidder may put a single bidder in a preferred position compared to others. Acquirers can prevent the competitive bidding process from fully unfolding when they can credibly show that they can transfer their own unique resources (e.g. complementary resources and absorptive capacity) to the target (Capron and Pistre, 2002). Despite evidence, this aspect is excluded from further analysis for two reasons. Firstly, the bidder's trust in the target's business, in the management and in the success of the transaction seems much more important because the risk associated with the target's business is transferred from the seller to the buyer; whereas the seller has riskless cash in its hands. Secondly, trust is measured with knowledge, reputation, experience of (target) management (on which see Section 2.4), and these variables are the same from either the bidder's or the seller's perspective. One cannot test two opposite directions of influence in the same regression analysis and therefore only trust from the bidder's perspective is taken into account.

2.3 QUESTION 2: WHICH FACTORS MAY PLAY AN ADDITIONAL ROLE WHEN THE TARGET IS AN INDEPENDENT PRIVATE FIRM?

To start the discussion, this section looks at the research existing on family business and the M&A process. One should remember that all independent private firms show characteristics of family firms, meaning the strong linkage between the (private) owners and the company.

Firstly one can say that differences between family and dependent private and public firms are discussed in two different streams of research. One argues that the private status itself influences the results of M&A transactions through e.g. the lack of public pressure. Ang and Kohers (2001) find for example higher premiums for privately held firms that are attributed to strong bargaining power and timing options resulting from a lack of public selling pressure.

The other stream of family business based literature assigns special characteristics to family businesses and investigates whether these characteristics lead to premium or discount valuation by interested investors. Authors argue that family businesses are special by their nature and culture compared to non-family businesses; they have unique strengths (and weaknesses) that characterize them. The mix of the personal sphere and the business sphere creates value; however, it could also create problems as family businesses are affected by relationships within and outside the family business. The European Foundation for the Improvement of Living and Working Conditions (EMC) (2002) presents a large stream of literature that discusses the economic performance of family businesses vs. non-family businesses with different approaches. One line of research, for example, simply quantifies the statistical performance differences between family businesses and non-family businesses based on measurable criteria like sales, number of employees, profit margins and others. Most studies show that family businesses outperform non-family businesses in the long run. In a comprehensive review, the

EMC identifies different key themes: ownership and control, management strategy and style, a company's strategic goals, succession and human resource characteristics.

Ownership and control: different studies and theories show that if ownership is concentrated in the hands of a family and the owner manages the company, then agency problems are naturally mitigated to a large extent. Even if the inherent conflict of interest is mitigated though constraints such as competition in the managerial labour market or threat of takeovers, family businesses experience cost advantages through low monitoring costs and controlling costs.[5] The study in Chapter 3 of the book shows that owner-management increases valuation. Agency cost efficiencies can not only be observed when the owner(s) is (are) the manager(s), but also in the case with external top-management. Lots of family businesses benefit from flat hierarchies, which shorten decision-making channels and this benefits customers, suppliers and employees alike.

Management style: family businesses are shown to experience a different management style, leading to a greater level of commitment and loyalty on the part of managers in these kinds of companies. The unique family-oriented atmosphere in the working environment may inspire greater motivation and trust in the owners' decisions. Tagiuri and Davis (1996) show that employees may feel very grateful to their family business, experience a greater sense of purpose leading to closer identification with the company and a lower managerial turnover. Both can affect the M&A transaction process: trust reduces expectation ambiguity and engenders a positive attitude of management towards their company, and towards the owner's decision; this makes the management a valuable asset for the potential acquirer.

Reduced ambiguity and a positively committed target management increase the target's value from the bidder's perspective, especially as competent top managers are a key asset for a company. Of course, to benefit from this asset, the new owner needs to replace the disciplinary effect of being like a family, to align the interest of managers to the new owner via other mechanisms like executive compensation packages, and to take action so as not to lose key employees who are likely to feel a much weaker bond with the new company heads. As stability in the managerial leadership serves to foster longer-running relationships of trust between family businesses and their clients and suppliers, the new owner needs to take steps to keep the trust of customers, as they are essential from the long-term perspective of the acquired company. The value of a company might decrease if the new ownership is not able to align the different interests and to strengthen its relations with key employees, managers and clients.

Strategic goals: many authors are of the view that family businesses have different time-horizons with respect to their business strategy. A survey in Germany analyzing 65 highly M&A active family firm companies shows that these companies are not as dependent as their public counterparts on short-term oriented profit expectations, but rather strategic motives such as sales growth, broadening the customer base or access to new technologies are the primary motives for bidders and targets in transactions (Ecker and Heckemüller, 2005).

The inseparability of private and business objectives within family businesses leads to a significant extension of the time-horizon when making strategic decisions. The long-term return focus, instead of emphasizing short-term profitability, can lead to an out-performance of these companies (EMC, 2002). On the other hand, some strategic goals of family business

---

[5] The organizational efficiencies of family businesses have been discussed in several studies. Daily and Dollinger (1992) analyze control and monitoring costs and Tagiuri and Davis (1996) show that efficiency is ensured through the use of "family language" in communication.

owners may cause value decreases, e.g. poor profit discipline when the members of a family business focus too much on quality or personal relationships.

Succession/selling motives: in addition, it has been shown that family businesses pursue goals such as maintaining or enhancing the lifestyle of the owners, and seek to maximize the well-being of current and future generations, not only of the family but also of the employees (Westhead and Cowling, 1997). Therefore, succession in family businesses differs from succession in non-family businesses. When selling the company more emotions are involved compared to purely strategic sell-outs and owners of family businesses are typically very keen to hand the company down to their descendants – selling to a non-family member is sometimes perceived as failure. In this context, researchers talk about emotional value and define it as the difference between the middle of the bandwidth of value according to valuation techniques (Fair Market Value, see Section 2.7) and the final price agreed for the company.

The emotional value strongly depends on several factors;, including pride (the certainty that firms stays within family), securing retirement, continuation of firm traditions (e.g. name, location) and compensation of other family members (justice for those family members not taking over the firm) and therefore the emotional value strongly depends on the kind of acquirer: there appears to be substantial price difference between succession within the family or succession externally. According to study results in the Netherlands (found in Flören, 2002), the kind of acquirer strongly influences the final price at which family owners sell their firms; when selling the company within the family or to a friendly buyer, owners seem to accept substantial price discounts to the Fair Market Value, with 25% of firms selling their company around or below 75% of Fair Market Value.

Selling to an external investor, it is crucial for the owners to see the company in good hands. As they had a long-term view when they ran the business and made managerial decisions, they also keep their long-term perspective beyond the disposal ensuring that the future is secured in the long term. Therefore, the owner of a family business might be quite restrictive when it comes to the selection of a potential acquirer, or sell to a particular kind of acquirer only if it is absolutely necessary, for example, where the financial situation of the company makes fresh equity necessary.

Empirical research shows that succession problems (where the owners do not have siblings who can take over the firm) are a common reason why owner-managed companies are sold – these companies depend on the lifecycle of the family or founder. Only a third of the first-generation family businesses seem to be successfully passed down to the second generation (Leenders and Waarts, 2001). The average life of family businesses appears to be relatively short, with two-thirds of family businesses either collapsing or being sold off under the helm of the first generation. When the succession of a company is not planned in advance, it constitutes a selling pressure that might negatively influence the position of the selling company.

How can strategic goals and selling motives influence the transaction process and its outcome? Section 2.2.5 argued that the trust of a seller may also play a role in the transaction process as a trustworthy bidder may be preferred to others. But trust might play a more important role when owners of private companies want to secure the well-being of their company and its employees. Therefore, they need to trust that the acquirer is acting in the best interests of the firm and its employees. This may have two implications for the bid level and for the price development in a transaction process: (a) with a bid in line with the average bids, a trustworthy bidder will preferably be invited to the DD phase or to the negotiations, or even be invited if his bid is lower compared to those of the other bidders, and (b) this bidder might not feel the necessity to increase his offer after being invited to the due diligence phase or during the negotiations.

Human resource characteristics: research has noted as an example that family members often decide on new recruitment. Despite potentially lower recruitment and human resource costs, this is potentially damaging for many family businesses as these managers may not always possess the appropriate skills or be the best possible candidates for the position selected. The human resource aspect is hardly measurable and will not be taken into account any further.

Owner-management: family companies in which the owner(s) act(s) as active manager(s) might exert even a stronger influence on employees, suppliers and clients and also on a potential acquirer. This behaviour can be value-enhancing in an M&A transaction and thereafter. An owner-manager can help the acquirer to understand the target management system which is necessary for a successful transaction. An owner-manager might reduce the ambiguity of the other managers in an M&A transaction, of both the target's and the acquirer's managers, which is important when entering into negotiations during the transaction process; lower ambiguity of what the deal will mean for the bidder and the seller will reduce discussion on that issue (Jemison and Sitkin, 1986). Furthermore, the trust built is necessary for a successful integration phase after the deal. Successful integration has proven to be a prerequisite for value creation because value will not be created until capabilities are transferred and people from both organizations collaborate in order to create the expected benefits (Salama et al., 2003).[6] Therefore, expectation ambiguity can affect value creation.

When it comes to the trust which prevails between the transaction parties research points out that the reputation of family businesses and managers can be higher and more credible than that of non-family businesses. According to Lyman (1991), reputation for example has been proven to foster the trust that a bidder has in the target's company.

The characteristics attached to family firms and their potential influence on the transaction process can be summarized as follows: according to theory and empirical research the link between the owner and company exerts influence on the company's value either through the trust built within the workforce, the trust a bidder might have in the target's company, or in the success of the transactions. These aspects will be taken into account for the analysis of the trust prevailing between the parties in the transaction process. Therefore the depth of business relationship between the bidder and the seller, the reputation of the management and the management's commitment are included. Section 2.4.1 also includes the target managers' attitude towards the bidder(s) in the measurement of trust as one indication of the confidence a bidder might have in this management. All the components are analyzed as part of the trust factor in the multivariate setting in Section 2.5.6.

Furthermore, the owner–company relation might influence the preference for certain bidders and the trust the seller places in some bidders. This aspect is analyzed in Section 2.5.5.

All assumptions are summarized in Exhibit 2.3.

---

[6] The integration is dependent on human processes and to achieve an atmosphere suitable for the transfer of strategic capabilities, it is vital that employees from both firms understand each other and really want to work together.

Exhibit 2.3   An overview of factors and their potential influence

Factor	Potential influence
Selling motive	Financially motivated selling pressure negatively influences the price development from the indicative bid to the revised bid and from the revised bid to the purchase price.
Acquisition motive	Synergies positively influence the price development from the indicative bid to the revised bid and from the revised bid to the purchase price.
Competition	Competition positively influences the price development from the indicative bid to the revised bid and from the revised bid to the purchase price.
Transaction charges	Transaction charges (bidder) negatively influence the price development from the indicative bid to the revised bid.
Transaction charges	Transaction charges (bidder) positively influence the price development from the revised bid to the purchase price.
Transaction charges	Transaction charges (seller) negatively influence the price development from the revised bid to the purchase price.
Trust	Trust (bidder) positively influences the price development from the indicative bid to the revised bid and from the revised bid to the purchase price.
Owner-company relation	Employed managers show a stronger commitment to and a higher level of trust in the owners' decisions in the family firms than in other companies.
Owner-company relation	Owner-company relation fosters trust a bidder has in the target company with and in the transaction outcome and therefore positively influences the development from the indicative bid to the revised bid and from the revised bid to the purchase price.
Owner-company relation	A trustworthy bidder is preferably invited to the due diligence phase and negotiations by family firm owners and private equity is not assumed to be trustworthy.

2.4 QUESTION 3: HOW CAN THE INFLUENCE FACTORS BE ANALYZED – SETTING THE MODEL

The objective of this study is to find empirical evidence of the influence of factors on the transaction process that are not directly based on the target's financial metrics, but have their foundation in the interaction between the parties involved in such a process. This study aims to prove their influence on the development of offer prices and the negotiated selling price. The goal of the study is not to estimate any changes from the indicative bids to the revised bids or from the revised bids to the ultimate purchase price paid. Instead, the study tries to capture interactions and soft factors that are relevant for the transaction outcome.

The study presented here was undertaken in Germany. The ideas and results shown can be applied to private independent companies where the linkage between owner and companies is strong, so the results of the process analysis are usable by an international audience. The study focuses in particular on the identity of ownership and control, different management strategies and style (the great amount of commitment and involvement) and the long-term view. The M&A processes analyzed here are transactions which involve a controlled auction with a limited number of bidders after the first selection.

All analyzed transactions are executed with an investment bank as the advisor of the seller. The role of an investment bank in that process is not only to maximize the value of its respective client, but to increase the efficiency of the process, as outside groups (experts) that move in and out of the process can work independently and little communication occurs between these groups. An investment bank steers communication, reduces complexity and decreases uncertainty in the process. Therefore, its involvement influences the outcome of a transaction process.[7] However, the focus is not on the influence of the investment advisor on the process as this influence is the same for all transactions. Instead, the comprehensive information which an investment advisor has because transactions are documented from the bank's perspective is crucially important. The analysis is carried out within a multivariate setting that is based on different pillars. In Sections 2.2 and 2.3 factors were identified that are supposed to influence the transaction and the interaction between the parties involved. After identifying the factors, the focus is now on the underlying databases and the set-up of the quantitative study. The exact measurement of the factors is shown in Appendix A.

2.4.1 Methodology

As discussed before, the price paid in transactions can be regarded as a result of a set of variables including not only the characteristics of the target company itself, but also other factors determined by the parties involved. Starting from indicative offers, the differences between the indicative bids and the revised bids are analyzed, as well as the differences between the revised bids and the prices paid. Therefore two different dependent variables with different components need to be built. The first dependent variable encompasses the development of the offer price from the indicative bid to the revised bid. As a starting point, a positive development (upside) is assumed and therefore the first independent variable is measured as the difference between the revised and indicative bids noted $\Delta_{(revised - indicative)}$. Rather than the absolute difference, the relative difference to the indicative offering noted $\frac{\Delta_{(revised - indicative)}}{indicative\ bid}$ or $Delta_1$ is used as the dependent variable. The offering price in the indicative bid is the first component of this variable. The bid level depends mainly on the target's characteristics presented in the IM. Other factors like competition or transaction costs are not assumed to play a primary role in the first offering. It is reasonable to assume that bidders also take into account future transaction costs and that these influence the price offered but these gain more influence in the course of the M&A process. In addition, the considerations of bidders prior to the indicative bid are hard to quantify.

The second component is the offering price stated in the revised bid. On the basis of the information in the IM, the bidder gathers during the DD phase intensive information about the target in the areas described in Section 2.1. The revised bid accounts for this information and is also dependent on the influencing factors described in Sections 2.2.1 to 2.2.5. As the same information concerning the target is presented to all bidders, differences between the single bids should not, or not only, be attributable to the target metrics, but (mainly) depend on other (soft) factors.

The second dependent variable encompasses the development of offer prices from the revised bid to the purchase price. It is again assumed that the development is positive and measures

---

[7] By analyzing the German M&A market, Beitel and Schiereck (2003) find that German acquirers pay higher acquisition premiums and transaction multiples in transactions advised by investment banks. These results become insignificant when other variables like transaction volume or the business focus of the target in the regression analysis are taken into consideration.

the upside as the difference between purchase price and revised bid noted as $\Delta_{(purchase - revised)}$, and the respective dependent variable as the relative difference noted $\frac{\Delta_{(purchase - revised)}}{revised\ bid}$ or $Delta_2$. The purchase price is the last component of the second dependent variable, stated in the SPA at the signing and mirrors the target at that date. As mentioned in Section 2.1, the SPA imposes conditions under which the purchase price can be changed referring to, e.g., significant changes in balance sheet positions of the target. As a consequence, the transaction value might change between signing and closing the deal. As these changes are technically and simply mathematically deducted from the financials, the closing price is not taken into account as it is reasonable to assume that the soft factors of interest do not exert any influence between signing and closing. Both independent variables, $Delta_1$ and $Delta_2$, are measured at the Enterprise Value (EV) level.

The EV (in some textbooks/studies referred to as "deal value") represents the entire economic value of a company. More specifically, it is a measure of the theoretical takeover price that an investor pays to acquire a particular firm. The EV considers the fact that an acquirer must also shoulder the cost of assuming the acquired company's debt. Additionally, the EV incorporates the fact that the acquirer would also receive all of the acquired company's cash. This cash would effectively reduce the cost of acquiring the company. The EV calculation used in this paper is market capitalization (number of shares outstanding multiplied by their current price per share) + total interest bearing debt – cash. As private companies have no publicly traded securities, the market cap is approximated by the consideration paid for the equity value (assuming a 100% acquisition).

In contrast to the EV, the equity value represents the economic value for the shareholders and is calculated indirectly using the EV minus the net debt (+ total interest bearing debt – cash) or directly via market capitalization. Because the upsides on equity value level are distorted by changes in the target company's financing, the deltas based on EV noting, $Delta_{1EV}$ and $Delta_{2EV}$, are used. This is consistent with the information presented in the SPA as the purchase price agreed on is free of debt and cash, so technically it is an EV.

The influence of k different factors is tested performing two multivariate regressions as specified in Equation 2.1 and Equation 2.2:

$$Delta_{EV1,i} = b_0 + = \sum_{k=1}^{K} b_k^* F_k \ \forall i = 1 \ldots 102 \tag{2.1}$$

$$Delta_{EV2,i} = b_0 + = \sum_{k=1}^{K} b_k^* F_k \ \forall i = 1 \ldots 40 \tag{2.2}$$

Each F_k contains a set of factors influencing the two dependent variables described in Exhibit 2.4. The number of cases i depends on the number of revised bids received (102) and on the number of transactions analyzed (40). All the transactions are based on the viewpoint of the seller and its advising investment bank. All documents relating to the transaction are gathered there and information is documented at the seller's advising bank. This single source allows for a comprehensive picture of the M&A transactions and increases the reliability of data. As one can see from Exhibit 2.4, most factors are measured using a (linear) combination of different variables. For example, "Selling pressure" is built as the sum of two other variables "Financial distress" and "Lifeline motive". For details see again Appendix A.

Instead of using linear combinations of variables, the influence factors *Competition, Transaction Charges (bidder)* and *Trust (bidder)* constitute statistical constructs and were built using factor and reliability analyses. The result of the procedure is the extraction of statistical factors which represent the constructs and constitute the information of the variables that were

Exhibit 2.4   Regression – summary of factors F_k

Factor	Part of F_k for		Measurement	Components (Variables)
	$Delta_{1EV}$	$Delta_{2EV}$		
Selling pressure	✓	✓	0;1;2	*Selling pressure* consists of the sum of two binary variables *Financial distress* and *Lifeline motive*
Synergies	✓	✓	0;1;2;3	Synergies consists of the sum of the two variables *Synergy motives* (binary) and *Synergy possibilities* [0;1;2]
Awarness (part of Competition)	✓		Construct	*Competition* is a influence factor which constitute of two constructs: *Awareness*
Rivalry (part of Competition)	✓	✓		and *Rivalry*. *Awareness* constitutes of the variables *Bidders on shortlist*, I*ndicative bids*, *Market echo* and *IM response quote*. *Rivalry* consists of *Parties in DR*, *Binding offers*, *Binding bid quote* and *Process quote*. The coefficients are determined by the factor scores shown in Exhibit 2.27. The items are standardized (z-transform) variables
Transaction charges (bidder)	✓	✓	Construct	Transaction charges (bidder) is computed as a weighted combination of Information desire and Complexity. Information desire and Complexity are two constructs derived from the factor analysis in Exhibit 2.28 and Exhibit 2.29
Transaction charges (seller)		✓	Linear combination	*Transaction charges (seller)* is the weighted combination of *Process length* and *People to handle*
Trust (bidder)	✓	✓	Construct and linear combination	*Trust (bidder)* is a weighted combination of *Knowledge, Reputation* and *Attitude*. *Knowledge* consists of the variable *Years of BR* as the variable *Stake* is not included in the analysis due to missing values. *Reputation* is a construct derived in the factor analysis in Exhibit 2.30. *Attitude* is a variable as specified in Appendix A.V
Owner-manager	✓		0;1	Binary variable

identified in Sections 2.2.3, 2.2.4, and 2.2.5. Each factor summarizes only part of the information of the variables which has been shown in Exhibit 2.5 for the influence factor *Competition* in the column label "Loadings". The complete procedure for the constructs competition, transaction charges and trust is described in detail in Appendix A. Exhibit 2.5 shows that the influence of the competition can be measured by quantifying two statistical factors.

Concerning the influence factor *Transaction charges (bidder),* the variables specified in Appendix A.IV are used and it is possible to identify two statistical factors in Exhibit 2.6.

Exhibit 2.5   Measurement of Competition

Competition	Number of statistical factors: 2	Rivalry		Awareness	
		Item list	Loadings	Item list	Loadings
Name of stat. factor 1:	Number of items:	Parties in DR	0.546	Bidders on shortlist	0.756
Rivalry	4	Binding offers	0.897	Indicative bids	0.868
Name of stat. factor 2:	Number of items:	Binding bid quotc	0.631	Market echo	0.706
Awarness	4	Process quote	0.870	IM response quote	0.861
Column number:	2	3	4	5	6

Operationalization of the influence factor Competition after explorative factor analysis in Appendix A.III. Two statistical factors have been extracted. The first statistical factor contains the four items Parties in DR, Binding offers, Binding bid quote and Process quote. These items describe the competitive intensity in the due diligence phase of the process, and subsumed under the expression "Rivalry" – as described in Section 2.2.3. The relationship of the statistical factor to the items is described in the fourth column of the table, and this indicates a positive relationship with values of 0.546, 0.897, 0.631 and 0.870. The second statistical factor contains the items Bidders on shortlist, Indicative bids, Market echo and IM response quote which can be regarded as some kind of opinion how the attractiveness of the target company is perceived by the market participants. According to column six of the table the relationship of the factor to the selected items is relatively strong (loadings: 0.756, 0.868, 0.706 and 0.861) and the statistical factor is included in the data set under the name "Awareness".

Exhibit 2.6   Measurement of Transaction charges (bidder)

Transaction charges	Number of statistical factors: 2	Complexity		Information desire	
		Variable list	Loadings	Variable list	Loadings
Name of stat. factor 1:	Number of variables:	DR availability	0.815	Man-days in DR	0.764
Complexity	3	Facilities	0.620	People involved	0.654
Name of stat. factor 2:	Number of variables:	Days IM to signing	0.802		
Information desire	2				
Column number:	2	3	4	5	6

Operationalization of the influence factor Transaction charges (bidder) after explorative factor analysis in Appendix A.IV. Two statistical factors have been extracted. The first factor is, according to column four, strongly related to the three items DR availability, Facilities and Days IM to signing (loadings: 0.815, 0.620 and 0.802) which describe the access to the data room and process length. In Appendix A.IV those are regarded as an expression of the complexity the bidder faces and therefore the first statistical factor is called "Complexity". The second factor contains the items Man-days in DR and People involved (loadings: 0.764 and 0.654), which assesses the effort a bidder undertakes to gather information on the target. Therefore, the second statistical factor is called "Information desire".

Exhibit 2.7   Measurement of Trust (bidder)

Trust (bidder)	Number of statistical factors: 1	Reputation	
		Variable list	Loadings
Name of stat. factor 1: Reputation	Number of variables: 4	Market leadership seller	0.795
		Years in firm	0.754
		Years in industry	0.748
		Manager reputation	0.412
Column number:	2	3	4

Operationalization of the influence factor Trust (bidder) after explorative factor analysis in Appendix A.V. One statistical factor has been extracted that contains the items Market leadership seller, Years in firm, Years in industry, and Manager reputation (loadings: 0.795, 0.754, 0.748 and 0.412) which describe the reputation of the target to some extent. Therefore, the items are subsumed under the statistical factor "Reputation".

For the influence factor *Trust (bidder,)* the variables specified in Appendix A.V are used as a starting point and one factor could be identified as shown in Exhibit 2.7.

In Appendix A.V two additional variables are specified which may measure the trust a bidder has, meaning *Years of BR* (Business relationship) and *Attitude.* There are not included in the above statistical factor but are still important aspects. Therefore a linear combination of the statistical factor *Reputation,* together with *Attitude* and *Years of BR* is used to quantify the concept of *Trust (bidder).*

The complete set of variables that is used to build the factors is given in Exhibit 2.32 in Appendix A.V.

2.4.2   Data Set

The analyzed data consists of 40 transactions involving German target firms between 2001 and 2006. Target companies were 20 independent private (Mittelstand[8]) companies and 20 dependent private firms. Deals include 19 domestic and 21 cross-border transactions with 12 European buyers, five buyers from the US, two buyers from the UK and two Asian buyers. Buyers include strategic buyers as well as financial investors from the private equity or venture capital industry. For confidentiality reasons, no names or other information which could identify the targets or the bidders are published in this study. Exhibit 2.8 gives an overview of the transactions used in the quantitative analysis.

2.5   STUDY RESULTS

This chapter shows the results of the univariate analyses and multivariate regression with focus on the single deal level. In addition, separate analyses are performed for each of the different factors shown in Section 2.4.1. Exhibit 2.9 summarizes the numerical results of the analyses at the level of the single transactions.

---

[8] Mittelstand refers to a class of independent private companies in Germany with a close link between owner and company (similar to a family firm). A detailed description of the Mittelstand is given in Section 1.3.

Exhibit 2.8 Overview of transactions

Target industry group	Acquiror industry group	Independent private (Mittelstand) (yes=1)	Owner-managed (yes=1)	Target turnover (EURm)	Stake aquired	Year completed	Private equity acquirer (yes=1)	Payment method	Same industry (yes=1)
Services	Services	0	0	61	64%	2004	0	cash + shares	1
Manufacturing	Finance	1	1	27	100%	2005	1	cash	0
Manufacturing	Manufacturing	0	0	244	100%	2004	0	cash	1
Services	Construction	0	0	168	100%	2002	0	cash	0
Manufacturing	Finance	0	0	52	100%	2005	0	cash	0
Agriculture	Finance	0	1	290	100%	2005	1	cash	0
Trade	Trade	1	1	291	100%	2005	0	cash	1
Services	Manufacturing	1	1	270	100%	2002	0	cash	0
Construction	Construction	0	0	312	100%	2002	0	cash	1
Manufacturing	Finance	1	0	56	100%	2003	1	cash	0
Manufacturing	Manufacturing	1	0	147	100%	2006	0	cash	1
Real Estate	Real Estate	1	1	23	100%	2002	0	cash	1
Manufacturing	Manufacturing	1	0	45	75%	2003	0	cash	1
Services	Services	1	1	17	100%	2002	0	cash	1
Services	Finance	0	0	156	100%	2004	1	cash	0
Manufacturing	Manufacturing	1	0	43	100%	2001	0	cash	1
Manufacturing	Finance	1	1	165	50%	2001	1	cash	0
Trade	Finance	1	1	26	100%	2002	1	cash	0
Manufacturing	Manufacturing	1	0	8	100%	2001	0	cash	1
Manufacturing	Manufacturing	1	1	166	100%	2002	0	cash	1
Manufacturing	Finance	0	0	251	100%	2003	1	cash	0
Transportation	Manufacturing	1	0	45	89%	2004	0	cash	0
Manufacturing	Manufacturing	1	0	10	100%	2004	0	cash	1

Industry	Industry								
Manufacturing	Finance	0	0	269	100%	2002	1	cash	0
Manufacturing	Services	0	0	84	100%	2002	0	cash	0
Manufacturing	Manufacturing	0	0	144	100%	2005	0	cash	0
Real Estate	Finance	0	0	184	100%	2006	1	cash	0
Manufacturing	Finance	0	0	164	100%	2006	1	cash	1
Manufacturing	Manufacturing	1	1	500	100%	2002	0	cash	0
Manufacturing	Finance	0	0	130	100%	2004	1	cash	1
Services	Services	1	1	14	100%	2001	0	cash + shares	1
Manufacturing	Manufacturing	0	0	54	100%	2002	0	cash	1
Manufacturing	Manufacturing	1	1	41	100%	2004	0	cash	1
Manufacturing	Finance	0	0	149	100%	2004	1	cash	0
Manufacturing	Finance	0	1	274	100%	2005	1	cash	0
Manufacturing	Manufacturing	0	0	102	49%	2002	0	cash	1
Manufacturing	Manufacturing	0	0	148	100%	2006	0	cash	1
Manufacturing	Finance	1	0	229	100%	2006	1	cash	0
Manufacturing	Finance	1	1	102	100%	2006	1	cash	0
Transportation	Transportation	0	0	460	100%	2006	0	cash	1
		20	12	148	96%	80141	16	NA	18

Average deal size (EURm)	133.7
Average target turnover (EURm)	145.3
Mittelstand	50.0%
thereof owner-managed	60.0%
Average target Debt/Equity	2.91
Average target Equity/Total assets	0.34
Share private equity investor	40.0%
Share cash payment	100.0%

The sample consists of 40 completed majority-ownership transactions between January 2001 and June 2006 with German target companies. For all these transactions, comprehensive inside information is available that has been gathered by the investment advisor of the seller in these transactions. The table reports some of the main characteristics of these transactions. One can see that 50% of the transactions (20) involve Mittelstand companies, of which around 60% are owner-managed. 40% of the acquirers are from the private equity industry. With 100% cash deals, the payment method as a potential influence factor is not included in the forthcoming study in Section 2.5.

Exhibit 2.9   Univariate analyses – transaction characteristics

Mittel-stand	Owner-managed	Industry	Selling pressure	Bidder submitting revised offer	Private equity bidder	SI with synergy motives	Bidder with synergy motives	Bidder with similar companies	Bidders on shortlist	IM sent out	Indicative bids	Management presentations
0	0	Services	0	3	0	0	0	0	18	7	6	3
1	1	Manufacturing	0	4	4	0	0	1	25	16	12	6
0	0	Manufacturing	0	4	0	1	1	0	62	23	15	8
0	0	Services	1	3	1	2	2	1	17	11	8	3
0	0	Manufacturing	0	3	0	3	3	0	59	14	8	5
0	0	Agriculture	0	1	1	0	0	1	43	22	16	3
1	1	Trade	0	2	0	0	0	1	48	15	4	2
1	1	Services	0	4	1	1	1	0	18	12	6	4
0	0	Construction	1	3	0	1	1	0	46	11	6	3
1	0	Manufacturing	0	3	2	0	0	2	49	34	7	6
1	0	Manufacturing	0	4	3	1	1	1	55	26	7	5
1	1	Real Estate	0	3	0	0	0	0	26	18	8	6
1	0	Manufacturing	0	2	0	2	2	0	20	18	6	2
1	1	Services	0	1	0	1	1	0	25	18	16	2
0	0	Services	0	1	1	0	0	0	14	10	5	3
0	0	Manufacturing	0	3	0	0	0	0	30	24	3	3
1	1	Manufacturing	1	1	0	0	0	1	33	18	14	3
1	1	Trade	0	4	4	0	0	1	48	16	5	3
1	0	Manufacturing	1	2	0	0	0	0	26	18	6	2
1	1	Manufacturing	0	3	2	0	0	2	27	15	12	3
0	0	Manufacturing	1	3	3	0	0	0	28	17	3	4
1	0	Transportation	1	3	0	3	3	0	19	10	6	2
1	0	Manufacturing	0	3	0	2	2	0	16	10	4	3
0	0	Manufacturing	0	2	2	0	0	2	26	18	6	6
0	0	Manufacturing	0	1	0	0	0	0	17	11	10	3
0	0	Manufacturing	0	3	2	0	1	1	37	19	11	7
0	0	Manufacturing	0	5	4	0	1	2	10	9	7	5
0	0	Real Estate	0	2	1	0	0	0	35	18	14	3
0	0	Manufacturing	0	2	2	0	0	1	38	38	10	4
1	0	Manufacturing	1	3	1	1	1	1	13	13	7	3
0	0	Manufacturing	1	3	0	0	0	1	51	35	4	3
1	1	Services	1	1	0	0	0	0	34	28	3	1
0	0	Manufacturing	1	2	0	0	0	0	22	13	4	3
1	1	Manufacturing	2	3	0	2	2	0	14	9	6	3
0	1	Manufacturing	0	3	3	0	0	2	14	10	7	4
0	0	Manufacturing	2	3	3	0	0	2	24	12	8	5
0	0	Manufacturing	0	1	0	0	0	0	17	10	3	3
1	0	Manufacturing	2	2	0	1	1	0	22	10	8	5
1	0	Manufacturing	0	1	0	1	1	0	17	11	5	3
1	1	Manufacturing	0	2	2	0	0	0	35	15	5	5
20	12	Average	0	3	1	1	1	1	29	17	8	4
		Min	0	1	0	0	0	0	10	7	3	1
		Max	2	5	4	3	3	2	62	38	16	8
		Sum	16	102	42	22	24	23	1177	663	301	150

The sample consists of 40 completed majority-ownership transactions between January 2001 and June 2006 with German target companies. For the entire set of transactions comprehensive inside information is available that has been gathered by the investment advisor of the seller in these transactions. The table reports selected variables specified in Appendix A.

2.5.1   The Seller – Disposal Motives

Financial selling pressure measured as a combination of stated disposal motive and weak financials exists in 13 (33%) of the 40 transactions, and in 7 (35%) of the 20 transaction involving a Mittelstand company, which is a difference that has statistically not proven to have any significance.

Selling pressure may negatively influence both the dependent variables, $Delta_1$ and $Delta_2$. Exhibit 2.10 analyzes this relationship and finds that the pricing deltas depend on the level of selling pressure. Without any selling pressure, the upside offered in the first stage is around

Parties in DR	Binding offers	DR size	Facilities	Man-days in DR	People invovled	Process length (days)	People to handle	Business relation	Years of BR	Stake in target	Years in firm	Years in industry	Commitment after disposal
3	3	23	8	4	9	208	22	0	1	0	13	13	0
4	4	8	95	3	7	162	10	0	0	0	14	14	0
4	3	25	12	3	6	395	26	3	1	0	5	20	0
3	3	23	5	5	10	146	17	2	2	0	15	20	0
4	2	17	3	4	9	535	16	0	1	0	10	27	0
2	1	31	12	8	20	208	31	0	0	0	10	20	0
2	2	21	14	4	9	182	13	0	1	0	32	33	0
4	4	24	9	3	10	277	19	1	2	0	8	20	1
3	3	150	60	28	46	208	54	2	7	1	10	28	0
3	3	17	2	5	10	231	12	0	0	0	19	24	0
5	4	15	3	4	9	449	12	0	0	0	4	20	0
6	3	10	5	2	7	357	17	0	0	0	15	15	1
2	2	7	1	3	8	305	13	1	2	0	24	24	0
2	1	6	1	3	8	109	13	0	1	0	20	27	0
2	1	7	1	3	7	118	16	0	0	0	10	15	0
3	3	14	1	12	13	446	18	2	3	0	7	19	0
2	1	13	17	4	9	404	21	0	0	0	15	17	0
2	1	10	4	4	7	251	15	1	0	0	24	26	1
2	2	10	3	4	8	313	16	0	1	0	2	15	0
3	3	11	3	3	6	214	10	0	0	0	13	23	1
2	1	60	19	9	5	125	10	2	1	0	16	27	0
2	1	12	1	4	8	68	13	3	8	0	7	12	0
3	1	10	4	5	9	130	14	3	5	0	14	16	0
2	2	40	19	3	11	331	14	0	0	0	14	25	0
2	1	7	1	3	8	217	11	1	10	0	15	20	0
3	3	13	8	3	13	196	35	1	1	0	3	18	0
5	5	23	8	10	12	67	34	1	1	0	4	18	0
3	2	10	5	2	8	182	11	0	1	0	5	15	0
2	2	12	102	6	15	106	19	0	0	0	2	21	0
3	3	80	40	3	10	396	13	0	0	0	0	25	0
3	3	28	7	4	10	518	15	0	0	0	9	24	0
1	1	7	0	3	8	397	13	0	0	0	5	10	0
3	2	15	3	3	10	304	19	0	0	0	3	13	0
3	1	7	3	4	5	296	13	0	1	0	12	23	0
4	3	25	7	3	10	426	14	0	0	0	19	28	1
3	3	11	86	14	15	135	20	0	0	0	10	20	0
3	1	7	1	3	8	385	10	0	1	0	11	31	0
3	1	12	1	4	8	78	13	2	9	0	7	12	0
3	1	11	6	7	10	98	15	1	2	0	14	16	0
2	1	9	4	5	5	94	10	2	4	0	23	27	0
3	2	21	15	5	10	252	17	1	2	0	12	20	0
1	1	6	0	2	5	67	10	0	0	0	0	10	0
6	5	150	102	28	46	535	54	3	10	1	32	33	1
114	86	841	584	206	404	10067	684	28	64	1	463	817	5

13% on EV (*Delta$_{1EV}$*), and in the later stage of the process there is an average upside of 11% (*Delta$_{2EV}$*) negotiated with the final bidder in contrast to situations with existing selling pressure where the upside decreases to 2% on *Delta$_{1EV}$* and 1% on *Delta$_{2EV}$*.

In addition to pure financial selling pressure, there are often succession problems imminent when owners of private firms sell their companies. Information on selling motives was gathered and we investigated how long the owners were able to serve their former companies after disposal. The last column in Exhibit 2.9 "Commitment after disposal" shows that five out of the 12 owner-managers state that they will stay with the firm for at least one year after disposal. Three out of the remaining seven state financial pressure as a selling motive; none of

Exhibit 2.10 $Delta_1$ and $Delta_2$ depending on the selling pressure

Dependent Variable	Eta	Eta^2	N	Selling Pressure			F-Value	Significance
				No	Low	High		
$Delta_{1EV}$	47.2%	22.2%	102	12.7%	3.7%	1.6%	3.86	2.4%
$Delta_{2EV}$	50.4%	25.4%	40	11.1%	6.7%	1.5%	3.91	1.8%
Column number:	2	3	4	5	6	7	8	9

The sample consists of 40 completed majority-ownership transactions between January 2001 and June 2006 with German target companies. The table reports the dependency of the deltas on the different levels of selling pressure using contingency tables and analyses of variance (ANOVA). Columns 5–7 show mean differences for the dependent variables with respect to the different degrees of selling pressure. The second and the third columns report the eta and eta² as association ratios between the deltas and the three different intensities of selling pressure. Eta equals the square root of the between-groups sum of squares divided by the total sum of the squares. In the case of a relation, the nominator will be as large as the denominator, and the eta will approach 1.0. Eta² can be interpreted as the percentage of variance in the dependent variable explained by the independent variable. The F-value gives the result of the analysis of variance with the respective significance level reported in the last column. One can see that the pricing deltas differ across the levels of selling pressure. The higher the selling pressure is, the lower are the upsides. Furthermore, one can see in the eta² in column 3 that a significant percentage of variance in $Delta_{1EV}$ and $Delta_{2EV}$ is explained by the selling pressure.

the owner-managers mentioned succession problems as the selling motives. One can conclude that none of the sellers waited until the situation at the company became somehow critical before they disposed of the company. Therefore, this motive only plays a secondary role and the resulting selling pressure remains low compared to the situation of financial pressure.

The results of the multivariate regressions as specified in Equations 2.1 and 2.2 are shown in Exhibit 2.11, which displays the influence of the factors on the development between

Exhibit 2.11   Results of the regression analysis

$Delta_{1EV}$	Coefficient	T-Value	Significance	$Delta_{2EV}$	Coefficient	T-Value	Significance
(Constant)	0.033	1.544	12%	(Constant)	0.046	1.776	10%
Selling pressure	−0.169	−1.648	10%	Selling pressure	−0.142	−1.833	10%
Synergies	0.141	2.145	5%	Synergies	0.230	3.012	1%
Awareness	0.137	2.099	5%	Rivalry	0.173	2.436	5%
Rivalry	0.101	2.081	5%	Transaction charges (bidder)	0.081	1.422	15%
Transaction charges (bidder)	−0.097	−1.883	10%	Transaction charges (seller)	0.051	1.155	20%
Trust (bidder)	0.230	2.216	5%	Trust (bidder)	0.129	2.006	5%
Owner-manager	0.094	1.314	15%				
R^2	21.1%			R^2	11.6%		

The sample consists of 40 completed majority-ownership transactions between January 2001 and June 2006 with German target companies. The number of cases to be analyzed depends on the number of revised bids received during the transaction process, leading to 102 cases to be included in the regression analysis on $Delta_{1EV}$ and 40 cases for $Delta_{2EV}$. The table reports the results of the stepwise linear regression computed according to Equations 2.1 and 2.2. The dependent variable consists of the relative change from the indicative bid to the revised bid measured on EV (left hand side) and the relative change from the revised bid to the price paid measured on EV (right hand side). The set of independent variables correspond to the influence factors shown in the first column of Exhibit 2.4.

the indicative bids to the revised bid $Delta_{1EV}$ (left) and the influence of the factors on the development between the revised bids to the purchase price $Delta_{2EV}$ (right).

With a regression coefficient of −0.169, this variable selling pressure is significant at the 10 % level and influences significantly the development from the indicative bid to the revised bid. In addition, with a coefficient of −0.142 and a 10% significance level, selling pressure influences the development from the revised bid to the purchases price negatively. This result is in line with the finding in Exhibit 2.10 which shows significant differences between the dependent variables across different levels of selling pressure.

2.5.2   The Bidder – Acquisition Motives

With regard to the acquisition motive, Exhibit 2.9 shows synergies as the main reasons for acquisitions: around 24% of the 102 bidders (37% of the strategic bidders and 5% of the private equity firms) mentioned synergies as their primary motive. Investigating synergies further, Exhibit 2.9 shows that 23 (55%) of the 42 private equity investors which submitted a revised offer had at least one company in the portfolio which provides synergy possibilities for the private equity firm after a successful acquisition. Exhibit 2.14 shows that the concentration of private equity firms is especially high in the trade and manufacturing industry; 67% (46%) of the bidders in the due diligence phase of the process (submitting a revised offer) are private equity firms, in contrast to no bids from private equity firms for the two targets from the construction and transportation industry.

Exhibit 2.12 shows that synergy possibilities can increase $Delta_1$ and $Delta_2$. In particular the up-trade in the negotiation phase differs depending on the availability of synergies. $Delta_{2EV}$ varies significantly from −2% (no synergies) to +24% (high synergies).

As $Delta_1$ depends on the level of indicative bids and $Delta_2$ on the level of the revised bids, the average bids from acquirers with synergy vs. the average bids without synergies are compared for all 40 transactions. According to the analysis in Exhibit 2.13, systematic differences in the indicative bid levels cannot be found.

The results of Exhibit 2.12 are supported by the regression coefficients in Exhibit 2.11: synergies positively influence the development from the indicative to the revised bids, with

Exhibit 2.12 $Delta_1$ and $Delta_2$ depending on the synergies

Dependent Variable	Eta	Eta^2	N	No	Low	Medium	High	F-Value	Significance
				Synergies					
$Delta_{1EV}$	39.1%	15.3%	40	−0.6%	0.7%	2.6%	5.0%	3.23	4.9%
$Delta_{2EV}$	72.8%	53.0%	102	−2.1%	3.7%	7.5%	24.0%	4.65	0.8%
Column number:	2	3	4	5	6	7	8	9	10

The sample consists of 40 completed majority-ownership transactions between January 2001 and June 2006 with German target companies. The table reports the dependency of the deltas on the different levels of synergies using contingency tables and ANOVA. Columns 5–8 show the mean differences for the dependent variables with respect to the different degrees of synergy. The second and the third column report the eta and eta^2 as association ratios between the deltas and the three different synergy levels. The F-values display the results of the analysis of variance with the respective significance levels reported in the last column. One can see that the pricing deltas differ across the levels of synergies. The higher the synergies, the higher are the upsides. Furthermore, one can see in the eta^2 in column 3 that a significant percentage of variance in $Delta_{1EV}$ and $Delta_{2EV}$ is explained by the selling pressure; in particular $Delta_{2EV}$ differs significantly given the three levels of synergy.

Exhibit 2.13   A comparison of bid levels

Mean bid level on:	Synergies						
	No	Low	Medium	High	Eta^2	F-Value	Significance
Equity Value (indicative offer, EURm)	69.2	73.3	62.2	85.5	2.3%	0.77	51%
Equity Value (revised offer, EURm)	69.5	75.5	50.6	85.4	2.5%	0.82	48%
Enterprise Value (indicative offer, EURm)	91.1	90.4	78.5	95.2	2.0%	0.65	58%
Enterprise Value (revised offer, EURm)	91.2	91.2	80.4	93.0			
Total	87.2	88.5	112.3	113.4			
Column number:	2	3	4	5	6	7	8

The sample consists of 40 completed majority-ownership transactions between January 2001 and June 2006 with German target companies. The table reports the median equity and EVs offered in the 102 indicative bids for the different levels of synergies. Column six reports the eta^2 as association ratio between the bid level and the three different synergy levels. The F-values in column seven display the results of the analysis of variance with the respective significance levels reported in the last column. One can see that the Equity Value and the EV do not differ across the levels of synergy as the eta^2 in column six only is very low and the F-values not significant.

a coefficient of 0.141 at a 5% significance level, and the development from the revised bid to the price paid with a coefficient of 0.230 at a 1% significance level. As shown in Section 2.2.2, synergy benefits can either be general or individual depending on the individual fit (organizational or strategic). From Exhibit 2.12, one can see that bidders with synergy possibilities offer higher upsides than others. The analysis in Exhibit 2.9 shows that 55% of the private equity bidders have at least one company in their portfolio. The gathered management experience with a similar company together with the synergistic fit of the portfolio companies themselves may lead to a unique synergy potential. This is perhaps the reason why private equity investors in the sample focus mainly on manufacturing industry. This also holds true for strategic buyers, of which 37% name synergies as a primary motive for an acquisition.

2.5.3   Competition

Concerning the awareness of the targets in the marketing phase of the transaction process, Exhibit 2.9 shows that the absolute number of potential bidders ("bidder universe") on the shortlist varies from 10 up to 62. From a closer look at the target industries in Exhibit 2.14 one can conclude that the deals in the service industry attract special interest from potential investors, whereas financial sponsors seem to focus on targets from the trade and manufacturing industry.

The market echo, meaning the percentage of bidders on the shortlist that signed a CA to receive an IM, is especially high for transactions in the service industry (69%) compared to a market echo of 59% in the manufacturing industry and 32% in the trade industry. The deal in the construction industry only generates low bidder attention in the sample and the market echo for the deal in the transportation industry is in between. Depending on the nature of the sample, it is difficult to generalize the results that differentiate by industry; it may only be possible for the 33 deals in the manufacturing industry.

As seen in Exhibit 2.9, 663 of the 1,117 bidders approached on the shortlist signed a confidentiality agreement to receive an information memorandum, leading to a market echo of 56% with an average of 15 IM sent out per transaction. This leads to an IM response quote

Exhibit 2.14 Bidders and transactions across industries

	Agriculture	Construction	Manufacturing	Real Estate	Trade	Services	Transportation
Number of private equity bidders	1	0	33	1	4	3	0
Number of bidders	1	3	71	5	6	13	3
Share of private equity bidders	100%	0%	46%	20%	67%	23%	0%
Number of transactions	1	1	27	2	2	6	1
Average number of bidders	1.0	3.0	2.6	2.5	3.0	2.2	3.0
Market echo (average)	51%	24%	59%	60%	32%	69%	53%
IM response quote (average)	75%	55%	42%	61%	29%	51%	60%

The sample consists of 40 completed majority-ownership transactions between January 2001 and June 2006 with German target companies. For these entire transactions comprehensive inside information is available. The table reports different metrics across the targets' industry groups. The industries have been classified using the 4-digit SIC code.

of 47%, with an average of seven indicative bids received per transaction. Therefore, in total 27% of potential bidders complete the marketing phase of the transaction process and submit an indicative bid on the target company. These ratios can be interpreted as a first indication for the competitive position the seller has in the following DD phase of the process, assuming that a strong seller position is a good prerequisite to create buyer competition in the later (DD) stage. On average, the seller is able to choose between seven bidders that can be invited in the DD stage; this number can be regarded as sufficient to generate competition.

More information on the competition between bidders in the DD phase of the process can be gathered by looking at the number of management presentations held, the number of parties in the data room and from the ratio of the number of binding offers compared to the number of indicative bids. Although there is no open communication between the bidders involved at that stage in the process, the bidders are usually aware that there are other parties involved, either from earlier experience or because the advising bank indicates that there are other interested parties. In this advanced stage of the process, competitive pressure becomes more latent, and from the results in Exhibit 2.9, one can see that competition generally unfolds for all deals because several bidders participate in each of the transactions. On average, management presentations are given to four bidders, from which three (75%) also undergo the DD process in the data room and submit a revised offer. In only one transaction, however, just one bidder went to the DD stage of the transaction process. On average, three bidders submit a revised bid, which is a good basis for the subsequent negotiation phase, despite there being eight transactions in which only one bidder submits a revised offer.

Section 2.2.3 argues that the awareness of the target and rivalry positively influences the price development ($Delta_1$ and $Delta_2$). Exhibit 2.15 analyzes these dependencies in a

Exhibit 2.15   The correlation between $Delta_{1EV}$, $Delta_{2EV}$ and competition

Dependent variable	Statistics	Bidders on shortlist	IM sent out	Indicative Bids	Management presentations	Parties in DR	Revised bids
$Delta_{1EV}$	Pearson Correlation	0.121	0.176	0.213	0.255	0.201	0.192
	Sig. (2-tailed)	22.66%	7.75%	3.12%	0.98%	4.67%	5.32%
	N	102	102	102	102	102	102
$Delta_{2EV}$	Pearson Correlation	0.180	−0.197	0.268	0.179	0.284	0.306
	Sig. (2-tailed)	26.52%	22.24%	9.51%	27.04%	8.42%	6.17%
	N	40	40	40	40	40	40

The sample consists of 40 completed majority ownership-transactions between January 2001 and June 2006 with German target companies. The table reports correlations between the dependent variables $Delta_{1EV}$ and $Delta_{2EV}$ and different variables that measure the construct competition (as shown in Exhibit 2.5). The number of cases N differs because $Delta_{1EV}$ is measured on the level of revised bids received (102) and $Delta_{2EV}$ depends on the number of SPA signed. The correlation coefficients between the number of IM which have been sent out and the number of indicative bids to $Delta_{1EV}$ are positive and significant (0.176 at 10% level and 0.213 at 3% level). The correlation coefficients between the number of parties in the data room, the number of binding offers and the upside negotiating ($Delta_{2EV}$) are positive and significant (0.284 and 0.306 are significant at the 10% level). Both independent variables influence the $Delta_{1EV}$ significantly (at the 5% and 10% levels respectively with correlation coefficients of 0.201 and 0.192)).

univariate framework using correlation coefficients between the items that constitute the factor competition and the dependent variables $Delta_{1EV}$ and $Delta_{2EV}$.

One can see that the awareness of the target (measured by the number of bidders on the shortlist, the number of IM which have been sent out and the number of indicative bids) influences the up-trade from the indicative to the revised bid at the due diligence stage of the process. Furthermore, it seems that the last bidder (and later acquirer of the target) is still under the impression that there is a potential threat from other bidders. Even when he has started bilateral negotiations with the seller, there is a positive correlation between the number of parties in the data room, the number of binding offers and the upside negotiated ($Delta_{2EV}$).

The influence of competition is confirmed by the results of the regression analysis in Exhibit 2.11: both the target's awareness as well as the bidder rivalry in the due diligence phase exert a positive influence on the development of the indicative to the revised bids. With a coefficient of 0.137 and 0.101 for *Awareness* and *Rivalry*, respectively and a 5% significance level, both factors significantly influence $Delta_{1EV}$. Competition also exerts a positive influence (coefficient of 0.173 at a 5% significance level) on the difference between the revised bids and the purchase price.

2.5.4   Transaction Charges

The transactions are analyzed further with respect to the transaction charges that the bidders incur. These are higher with the increasing complexity the bidder faces. The analysis of transaction charges is undertaken in Exhibit 2.9 and Exhibit 2.16 which show the measurement of the factor and how the single variables are related to each other. The analysis of correlation coefficients supports the interpretation of the result in Exhibit 2.9. Exhibit 2.9 shows that the number of facilities to be analyzed (and sometimes visited) varies from 0 to 102 with an average data room consisting of 13 binders to be analyzed in the due diligence, despite the fact that there is quite a wide range from a minimum of six to a maximum of 150. An increase in facilities does not necessarily lead to more complex information (correlation coefficient of 0.303 between both variables in Exhibit 2.16).

Exhibit 2.16   Correlation coefficients for Transaction charges (bidder)

	Target turnover	Folders DR	Day DR opens	Facilities	Days IM to signing	Man-days in DR	People involved	Days process	People to handle
Target turnover	1.000								
Folders DR	0.530	1.000							
Day DR opens	0.431	0.592	1.000						
Facilities	0.264	0.303	0.490	1.000					
Days IM to signing	−0.227	0.012	−0.227	−0.212	1.000				
Man-days in DR	0.168	0.705	0.567	0.395	−0.139	1.000			
People involved	0.320	0.773	0.493	0.399	−0.014	0.862	1.000		
Days process	−0.210	−0.014	−0.187	−0.230	0.890	−0.213	−0.083	1.000	
People to handle	0.104	0.440	0.503	0.105	−0.065	0.523	0.496	−0.116	1.000

The sample consists of 40 completed majority-ownership transactions between January 2001 and June 2006 with German target companies. The table reports correlation coefficients between the variables that measure the factor "Transaction charges".

According to Exhibit 2.9, the number of man-days in the data room varies between two and 28 and is positively related to the amount of information presented, indicated by a correlation coefficient of 0.705. The bidder's deal time size (*People involved*) varies between five and 46 people with an average of nine. The variable is significantly related to the days in the data room (correlation coefficient of 0.862) and the amount of information presented (correlation coefficient of 0.773) meaning that the parties involved spend relatively more time in the data room and execute due diligence with an increased workforce. In addition, *People involved* has a positive relation to the target size (correlation coefficient of 0.320). This might indicate that bidder attention increases with target size in terms of the people involved on the bidder's side. The target's size (turnover) itself has no clear relation to the due diligence effort (correlation coefficient to days in data room of 0.168) meaning the bigger deals are not necessarily more complex or screened with more scrutiny.

According to Exhibit 2.9, the average transaction process takes seven months; the process length varies from a minimum of two months up to 1.5 years for selling a small manufacturing division with EUR 52m turnover, and is significantly correlated to the days the seller needs from obtaining the IM to expected signing (correlation coefficient of 0.890). The seller and its advisors need to handle an average of 14 people with a maximum team size of 54 people, including its own legal and tax advisors. The number of people to handle is not significantly correlated with the target's size (correlation coefficient of 0.104), but is naturally significantly correlated with the deal team size of the bidder (correlation coefficient of 0.496).

According Exhibit 2.11, transaction charges negatively influence the development from the indicative to the revised bid. With a coefficient of −0.097, this factor is significant at the 10% level. Lower transaction charges can lead a bidder to revise his bid positively without giving too much shareholder value away. At the same time, higher transaction costs take this flexibility away from the bidder and lead him to be more cautious with the update he offers in the revised bid. The coefficient and the significance level show that the influence of the transaction costs is not as strong as e.g. the influence of competition. It is reasonable to assume that some bidders have the possibility to increase their revised bids due to the lower costs they face (and also for other reasons), but they do not pass these savings on to the seller, even though they face competitive bids.

According to Exhibit 2.11, transaction charges have no influence on the development from the revised bid to the purchase price, either on the bidders or on the seller's side. Neither factor is significant (15% and 20% significance level).

The pressure of incurred transaction charges does not make the bidder negotiate on an update because he faces increased pressure to close the deal. A potential explanation could be that the bidder has agreed with the seller in the LOI to the absorption of some of his costs by the seller. Another explanation might be that after going through the complete process other factors may influence the negotiation phase of the process and the actions of the bidder and the seller.

From the seller's perspective, an allowance negotiated on the purchase price might not be primarily driven by transaction charges but more by other aspects that cannot be accounted for in the regression. This is expressed by a lower adjusted R^2 compared to the regression on $Delta_{1EV}$.

2.5.5   Trust in the Respective Counterparts

Trust is an important factor in the transaction process and potentially influences even the prices offered and agreed on in the SPA. A prerequisite of trust is knowledge through a (business) relation and reputation. According to Exhibit 2.9 around 27% of the sellers have a business relationship with the potential acquirers left in the due diligence phase of the process which on average lasts for about two years. According to Exhibit 2.9, in only one transaction a bidder is involved who has a stake before approaching the company. Therefore, this variable is excluded from further analysis. The average selling management team is quite familiar with its company and relatively experienced, with an average of two years in the firm and 10 years in the industry. The years of industry experience range from a few months to 10 years in the firm, and a maximum of 32 years in the industry. It will be investigated whether those differences might influence the confidence of a bidder in the target's management by including them in the trust factor.

Exhibit 2.11 confirms with a coefficient of 0.230 and a significance level of 5% that trust positively influences the development from the indicative to the revised bid. Section 2.2.5 argued that trust exerts influence via knowledge and reputation, and that the seller's top management is a key asset in whose commitment and experience the bidder needs to trust. According to Exhibit 2.9, 28 of 102 bidders have a prior relationship with the target's company. The factor trust also reveals its influence on the development for the revised bid to the purchase price with a coefficient of 0.129 at the 5% significance level.

Owner – Company Relation – the "Family Factor"

The personal relationship of (family) owner(s) to the company exerts influence in different areas which might impact on the transaction process and the influence is exerted through ownership and control, management strategy and style, the company's strategic goals, selling motives and active owner-management. Some of those might influence the trust prevailing between the bidder and the seller and one can conclude that the trust a bidder has in the company and the management during the transaction and the sustainability of the target's business is higher if the target is a family company. The "family factor" may also impact on the transaction process via strategic goals that are not primarily related to maximizing the purchase price of the company, but relate to the general well-being of the company and

Exhibit 2.17   Management involvement

IV. Overall strategy and management involvement

From our meetings with the management team we have reinforced our adhesion to the strategy sucessfully implemented by Seller relying on a strong home market position and of expanding on an international basis, with a strengthened R&D capacity and through a combination of internal and external growth strategy.

We understand that the management team is strongly motivated to continue with Seller and that they would favourably view an acquisition led by the Bindder. Consequently, we do not foresee any difficulties in reaching an agreement with them on the terms of their association in the project.

Extract from indicative offer letter from a private equity investor addressed to the transaction advisor of the seller. It emphasizes the importance of the management at an early stage of the transaction. For confidentiality reasons, the names of the bidder and the seller have been replaced.

its employees. Furthermore, the management might show greater commitment and a more positive attitude in family companies.

The sample is split and Exhibit 2.21 finds that the average number of years top management stays with the firm is longer for Mittelstand companies than for other firms.[9] One can also see that managers stay on average for 13.6 years compared to 8.7 years in other private and public companies. Mittelstand companies with an owner-manager show even more years of management commitment (16.5 years[10]) than the rest of the Mittelstand (9.3 years). In addition, the attitude of the target's management towards the bidder seems more positive for Mittelstand than for non-Mittelstand companies.

Key managers are a core asset for the firm. Management commitment and involvement is appreciated by interested bidders (see example in Exhibit 2.17).

Other bidders see management commitment as an important requirement to proceed further with the transaction and management forms part of future DD (see example in Exhibit 2.18).

An analysis of 35 revised offer documents (LOIs) that have been available and the comments on the role of the old management shows that nearly 85% of the bidders view the management as crucially important (see example in Exhibit 2.19).

Furthermore, the final bidder stated in 28 cases that a management participation scheme would be offered after acquisition (without giving any further details on concrete implementations). This information is crucially important for the seller and advisors often include these explicitly in presentations they give to the seller's management and/or owners (see example in Exhibit 2.20).

To align the interests between management and the new company owner, bidders offer more incentive programs to the management of Mittelstand companies (75%) than to other companies' management (65%). Given the management's key role and its potential influence on the transaction process and outcome (in terms of purchase price), the management commitment in later years and the attitude towards a bidder are crucial elements of the factor trust (see Appendix A.V).

The relationship between the owner and the company might positively influence the business relationship to suppliers and other companies in the market. Exhibit 2.21 investigates the differences in the length of the business relationship to the bidder between both company

---

[9] Again, Mittelstand companies represent independent private companies in Germany with a close link between owner and companies (similar to a family firm). A detailed description of the Mittelstand is given in Section 1.3.

[10] Thereby excluding the owner-manager(s).

Exhibit 2.18   Requirement for management involvement

Basis of Indicative offer

In order to firm up **B's** view on pricing, and whilst not an exclusive list, there are four principal areas **B** will focus in the next stage of its due diligence:

- Management's appetite to take part in a buyout transaction and substantially roll over their existing stakes in the business;

- Confirmation that the business is not reliant on the exiting shareholders, in particular **Existing Owner;**

- The ability of the business to continue to grow (as projected) well in excess of projected market rates, notwithstanding the risk of a construction sector slowdown in the business' core European market; and

- The working capital profile of the business, given the "trading" nature of a material part of the Company's operations.

Extract from indicative offer letter from a private equity investor addressed to the transaction advisor of the seller. It emphasizes the importance of the management at an early stage of the transaction and requirement for further DD on the management commitment and its involvement. Furthermore, the new potential owner is concerned about the dependency of the target on the existing shareholder, in this case a family owner. For confidentiality reasons, the names of the bidder (B) and the seller (S) have been replaced.

classes. Mittelstand companies have on average a 1.1-year relationship to the final bidder, and non-Mittelstand companies have a 1.5-year relationship. This difference is driven by owner-managed companies that generally have a shorter (0.6 years) relationship with their bidders. The business relationships of non-owner-managed Mittelstand companies last longer (1.7 years). In the sample, the length of the business relationship is not positively influenced by the linkage between owner and company.

Exhibit 2.19   Revised bid and signing requirements

V. Conditions to Signing and Closing

This Confirmed Offer is subject to:

1. Access to all information with respect of the Transaction and the Company, its subsidiaries and its management team.
2. Bidder's satisfaction with the outcome of a confirmatory due diligence investigation into the state of affairs of the Transaction and the Company. These investigations will include:

    - a confirmatory financial due diligence (including IT, taxes and pension);
    - a review of a revised business plan based on the recurring business;
    - a confirmatory market due diligence;
    - a confirmatory legal due diligence;
    - a confirmatory environmental due diligence; and
    - an insurance review.

    We will be able to finalize our confirmatory due diligence within three to four weeks, depending on the availability of the management team.

3. The full co-operation of the Company's management team with the contemplated transaction.
4. Bidder's satisfaction that all parties have complied with all applicable laws and regulations with respect to this Transaction. In this regard, Bidder may be required to obtain clearance from the anti-trust authorities, although as a financial investor it does not foresee any substantial competition or anti-trust issues which could prevent completion or materially delay the Transaction.

Extract from a revised offer letter from a private equity investor addressed to the transaction advisor of the seller. It shows that the ongoing commitment of the senior management to the transaction as a requirement for the subsequent signing and closing. For confidentiality reasons, the names of the bidder and the seller have been replaced.

Exhibit 2.20 Revised offers – summary presentation

Investor	Valuation		Assumptions	Due Diligence	Timing	Comment
Private Equity	Enterpr. Value	105.000 mn	– Offer based on BS 12/03	– Financial (incl. tax)	– MP, DR, SV start end of July	– Letter of support financing bank
	Cash	+0.600 mn	– 2003 EBITDA will be achieved	– Commercial (incl. customer referencing)	– **Access to management (also on informal basis)**	– **Management to remain in the company**
	Lt. debt	–9.942 mn	– Leases will not be "Financial Lease"	– Environmental	– Site visits	– **Management to reinvest substantially**
	St. debt	–11.330 mn	– Deliverability of forecasts	– Insurance	– No exclusivity for next round	
	Shareholder loan	–13.556 mn	– Act. business meets monthly forecasts	– **Management/Corp. Governance**		
	Lease financing	n.a.	– Sufficient working capital	– Legal		
	Tax liabilities	0,000 mn	– No 3rd party complaint			
	Cash-effective Provisions	n.a.				
	Equity Value	70.772 mn				
	Revised offer	up to 120 mn				

Extract from a presentation that summarizes the status of revised bids and further procedure based on the offers received. The presentation has been prepared by the seller's transaction advisor for a meeting with seller. For confidentiality reasons, the names of the bidder and the seller have been replaced (BAS stands for Balance Sheet, MP stands for Management Presentation, DR for Data Room and SV for Site Visits).

Exhibit 2.21 Split sample analysis

Target Status	Owner-manager	Trans-actions	Years in firm	Years in industry	Attitude (towards bidder)	Years of BR	Market share	Manager reputation	Reputation seller (firm)	Non-pecuniary goals	Share of private equity	Number of bidders	Average of revised bid (EV)	Days IM to signing	Particpation schemes	Years of commitment	Corr. (Market leadership bidder, EV revised)
Other	No	20	8.7	19.9	1.6	1.5	19%	1.2	1.9	NA	34%	50	121	189	13	NA	0.09
Mittelstand	No	8	9.3	20.0	1.7	1.7	18%	1.8	1.8	NA	43%	21	169	190	6	NA	−0.15
Mittelstand	Yes	12	16.5	21.9	2.5	0.6	12%	2.0	2.1	0.6	52%	31	64	186	9	3	−0.14
Mittelstand	Both	20	13.6	21.1	2.2	1.1	14%	2.0	2.0	0.6	48%	52	106	189	15	NA	−0.33
Column number:	2	3	4	5	6	7	8	9	10	11	12	13	14	15	16	17	18

Share of PE investors

Selling pressure	Owner-managed	Non-owner-managed	Non-Mittel-stand
0	61.5%	45.5%	39.4%
1	0.0%	50.0%	7.1%
2	0.0%	0.0%	100.0%

The sample consists of 40 completed majority-ownership transactions between January 2001 and June 2006 with German target companies. The upper part of the table reports the differences in the dependent variables between owner-managed Mittelstand, non-owner-managed Mittelstand and non-Mittelstand, companies. The third last column measures the number of bidders which explicitly state the intention to offer a participation scheme to the targets' management after the acquisition. The second last column measures the average number of years those 12 owner-managers intend to work for the new company who stated that they will stay after acquisition. The last column reports the median correlation coefficients between the level of revised bids and the reputation of a bidder. The coefficients are computed for each transaction separately, but only when at least three revised bids were received. The lower part of the table reports the share of private equity investors after the indicative bids are submitted across different levels of selling pressure. The figures are computed as medians for each class of target companies.

The influence of owner-management is analyzed separately and included as an independent variable into the regression on $Delta_{1E}$ (due to the limited number of cases in the regression on $Delta_{2EV}$) despite the fact that this variable is correlated to other independent variables (e.g. to *Years in firm*). According to Exhibit 2.11, $Delta_{1EV}$ is positively influenced by owner-management (coefficient of 0.094), but the influence is not significant; therefore the inclusion of this variable does not increase the explanatory power of the regression.

The owner-manager identity may somehow influence the market position of the firm through reputation within the industry. A positive relation cannot be shown in Exhibit 2.21. Non-owner-managed companies have higher market shares than other companies, the market share of owner-managed companies stays below those of the rest of the companies. The relation might be spurious anyway.

Section 2.3 hypothesizes that the reputation of managers and firms might be higher in the case of Mittelstand companies. According to Exhibit 2.21, there are differences in the measured grade of reputation of the management between those companies, and the grade is higher for Mittelstand (2.0) than for other companies (1.2). With respect to firm reputation, there are only minor differences.

According to theory, some owners of private companies pursue non-pecuniary goals, i.e. they want to give the firm away into "good" hands and invite only trustworthy bidders with a reluctance to sell their companies to private equity firms. But in the split sample in Exhibit 2.21, one can see that the share of private equity bidders invited to submit a revised bid is higher for Mittelstand companies (the average percentage of private equity bidders in the later stage is 48%) than for others (the average percentage of private equity bidders in the later stage is 34%) and even higher for owner-managed firms (the average percentage of private equity bidders in the later stage is 52%). This relationship is independent from the selling pressure the companies face as shown in the lower part of Exhibit 2.21. Even where there is high pressure, no private equity investors are in the process at all when owner and non-owner-managed Mittelstand companies are sold. The level of indicative bids of private equity investors compared to strategic investors is analyzed for those transactions where both kinds of investors have been approached. It appears that there is no difference in indicative bid levels.[11] According to the data, no kind of bidder is preferably invited by Mittelstand sellers into the process. Interestingly, in the end six Mittelstand companies (16 companies in total) are acquired by private equity investors.

2.5.6   Study Results – Summary of Findings

Exhibit 2.22 below summarizes the results of the preceding section.

According to Exhibit 2.22 selling motives, acquisition motives, competition, trust and transaction charges influence the transaction process.

Financial pressure as selling and synergies as acquisition motives influence the dependent variables; whereas selling pressure exerts negative influence, the synergy motive exerts positive influence.

The concept of *Competition* consists of two factors, which are summarized under *Awareness* and *Rivalry*. *Awareness* includes items like *Bidders on shortlist*, *Market echo* or *IM response quote*, which describe how the target's attractiveness is perceived by the market. *Rivalry*

---

[11] The analysis shows that in transactions with Mittelstand companies where both kinds of investors have been approached (nine in total), the bids of private equity investors are on average 1% higher than those of strategic investors.

Exhibit 2.22   Results summary

Factor	Result
Selling motive	Financially motivated selling pressure negatively influences the price development from the indicative bid to the revised bid and from the revised bid to the purchase price
Acquisition Motive	Synergies positively influence the price development from the indicative bid to the revised bid and from the revised bid to the purchase price
Competition	Competition positively influences the price development from the indicative bid to the revised bid and from the revised bid to the purchase price
Transaction charges	Transaction charges (bidder) negatively influence the price development from the indicative bid to the revised bid
Transaction charges	Transaction charges (bidder) do not positively influence the price development from the revised bid to the purchase price
Transaction charges	Transaction charges (seller) do not negatively influence the price development from the revised bid to the purchase price
Trust	Trust (bidder) positively influences the price development from the indicative bid to the revised bid and from the revised bid to the purchase price
Owner-company relation	Employed managers show stronger commitment and higher trust in the owner's decisions in Mittelstand than in other companies
Owner-company relation	Owner-company relation fosters trust a bidder has in the target company with higher (seller) management commitment and reputation and in the transaction outcome and therefore positively influences the development from the indicative bid to the revised bid and from the revised bid to the purchase price.
Owner-company relation	A trustworthy bidder is not preferably invited to the due diligence phase and negotiations by family firm owners and private equity is treated equally to other bidders.

includes items like *Parties in DR*, *Binding offers* or *Binding bid quote*, which describe the competitive intensity in the due diligence phase of the process. The threat of competition makes a buyer increase its offer; both in the DD phase and in the negotiation phase of the process. The analysis revealed an overall *IM response quote* of 47%; the seller can choose on average between seven bidders for invitation to further due diligence, a number which can be regarded as sufficient to generate competition in the DD phase. To generate a certain level of competition, the seller should therefore aim to send out at least 10 to 15 IMs, meaning that the bidder universe should consist of around 25–30 addressees. In the data set, the seller was able to generate competition between an average of four bidders in the due diligence phase, of which 75% submitted a revised offer. With the choice between on average two bidders, the sellers and their advisors are able to put some pressure on the final bidder to sign-off the deal after a little upside has been negotiated, and to at least have a choice between two bidders in the negotiation phase, it is recommendable to obtain at least seven indicative bids out of the marketing phase. This is because an average of one revised bid is received from two to three bidders which have made an indicative offer (*Process quote* of 29%).

Transaction charges are related to the information desire of a bidder and complexity of the process. The influence of transaction charges is only significant in the due diligence phase of the process, and the lower the charges are, the more willing bidders are to offer more in their revised bids. It has been shown that the deal team size of the bidder varies between 5–46 people and that the data room is the place the bidder spends most effort on. Both items characterize the information desire and they influence the transaction charges. Because the seller cannot close down its facilities to keep its business lean, it needs to focus on a lean presentation in the data room, easy access to information (e.g. electronic data room) and structured set-up of the due diligence process.

The concept of *Trust* comprises the aspects of *Knowledge*, *Reputation* and *Attitude*. The firm's and management's reputation, as well as prior knowledge of the respective counterparts and a positive attitude of the target's management seem to be valuable from the bidder's perspective as these items are constituents of the concept of *Trust* that influences the change from the indicative over the revised bids to the purchase price negotiated. Given the influence of the trust factor, it is recommended that the seller and its advisors approach a high percentage of bidders that are familiar with the target although they might be competitors. According to Exhibit 2.31, the factor *Reputation* consists of the market leadership of the seller's firm and the management commitment and experience. As the seller cannot change these parameters before starting the transaction it is recommended to incentivize the senior management to the extent that they stay with the company and work with the bidder towards the success of the transaction.

The linkage between owners and firms influences the transaction process and result. A more positive manager attitude in general and towards the transactions, a longer commitment of key managers, a higher reputation and therefore a higher degree of trust on the side of the bidder in the transaction and the target are characteristics for transactions involving Mittelstand companies, whereas other prejudices like the reluctance to sell to a special investor group could not be proven true.

2.6 STUDY ASSESSMENT

Prior research on private firms can be divided into two streams. The first examines performance differences between family and non-family business using only simple statistical measures of performance like sales growth, number of employees and profit margins, and they examine whether differences are statistically significant. These studies have shown a diverse range of results: some authors state clearly that non-family businesses outperform family businesses in sales growth and productivity (Binder, 1994). Others report higher sales growth and profitability of family businesses (Anderson and Reeb, 2003). Some studies conclude that these show no significant differences (Westhead and Cowling, 1997). None of the studies attempts to explain the causes of the differences.

The second stream focuses on M&A transactions and finds evidence that the linkage between ownership and company influences the relationship between the seller and the bidder, the behaviour of the target's management during a transaction, and the bargaining tactic. The research concludes that this linkage between ownership and company causes valuation differences, but it lacks empirical evidence for the performance differences between family and non-family firms. Some researchers are able to show performance difference but the explanatory variable is constituted by the intensity of the linkage between the owner and the manager itself. Therefore these studies could not show how the influence is exercised. Engelskirchen (2007) analyzes a sample of 226 transactions of family and non-family firms acquiring public targets in Germany. He tests concrete hypotheses on the outperformance of acquisitions undertaken by family businesses. He includes in his setting, next to some controlling variables, the share of family ownership of voting rights, the presence of the family on the supervisory board and its presence on the management board and tests as a dependent variable (outperformance) the two-day abnormal return for the bidder on the day of the announcement of the transaction. He finds higher abnormal returns for family businesses compared to non-family businesses but could not link this outperformance to factors other than the ownership structure itself.

This study tries to align both streams of research and investigates how non-performance-related characteristics influence the transaction process and the purchase prices finally agreed on. In the course of this question, the study tries to find out, how the linkage between owner and enterprise might influence the transaction process and the final value for the disposed company by looking at the transaction process in detail. Furthermore, the study aims to measure variables that capture the influence of the linkage between owner and company, as well as the influence of other factors that are not related to the target's financial characteristics. These variables are linked to the prices offered during the transaction process and examine how they influence the outcome in a multivariate setting. Although the study is done in Germany, the setting of the study (and the international character of the transactions themselves) makes the results applicable for an international audience. As data include transactions from 2001–2006, the data set feels a little outdated given the dramatic changes in the market environment in the last few years. But one should note that this study does not try to estimate a purchase price, to value a company, or to explain the absolute amount of the purchase price, but to identify key factors (next to the market environment and target's financial characteristics) that influence the development from the indicative offer to the binding offer and to the agreed purchase price. Furthermore, the period 2001–2006 includes two different market environments; 2001–2003 with a strong M&A downturn and the period between 2004 and 2006 with a strong recovery of M&A markets.

Overall, this analysis confirms that the process view is a realistic view of the M&A process and could show the reader some key elements of the process that directly influence the pricing outcome.

2.6.1   Limitations of the Study

This study cannot explain why private firms are traded at discounts relative to public companies. This explanation does not constitute either the motivation or the goal of the previous analyses. The focus is only on factors beyond financial target characteristics in particular how special characteristics of independent private firms influence the purchase price agreed.

The study is set up in such a way that it only captures the influence of those factors that are based on the interaction of the parties and characteristics of the process. But one cannot deny that characteristics of the targets themselves or the market environment influence the dependent and independent variables. For instance, one could say that the industry, the market position or the size of a target influence the numbers of potential bidders or the bids received. Or that the numbers of bidders which are still interested in the later stages of the process are related to the general market sentiment (M&A environment). Some of these issues have been addressed, e.g. the relationship between the number of bidders on the shortlist and both the target's size and the target's industry has been cross-checked, but this relationship does not show any statistical significance. Other influences still exist – the study cannot completely disregard the interdependencies between some target characteristics and the independent variables in the regression set-up. Although a strong relationship between the items and the constructs exists, other items may contain aspects that are not directly linked to the process, the interactions and the concepts quantified. Given the relatively low R^2, especially of the regression on Delta_{2EV}, the robustness of the approach can be improved by including some more transactions.

Depending on the nature of the study, it is not possible to predict how trust or competition influence single actors in the process, and why these factors are more important within one process than in the other. The reader needs to be aware that the results of this study are not directly comparable to the findings in Chapter 3 of the book; the previous study does not focus on final transaction prices and does not seek to estimate price difference between private and public companies.

2.7 RELATIONSHIP BETWEEN THE STUDY, VALUATION CONCEPTS AND THE CONTROL PREMIUM DISCUSSION

To understand the relationship, this section will briefly discuss (1) the function of private company valuation in the M&A process and (2) some standards of value (their usage and definition).

Valuation (including private company valuation) serves different functions and therefore the same company may be assessed differently depending on the situation in question, the purpose of the valuation and the party that executes the valuation. Distinct concepts lead to significant value differences during the course of an M&A process. A deep understanding of potential implications is crucial for the management and monitoring of an M&A transaction. Corporate valuation in the M&A process is often used for the appraisal of a comprehensible starting base for the proceedings between the parties. The appraisal of value is different from the buyer's and the seller's perspectives. According to valuation theory, the indicative bid of a potential buyer should state a value that is related to the Investment Value of the target from the viewpoint of the buyer which is different from the Fair Market Value concept generally used by a seller, see Exhibit 2.23.

Fair Market Value (FMV): the Fair Market Value of the target means "a price at which the property (here the target company) changes hands between a willing buyer and willing seller, neither being under any compulsion to buy or sell and both having reasonable knowledge of the

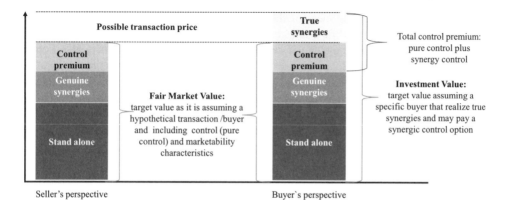

Exhibit 2.23   Valuation concepts and perspectives

relevant facts."[12] This concept of values assumes the target company as it is including control and liquidity aspects. In addition, a hypothetical transaction is assumed, so no synergetic control premium is included. The FMV constitutes the lower bound at which the seller is willing to give away his company.

Investment Value: The Investment Value means the value of the target to some particular buyer and might incorporate a synergy control premium the buyer is willing to pay for business opportunities and cash flow benefits that can be exploited post transaction. The Investment Value constitutes the upper bound a bidder is willing to pay; he only generates shareholder value by paying a price lower than the Investment Value.

How does the study set-up fit in? Only successful M&A transactions have been analyzed that end, self-evidently, with an agreement on the disposal of the target company at a certain purchase price to the acquirer. But often the purchase price does not lie in the range that is bound by the appropriate value concepts. By definition, the FMV as a hypothetical value is nearly impossible to hit in reality due to external and internal disturbances. The final price paid is first of all based on the fundamental characteristics of the target company. But as shown already, a seller who can create competition among bidders is likely to be able to achieve a higher transaction price than with only one seller in a one-on-one situation. The motives of seller and bidder influence the competitive position and their ability to negotiate the price they want to realize or are prepared to pay. The analysis shows the influence of the transaction process and explains some of the differences between initial and revised valuations and some reasons for the delimitation between valuation and selling price. As shown in Exhibit 2.24, the seller has an idea of the value of his company measured by the FMV; the bidders calculate the Investment Values as upper bounds for an indicative bid. In the course of the process, competition, selling pressure, transaction charges, trust, motives and other factors influence the seller's and buyer's value appraisal for the target company, shown in Exhibit 2.24 at the point where the revised bids are submitted: the transaction process influences the value appraisals displayed a shaded bars. As said, at this point, the value appraisal of the seller and bidder includes the influence of the transaction process and both appraisals are further influenced in the negotiation phase of the process. At the end, the price can be lower or higher or also lie within the range previously suggested by valuation analysis.

APPENDIX A   MEASUREMENT OF FACTORS

In this Appendix, the measurement of the independent variables (the influence factors) is shown. Some of these factors constitute constructs (e.g. competition, transaction charges and trust) and the Appendix formulates the items to operationalize the constructs based on the theory presented in Sections 2.2 and 2.3. In the following, the items are presented in detail and factor analyses and reliability analyses are used to: (a) select the items/confirm the pre-selected items, and (b) to compute the weight/coefficients with which the items load to the factors. The use of constructs is necessary as: (a) one cannot directly measure competition, transaction charges or trust, and (b) a reduction of data dimension for the regression model is required because only 102 ($Delta_{1EV}$) and 40 ($Delta_{2EV}$) cases are available.

---

[12] This definition was formulated by the United States Supreme Court in the Cartwright case: *United States v. Cartwright*, 411 U. S. 546, 93 S. Ct. 1713, 1716–17, 36 L. Ed. 2d 528, 73-1 U.S. Tax Cas. (CCH) 12,926 (1973) (quoting from US Treasury regulations relating to Federal estate taxes, at 26 C.F.R. sec. 20.2031-1(b)).

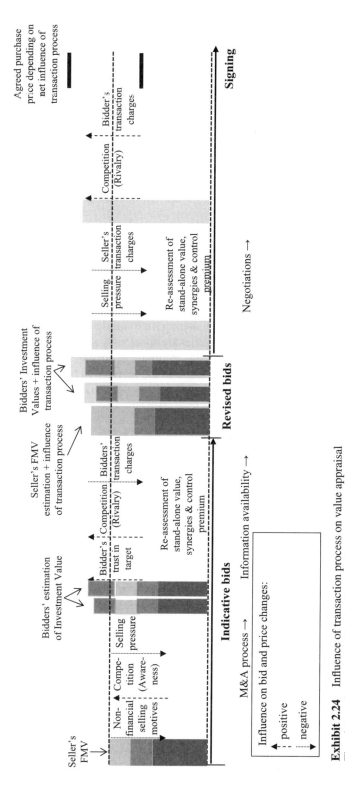

Exhibit 2.24 Influence of transaction process on value appraisal

The picture shows a possible development from valuations (bidders' Investment Values and seller's FMV) to the finally agreed purchase price. All components of the bar can change during the process as more and more information are revealed and the bidders learn more about the target's value. Furthermore the size of the bar is influence by the transaction process itself via factors which exert influence like competition, trust and motives.

I Measurement of Selling Pressure

Section 2.2.1 distinguishes different selling motives and states that selling pressure leads to an unfavourable bargaining position. Financial selling pressure is taken into account by analyzing the financial position of the selling company or the selling division (and its mother company if necessary). Furthermore, the motives stated by the management are included.

Selling pressure is gathered from the following variables:

1. Existence of financial distress (either of the target itself or the mother company) leading to a nominal variable *Financial distress* [0;1]. In the case of the 20 Mittelstand companies, the P&L and balance sheet are analyzed and financial distress is assumed to exist in either one of these cases:
   (a) Negative net income or operating profit for the last fiscal years and the next two subsequent years; or
   (b) Leverage (Debt/ Equity ratio) greater than 3.3 which constitutes the median leverage of all Mittelstand companies in Germany (analyzed in Exhibit 3.14 in Chapter 3)

      In the case of non-Mittelstand companies, a leverage ratio greater than 2.0 concludes that financial distress exists. In addition, the P&L and balance sheet data of the mother companies are analyzed, which were available in 12 of the 17 cases. In two of the five remaining cases, the financial statements of the subsidiary have already indicated financial distress. The remaining three might give room for potential errors.
2. Stated disposal motives: as financial difficulties are not directly addressed in the information memorandum, the advising bank gathers this information directly from the seller's management in the course of the preparation phase in the transaction process. The qualitative statements have been converted into a nominal variable *Lifeline motive* [0;1].

A linear combination of "Financial distress" and "Lifeline motive" forms the ordinal variable *Selling pressure* [0;1;2] with three different degrees of selling pressure included in the analysis in Section 2.5.

II Measurement of Synergies

Synergy motives may lead to possible pricing upsides compared to other bidders. It is reasonable to assume that true synergies depend on the nature of the acquirer. For example cost benefits though combined purchasing are typically associated with acquirers from the same industry, and supply efficiencies depend on the position in the value chain. This kind of fit can only be realized by strategic investors and the respective information on bidder characteristics is gathered. Concerning financial investors one can assume that those with unique idiosyncratic assets or capabilities may generate more value than their rivals can obtain when combining their own capabilities with those of the target and such an investor will be able to appropriate part of the economic value and generate abnormal returns. These capabilities include the private investor's organization, the (regional) focus, its experience in deal making and managing portfolio companies, and its network.

Hence, the existence of synergy motives is gathered, and supportive information for the existence of synergy possibilities is added:

1. Bidder motives and strategy are stated in the offering documents with respect to the indicative offer and also in the revised offer. The variable *Synergy motives* [0,1] is created and set to 1 if synergy motives are mentioned.

2. To assess the existence of synergy possibilities, some bidder characteristics are investigated. As mentioned in Section 2.2.2, some synergies can only be achieved by some of the investors, so it is necessary to distinguish between strategic and financial investors. For strategic investors, the industry of the acquirer and its position in the value chain compared to the target are investigated. This information is mainly available from internal documents: the advising investment bank summarizes and analyzes information on the bidders for the seller and makes a recommendation concerning the strategic fit of the transaction. These so-called "overview-of-bids-presentations" serve as the information basis to assess whether synergy possibilities exist for a bidder. In addition, publicly available sources like websites are used.

The same sources are used to assess synergy possibilities for financial investors as well. In this context, the focus is on the fit between the acquired company and the companies already in the portfolio. The private equity market in Germany shows a considerable variety of equity providers. There are differences with respect to fund size, financing stage (seed capital, early stage or growth stage financing) and acquisition size. In addition, they differ with respect to geographical focus and industry focus. Therefore, the type of private equity investor and the portfolio are analyzed. On the basis of the explanations in Section 2.2.2, the existence of acquirer-specific synergies is more likely when there is at least one company from the same industry sector in the portfolio, or when the private equity investor focuses on the target's country.

The variable *Synergy possibilities* [0;1;2] is created which adds up the information on the industry (same industry = "1") and the value chain (supplier, customer-relationship or competitors ="1") in the case of strategic investors and portfolio fit (at least one similar company ="1") and regional fit (main market of target company lies in the regional focus of the private equity investor = "1"). Then synergies are measured by adding up *Synergy motives* and *Synergy possibilities* to an ordinal-scaled variable *Synergies* [0;1;2;3] comprising no, low, medium, and high synergies.

With respect to motives, the existence of a hidden agenda/aspects which influence the value of target from a bidder's perspective is not considered because these aspects are hard to estimate. For example, different bidders may prefer different financing structures as some experience threats from a majority shareholder, from the ability to minimize taxes or from the financial feasibility of the transaction given the bidder's unused debt capacity. Despite some information being available in the data, hidden agenda aspects are not included in the analysis in Section 2.5.

III   Measurement of Competition

For the operationalization of competition, the intensity of competition during two phases of the process has been gathered: in the marketing phase of the process, the focus is on the target's attractiveness and the market's awareness of it. The amount of competition is measured by ratios that include the number of indicative bids or information memoranda sent out and received back. The higher these ratios, the higher the market awareness for the target is and the better is the seller's position to create competition in the transaction process. In the later DD phase of the transaction, the rivalry between bidders is monitored by ratios that include the number of parties in the data room or the number of binding offers. The higher these ratios, the weaker the bidder's position and the more competition exists in the DD phase of the transaction process.

To measure the attractiveness of the target and the rivalry among bidders, both factors are quantified with different variables. With respect to the target's market awareness, the following information has initially been gathered:

1. The number of bidders on the shortlist. This variable indicates the theoretical size of the bidders' universe and helps to interpret the IM response quote (see below). The size of the shortlist is summarized in the variable *Bidders on shortlist* [continuous];
2. The number of information memoranda which have been sent out to the bidders. This number indicates how many of the approached bidders on the shortlist have indicated interest in the target and the variable *IM sent out* [continuous] is created;
3. The number of indicative bids received (*Indicative bids*) [continuous]. The higher the ratio, the more bidders are interested in a target size and the higher the competition.

With this information, two variables are computed:

1. The ratio between the number of information memoranda sent out and the number of bidders on the shortlist. This variable is called *Market echo* [continuous] and it indicates the percentage of bidders with a general interest in the target. The higher the number the higher the target's attractiveness/market awareness;
2. The ratio between the number of indicative bids received and the number of information memoranda sent out. The variable is called *IM response-quote* [continuous]. After obtaining only very limited information on the targets in the first place, the IM gives potential acquirers the chance to obtain a completed and detailed picture about the target. Therefore, the IM response quote indicates how many bidders have a concrete interest in the selling company.

It is assumed that the higher the *Market echo* and the *IM response quote,* the higher the target's attractiveness and market's awareness of the target are. Both variables are assumed to influence the competition in the DD phase as they relate to the seller's ability to create more competition.

With respect to the rivalry between the bidders in the DD phase of the transaction process and the resulting competitive intensity, it is necessary to track the numbers of bidders in the DD phase ("number of players in the game") and examine how many of them go through the whole phase when making a binding offer for the target. To measure the rivalry aspects of the competition, the following information is gathered:

1. The number of parties in the data room. Only some of the bidders, those who passed the marketing phase, are invited to the data room to scrutinize the target company's situation in all aspects. Because of the sensitivity of information provided, these bidders are carefully selected by the selling company. A variable *Parties in DR* [continuous] is created;
2. The number of management presentations held. Although this variable is related to the number of parties in the data room, not all bidders invited to the data room are also invited to a management presentation since this presentation involves the senior management, and the attendees are therefore selected by the selling company. In addition, some bidders invited to the data room step out of the process when their findings are unsatisfactory. A variable *Management presentations* [continuous] is created;
3. The number of binding offers made. In the end, not all parties which have been given a management presentation will make a binding offer. The absolute number indicates the

seller's basis for the ongoing negotiation: the negotiating position of a seller with different binding offers at hand is stronger than for a seller who received only one binding offer. This information is summarized in the variable *Binding offers* [continuous].

With the information above, two variables are computed:

1. The ratio between the number of binding offers and the number of parties in the data room. This variable indicates how many bidders are left at the late stage of the DD phase. The higher the number, the more pass through the whole due diligence process and are very interested in the target; therefore, the greater the competition the seller was able to create between the bidders before they handed in the revised bid. The variable *Binding bid quote* is created as a percentage number [continuous];
2. The ratio between the number of binding offers and the number of indicative bids, which indicates how many interested parties went through the whole process until the negotiations. The variable *Process quote* as a percentage number [continuous] is created.

One can assume that the higher the numbers are, the greater the rivalry between the bidders and the greater the competitive intensity in the due diligence phase is. The more intensive the competition is, the greater the positive difference between indicative bids and revised bids ($Delta_{1EV}$) should be. In addition, the greater the rivalry and competitive intensity, the greater the difference is between the revised bid and price paid as they increase the competitive position of the seller in the subsequent negotiations ($Delta_{2EV}$). To quantify the factor "Competition" (explorative) factor analysis and reliability analyses are used including *"Bidders on shortlist"*, *"IM sent out"*, *"Indicative bids"*, *"Market echo"*, *"IM response quote"*, *"Management presentations"*, *"Parties in DR"*, *"Binding offers"*, *"Binding bid quote"* and *"Process quote"* (in the context of factor analysis there are called "items"). The goal of the analyses is to summarize these 10 items under the umbrella of common constructs. To detect the underlying structure in the data, factor analysis with principal axis factoring and a varimax rotation method is used. The initial solution shows two statistical factors with eigenvalues greater than one which explain 73% of the variance of the underlying variables. A comparison of the extracted communalities for the items and the analysis of the factor loadings shows that for the items *IM sent out* and *Management presentations* the loadings are relatively low compared to the others. In addition, the factor loadings were hard to interpret as both items did not load high on either the first or the second statistical factor. Furthermore, the Kaiser-Meyer-Olkin measure of sampling adequacy[13] indicates with a value of 0.53 that the proportion of variance in the variables that might be caused by underlying factors is not sufficiently high. Therefore, item to total correlations and Cronbach's alpha[14] are computed as an indication of the reliability of the scale. Those items are removed from the analysis that show a relatively low item-to-total correlation and an increased Cronbach's alpha if this item is deleted (see Exhibit 2.25).

Based on this result, the items *IM sent out* and *Management presentations* are removed from the analysis and the factor procedure is repeated. The result is shown in Exhibit 2.26.

Two statistical factors with eigenvalues significantly above 1 can be extracted. They account for 80% of the variance in the eight items. Although some information is lost, this result is

---

[13] The Kaiser-Meyer-Olkin Measure of sampling adequacy indicates the proportion of variance in the variables that might be caused by underlying factors. High values (close to 1.0) generally indicate that a factor analysis may be useful with the data. If the value is less than 0.50, the results of the factor analysis will probably not be very useful.

[14] The Cronbach's alpha is a coefficient of reliability (internal consistency) of a score as it generally increases when the intercorrelations among the items increase. Cronbach's alpha can be expressed as the ratio of the true-score and the total-score (error plus true score) variances. The closer the ratio is to one the more suitable are the items to measure the underlying score (factor).

Exhibit 2.25 Reliability of scale for construct Competition

Item	Item-to-total correlation	Cronbach's Alpha if item is deleted
Bidders on shortlist	0.468	0.610
IM sent out	0.018	0.719
Indicative bids	0.704	0.639
Market echo	0.318	0.620
IM response quote	0.370	0.639
Management presentations	0.070	0.708
Parties in DR	0.461	0.510
Binding offers	0.424	0.619
Binding bid quote	0.803	0.641
Process quote	0.351	0.665

The sample consists of 40 completed majority-ownership transactions between January 2001 and June 2006 with German target companies. The number of cases to be analyzed depends on the number of revised bids received during the transaction process, leading to 102 cases to be included in the factor analysis. The principal component analysis is used for factor extraction. The table reports the correlations and Cronbach's alpha as an indication of the reliability of the statistical factor. One can see that the items *IM sent out* and *Management presentations* both have low correlation coefficient with the other items (0.018 and 0.070) and that the Cronbach's alpha increases when these items are deleted.

good enough to work with, especially because another factor analysis with rotation could not improve the explained variance proportion.

Exhibit 2.27 shows that the first statistical factor loads especially high on the items *parties, DR, Binding Offers, Binding bid quote and Process quote* (loadings of 0.546, 0.897, 0.631 and 0.870). These items describe the competitive intensity in the DD phase of the process, and are

Exhibit 2.26 Competition – factor analysis final results

	Initial			Selected factors		
Component	Eigenvalue	% of Variance explained	Cumulative % of Variance explained	Eigenvalue	% of Variance explained	Cumulative % of Variance explained
1	3.326	46.8	46.8	3.326	46.8	46.8
2	2.441	33.3	80.1	2.441	33.3	80.1
3	0.913	9.9	90.0			
4	0.782	5.8	95.8			
5	0.654	2.2	98.0			
6	0.114	1.0	99.0			
7	0.052	0.6	99.7			
8	0.019	0.3	100.0			
Column number:	2	3	4	5	6	7

Competition
The sample consists of 40 completed majority-ownership transactions between January 2001 and June 2006 with German target companies. The number of cases to be analyzed depends on the number of revised bids received during the transaction process, leading to 102 cases to be included in the factor analysis. The principal component analysis is used for factor extraction. The table reports the results of the factor analysis for the construct *Competition* after excluding the items *IM sent out* and *Management presentations,* and it shows the percentage of variance of the items that is explained by all factors (columns 3–4) and by the two extracted statistical factors *Rivalry* and *Awareness* (the last two columns), which together explain 80% of the variance in the underlying data.

Exhibit 2.27   Factor statistics – construct Competition

Items	Factor 1 Loading	Factor 2 Loading	Cronbach's alpha	Kaiser-Meyer-Olkin	Approx. Chi-Square		Factor 1 scores	Factor 2 scores
Bidders on shortlist	0.273	0.756	Factor 1: 0.74	.736	Statistic	723.833	0.104	0.751
Indicative bids	0.361	0.868	Factor 2: 0.73		df	28.000	0.261	0.447
Market echo	0.116	0.706			Sig.	0.000	0.097	0.789
IM response quote	0.051	0.861					0.019	0.444
Parties in DR	0.546	0.315					0.208	0.114
Binding offers	0.897	0.266					0.342	0.089
Binding bid quote	0.631	0.003					0.240	0.001
Process quote	0.870	−0.331					0.331	−0.171
Column number:	2	3	4	5	6	7	8	9

The sample consists of 40 completed majority-ownership transactions between January 2001 and June 2006 with German target companies. The number of cases to be analyzed depends on the number of revised bids received during the transaction process, leading to 102 cases to be included in the factor analysis. The table reports the relation of the items and the two extracted factors. Column 2 and column 3 show how the first and the second statistical factor are related to the single items, columns 4 to column 7 indicate the quality of the factor model. The Cronbach's alpha of 0.74 and 0.73 for the first and the second statistical factor indicates a sufficient reliability of the scale. In addition, the Kaiser-Meyer Olkin measure in column 5 is above the critical value of 0.5. The significance of the Chi-Square statistic (Bartlett's test of sphericity) in column 7 shows the quality of the fit of the factor model. It tests the hypothesis that the correlation matrix is an identity matrix, which would indicate that the items are unrelated and therefore unsuitable. This test indicates the quality/fit of the factor analysis result, and the rejection of the hypothesis with small values (less than 0.05) of the significance level indicates that a factor analysis result is useful in connection with the data. The last two columns of the table show the computed factor score coefficients that are needed to compute the two new variables (*Awareness* and *Rivalry*) from the eight items that measure the construct Competition. The scores are multiplied by the cases' standardized item values to derive the factor values.

subsumed under the expression "Rivalry". The second statistical factor with loadings of 0.756, 0.868, 0.706 and 0.861 loads high on the items *Bidders on shortlist*, *Indicative bids*, *Market echo* and *IM response quote*. These items are summarized under the expression "Awareness".

Exhibit 2.27 shows in the last two columns the computed factor score coefficients. In the case of the constructs (factors) *Awareness* and *Rivalry,* these factor values constitute the values of awareness and rivalry (derived as a combination of eight items) for each case. The statistical factors and their factor values are saved as new variables *Awareness* and *Rivalry* in the data set.

IV   Measurement of Bidders' Transaction Charges

Transaction charges occur for the bidders and the seller. As one cannot measure direct costs incurred such as fees paid to the external advisors, transaction costs are measured by reference to the effort/time/manpower invested in the transaction process with different variables.

Thus it is reasonable to assume that transaction charges depend on the complexity of the target and the process and assume a positive relationship between the complexity and the transaction charges which occur for the bidder and seller. For the bidder, the complexity is measured with variables that focus on the amount of information that is presented and on the length of the process as follows:

1. The number of folders in the data room (the data rooms in the sample are physical not virtual). The information is gathered from the data room index and create the variables *DR size* [continuous];

2. The standard period (in days) the DR is open for each party and is called *DR availability* [continuous]. This information has been gathered from data room documentations, i.e. from timetables the advising investment bank creates;
3. The number of facilities as *Facilities* [continuous] of the target company. Next to the headquarters, production facilities are only taken into account in case the seller is from the manufacturing industry. For non-producing companies, all facilities except for local selling agencies are taken into account. For real estate, the number of residential buildings is counted;
4. The number of days the process lasts from receiving the information memorandum to the signing of the SPA. As only one bidder actually signs the contract, the date of the expected signing for the other bidders is used, which the bidders include in the revised bid documentation (LOI). As a proxy for the date the bidder receives the IM, the day the IM is sent out by the advising bank is used. Since only the final bidder signs an SPA, the estimated time to sign as stated in the revised offer document is taken as a proxy for the signing date. The difference between both dates is called *Days IM to signing* [continuous].

The first three variables measure the complexity of the target, the last one the complexity of the process itself. The higher the numbers are, the more complex the target/transaction is, and complexity is assumed to increase transaction charges. Transaction charges for a bidder are related to the complexity of the target, but they also depend on the diligence of the bidder and its involvement in the process. The committed manpower is measured using two different variables:

1. The number of man-days in the data room. This number is calculated using data room documentation as each person who enters the data room needs to register his entrance. As the concrete hours are not recorded, it is assumed that each registered person spends the same amount of time (a complete day) in the DR. The resulting variable is called *Man-days in DR* [continuous];
2. The number of persons involved. This information is gathered using a working parties list in which all persons involved in a deal are registered with full contact details and called *People involved* [continuous].

Both variables are positively related to transaction charges. Then factor "Transaction charges (bidder)" is quantified using factor analysis with the items "*Man-days in DR*", "*People involved*", "*DR size*", "*DR availability*", "*Facilities*" and "*Days IM to signing*". According to Exhibit 2.28, two statistical factors with an eigenvalue significantly above 1 can be extracted. They account for 75% of the variance in the six items.

Exhibit 2.29 shows that the second statistical factor loads high (factor loadings of 0.764 and 0.654) on the first two items, and that the first statistical factor loads high on the last three items (factor loadings of 0.815, 0.620 and 0.802). The item *DR size* has relatively high loadings on both factors, potentially because of its high correlation to *People involved*. The first two items both include the effort a bidder undertakes to gather information on the target. Both items are therefore subsumed under the term "*Information desire*" in the second statistical factor. The other three items describe the access to the data room and process length and characterize the complexity the bidder faces.

The last two columns in Exhibit 2.29 show the computed factor score coefficients. The statistical factors and their values are saved as the new variables *Information desire* and *Complexity* in the data set. For *Information desire* and *Complexity*, these factor values constitute

Exhibit 2.28   Transaction charges (bidder) – factor analysis final results

	Initial			Selected factors		
Component	Eigenvalue	% of Variance explained	Cumulative % of Variance explained	Eigenvalue	% of Variance explained	Cumulative % of Variance explained
1	2.497	41.6	41.6	2.5	41.6	41.6
2	1.627	33.1	74.7	1.6	33.1	74.7
3	0.887	12.6	87.3			
4	0.542	5.9	93.2			
5	0.398	4.5	97.7			
6	0.148	2.3	100.0			
Column number:	2	3	4	5	6	7

Transaction Charges

The sample consists of 40 completed majority-ownership transactions between January 2001 and June 2006 with German target companies. The number of cases to be analyzed depends on the number of revised bids received during the transaction process, leading to 102 cases to be included in the factor analysis. The principal component analysis is used for factor extraction. The table reports the results of the factor analysis for the construct *Transaction charges (bidder)* and shows the percentage of variance of the items that is explained by all factors (columns 3–4) and by the two extracted factors *Information desire* and *Complexity* (the last two columns) which together explain 74.7% of the variance of the underlying data.

Exhibit 2.29   Factor statistics – construct Transaction charges (bidder)

Items	Factor 1 loading	Factor 2 loading	Cronbach's alpha	Kaiser-Meyer-Olkin	Approx. Chi-Square		Factor 1 scores	Factor 2 scores
Man-days in DR	0.290	0.764	Factor 1: 0.70	.742	Statistic	177.708	0.116	0.496
People involved	0.328	0.654	Factor 2: 0.65		df	15.000	0.131	0.510
DR size	0.683	0.560			Sig.	0.000	0.314	0.347
DR availability	0.815	0.222					0.327	0.167
Facilities	0.620	0.365					0.248	0.275
Days IM to signing	0.802	0.095					0.321	0.072
Column number:	2	3	4	5	6	7	8	9

The sample consists of 40 completed majority-ownership transactions between January 2001 and June 2006 with German target companies. The number of cases to be analyzed depends on the number of revised bids received during the transaction process, leading to 102 cases to be included in the factor analysis. Column 2 and column 3 show how the first and the second statistical factor are related to the single items, columns 4 to column 7 indicate the quality of the factor model. The Cronbach's alpha of 0.70 and 0.65 for the first and the second statistical factor indicates a sufficient reliability of the scale for the first factor *Complexity* and acceptable reliability for the second factor *Information desire*. In addition, the Kaiser-Meyer Olkin measure in column 5 is above the critical value of 0.5. The significance of the Chi-Square statistic (Bartlett's test of sphericity) in column 7 shows the quality of the fit of the factor model. It tests the hypothesis that the correlation matrix is an identity matrix, which would indicate that the items are unrelated and therefore unsuitable. This test indicates the quality/fit of the factor analysis result, and the rejection of the hypothesis with small values (less than 0.05) of the significance level indicates that a factor analysis result is useful in connection with the data. The last two columns of the table show the computed factor score coefficients that are needed to compute the two new variables (*Information desire* and *Complexity*) from the six items that measure the construct *Transaction charges (bidder)*. The scores are multiplied by the cases' standardized item values to derive the factor values.

the values of information desire and complexity (derived as a combination of six items) for each case. The statistical factors and its factor values are saved as new variables "Information desire" and "Complexity" in the data set.

To measure the transaction charges for a seller, the following variables are gathered:

1. The number of days of the total process (from start of the beauty contest with financial advisors to signing). This number measures the complexity from the seller's point of view starting with the preparation phase. As a proxy for the start of the beauty contest the date on which the advising bank has been invited to the seller is used. The variable *Process length* [continuous] is created;
2. The number of people to handle. This number counts all people involved in the process: the people the respective bidder brings into the process and all advisors to the seller. This information has been gathered from the working group list that is prepared by the seller's advisor and contains all contact details of (a) parties involved and (b) people involved with these parties. The variable *People to handle* [continuous] is created, which increases the complexity of the process.

The incurred transaction charges for the seller are assumed to increase the seller's pressure to close the deal in the negotiation phase and therefore the two variables are used to analyze the influence of the seller's pressure on $Delta_{2ev}$. A linear combination of both variables is formed and equally weighted to end up with a variable *Transaction charges (seller)* [continuous].

V   Measurement of Trust

The existence of trust is assumed when either the parties know each other through a business relationship or a stakeholding before the transaction or one party has a special reputation. Therefore, the following information is gathered:

1. The existence of a business relationship: it is investigated whether either the seller or the buyer is a supplier, a customer, or if another relationship like a joint venture or partnership agreement exists. No distinction is made as to who is the customer and who is the supplier. With respect to Joint Ventures (JV) or other partnerships, only those JV or partnerships are included where both parties are equally participating.[15] This information is gathered mainly by analyzing the summaries of indicative offers the seller's advisor prepares, as this kind of information is recorded to better assess the single bidders. Knowledge in the case of a supplier, customer, JV or other relationship is assumed to exist leading to the variable *Business relation* [0;1];
2. The years of relation (*Years* [continuous]): in case of an existing relationship, the number of years this relationship existed has been gathered. It seems reasonable to assume that the longer the relationship exists, the better the partners know each other. In the analysis in Section 2.5, the variable *Years of BR* [continuous] is built as the product of the variables *Business relation* and *Years*;

---

[15] The argument with respect to influence is on the one hand related to trust and trustworthyl knowledge can only be assumed when one partner is not dominant over another. On the other hand, knowledge lowers information costs and can also be assumed when the bidder has a dominant position in a JV or partnership. However, this differentiation would not lead to any solid hypotheses about the amount of influence.

3. The stake of a bidder in the target: a stake may result in a competitive advantage compared to other bidders that is explained by lower information costs. It is measured, whether the bidder has a stake in the target or not, leading to the variable *Stake* [0;1].[16]

Altogether, a linear combination of *Years of BR* and *Stake* is used to quantify the variable *Knowledge*.

Concerning reputation, this factor is measured using four variables for the seller and two variables for the bidder [only No. 1 and No. 2]. The management and the company are differentiated to quantify reputation; therefore the reputation of the company itself is gathered in addition to information on the senior management, i.e. if it is experienced and well-known in the industry. The following variables are measured with respect to the company:

1. The market share of the company: information on the market share is gathered with focus on the companies' core region(s) or core technology leadership, i.e. in a case where a seller has a 30% market share in Germany and only 1% in North America only the 30% in Germany is taken into account instead of computing a weighted share. For a company with a core technology, the weighted sum of market share in the regions it distributes the product is computed. The information is gathered for the seller from the IM which includes a detailed description of the market position. For the bidder, this information is gathered from offer documents that include a detailed description of the bidder's enterprise and publicly available information. For financial sponsors as acquirers, an implied market share is calculated as a ratio between the number of companies a bidder has in its relevant portfolios and the number of all portfolio companies all relevant bidders have. The relevant bidders stem from all bidders which appear in one of the 40 transactions, as they seem to build the potential private equity universe for the mid-cap companies offered. Portfolio companies are only relevant if they relate to the target region or industry. Finally, the variable *Market share* [continuous] is created for the seller and the bidders;

2. The reputation the companies are credited with. This is a subjective estimate and the information thereon has been gathered from the presentations the advising investment bank prepared for the seller, e.g. the overview-of bids-presentation which presents the complete offer terms of all bidders and also the assessment of the potential fit to the target. One aspect of this fit is the credibility of the bidder which is categorized as low, medium or high leading to a variable *Reputation bidder* [1;2;3]. The assessment of the seller's reputation is also drawn from offer documents and comments from the bidders on the credibility of the seller leading to a variable *Reputation seller* [1;2;3]. For the analysis in Section 2.5 the variable *Market leadership seller* [continuous] is created as a product of *Market share* and *Reputation seller* and the variable *Market leadership bidder* [continuous] as a product of *Market share* and *Reputation bidder*.

3. The experience of the top management (only) of the selling company in years. This information is gathered from the IM with respect to (a) the years of experience in the company as an average of all top managers (*Years in firm* [continuous]) and (b) with respect to its experience in the industry as an average of all top managers (*Years in industry* [continuous]. Both variables serve as an indication for professional competences as indicators for (professional) reputation;

---

[16] Despite possible influence on the seller's or the bidder's trust, the stake that a seller might have in a bidding company is not analyzed due to missing information.

Exhibit 2.30   Trust (bidder) – factor analysis final results

Component	Initial			Selected factors		
	Eigenvalue	% of Variance explained	Cumulative % of Variance explained	Eigenvalue	% of Variance explained	Cumulative % of Variance explained
1	2.100	40.8	40.8	2.1	40.8	40.8
2	0.903	15.4	56.2			
3	0.928	15.5	71.7			
4	0.734	12.2	83.9			
5	0.591	9.9	93.8			
6	0.375	6.2	100.0			
Column number:	2	3	4	5	6	7

Trust
The sample consists of 40 completed majority-ownership transactions between January 2001 and June 2006 with German target companies. The number of cases to be analyzed depends on the number of revised bids received during the transaction process, leading to 102 cases to be included in the factor analysis. The principal component analysis is used for factor extraction. The table reports the results of the factor analysis for the construct *Trust (bidder)* and shows the percentage of variance of the items that is explained by all statistical factors (columns 3–4) and by the extracted statistical factor *Reputation* (the last two columns) which explains 40.8% of the variance of the underlying data.

Exhibit 2.31   Factor statistics – construct Trust (bidder)

Items	Factor loading	Cronbach's alpha	Kaiser-Meyer-Olkin	Approx. Chi-square		Factor scores
Years of BR	−0.290	0.581	.572	Statistic	87.296	−0.143
Market leadership	0.795			df	15.000	0.392
Years in firm	0.754			Sig.	0.000	0.372
Years in industry	0.748					0.368
Manager reputation	0.412					0.203
Attitude	−0.125					−0.062
Column number:	2	3	4	5	6	7

Trust
The sample consists of 40 completed majority-ownership transactions between January 2001 and June 2006 with German target companies. The number of cases to be analyzed depends on the number of revised bids received during the transaction process, leading to 102 cases to be included in the factor analysis. The table reports the relation of the items and the extracted factor. Column 2 shows how the statistical factor is related to the single items, column 3 to column 6 indicate the quality of the factor model. The Cronbach's alpha of 0.58 indicates a somehow sufficient reliability of the scale for the statistical factor *Reputation*. In addition, the Kaiser-Meyer Olkin measure in column 4 is above the critical value of 0.5. The significance of the Chi-Square statistic (Bartlett's test of sphericity) in column 6 shows the quality of the fit of the factor model. It tests the hypothesis that the correlation matrix is an identity matrix, which would indicate that the items are unrelated and therefore unsuitable. This test indicates the quality/fit of the factor analysis result, and the rejection of the hypothesis with small values (less than 0.05) of the significance level indicates that a factor analysis result is useful in connection with the data. The last column of the table shows the computed factor score coefficients that are needed to compute the new variable (*Reputation*) from the four items. The scores in column 7 are multiplied by the cases' standardized item values to derive the factor values. The construct *Trust (bidder)* is built as a linear combination of the construct *Reputation* together with the variables *Attitude* and *Years of BR*.

Exhibit 2.32 The set of variables included in the analyses

Factor / variable	Value	Description	Influence on	
			$Delta_{1EV}$	$Delta_{2EV}$
Selling pressure	0,1,2	Financial distress + Lifeline motive	−	−
Financial distress	0;1	'1' if financial metrics are worse, 0 otherwise		
Lifeline motive	0;2	'1' if stated disposal pressure 0 otherwise		
Synergies	0;1;2;3	Synergy motives + synergy possibilities	+	+
Synergy motives	0;1	'1' if stated synergy motives, 0 otherwise		
Synergy possibilities	0;1;2	SI: industry + value chain or PE: regional fit		
Regional fit (PE)	0;1	'1' if main market of target company lies in the regional focus PE		
Portfolio fit (PE)	0;1	'1' if at least one similar company in the portfolio		
Same industry (SI)	0;1	'1' if seller and bidder same industry		
Value chain (SI)	0;1	'1' if customer, supplier, JV or competitor		
Competition	Construct	See Exhibit 2.27	+	+
Market echo	Continuous	IM sent out / Bidders on shortlist		
IM response quote	Continuous	Indicative bids/ IM sent out		
Bidders on shortlist	Continuous	Number of bidders on shortlist		
IM sent out	Continuous	Number of information memoranda sent out		
Indicative bids	Continuous	Number of indicative bids received		
Binding bid quote	Continuous	Binding offers / Parties in DR		
Process quote	Continuous	Binding offers / Indicative bids		
Parties in DR	Continuous	Number of bidders in data room		
Management presentations	Continuous	Number of management presentations given		
Binding offers	Continuous	Number of revised offers received		
Transaction charges (bidder)	Construct	See Exhibit 2.29	−	+
Man-days in DR	Continuous	Cumulative number of days bidders spend in the data room		
People involved	Continuous	Number of people on the bidder's site involved		
Complexity	Construct	a_1 DR availability + a_2 Facilities + a_3 Day IM to signing		

(continued)

Exhibit 2.32 (*Continued*)

Factor / variable	Value	Description	Influence on Delta$_{1EV}$	Delta$_{2EV}$
DR size	Continuous	Number of folders in data room		
DR availability	Continuous	Standard period in days the data room is open		
Facilities	Continuous	Number of facilities except local agencies		
Days IM to signing	Continuous	Number of days the process takes from receiving the information memorandum to the estimated signing of the SPA		−
Transaction charges (seller)	Linear combination	0.5*Process length + 0.5*People to handle		
Process length	Continuous	Number of days from start of the beauty contest to signing SPA		
People to handle	Continuous	Number of all people involved in process		
Trust (bidder)	Construct	See Exhibit 2.31	+	+
Knowledge	Linear combination	[0.5*]Years of BR + [0.5*Stake]		
Years of BR	Continuous	Business relation * Years		
Business relation	0;1	'1' if customer, supplier, or JV at equal parts		
Years	Continuous	Number of years the business relationship exists		
Stake	0;1	'1' if bidder owns a stake in target before deal (excluded in Chapter 2.5 due to lack of cases)		
Reputation	Construct	a$_1$ Market leadership seller+ a$_2$ Years in firm + a$_3$ Manager reputation		
Market leadership seller	Linear combination	Market share (seller)* Reputation seller		
Market leadership bidder	Linear combination	Market share (bidder)* Reputation bidder		
Market share (measured for seller and bidder)	Continuous	Share in main market or main product or number of companies in portfolios compared to the number of portfolio companies of the relevant bidder set		
Reputation seller	1;2,3	Estimate of seller reputation 1 = low, 2 = medium (normal), 3 = high		
Reputation bidder	1;2,3	Estimate of bidder reputation 1 = low, 2 = medium (normal), 3 = high		
Years in firm	Continuous	Average number of years the top management is in the firm		
Years in industry	Continuous	Average number of years the top management is in the industry		
Manager reputation	1;2,3	Estimate of reputation of selling management, 1 = low, 2 = medium (normal), 3 = high		
Attitude	1;2;3	Estimate of attitude of seller's management towards bidder, 1 = negative, 2 = medium (normal), 3 = positive		
Owner-manager	0;1	'1' if owner is active manager in the company	+	+

4. The reputation of the seller's management, which is again subjective and gathered during the transaction process from discussion with the bidders. A "normal level" of reputation is assumed and only in the case of explicit comments on the quality of the management (either positive or negative) is this assessment categorized with "1" (negative comments – low reputation) or "3" (positive comments – high reputation), in contrast to the normal level "2", to compute the variable *Manager reputation*.

In addition to the information above, the attitude of the target's management with respect to a bidder is analyzed. This information is gathered from the advising investment bank directly from the management or company owner, or the selling company (in case of divestment). This information is categorized in the variable *Attitude* [1;2;3] where a "normal" level ("2") has been assumed again and only in case of positive or negative comments were category "3" or "1" respectively used.

To quantify the factor "Trust (bidder)", six items (*years of BR, Market leadership, Years in firm, Years in industry, Manager reputation and Attitude*) are included into the factor analysis. According to Exhibit 2.30, one statistical factor with an eigenvalue significantly above 1 can be extracted, which accounts for only 41% of the variance in the six items.

The statistics in Exhibit 2.31 show that the extracted factor loads high on *Market leadership, Years in firm, Years in industry* and *Manager reputation*, which are components/an expression of reputation. As the remaining items *Years of BR* and *Attitude* are not represented by the statistical factor "Reputation", *Trust (bidder)* is implemented as a combination of the construct Reputation measured by the analyses in Exhibit 2.31 and the variables *Years of BR* and *Attitude*.

This quantification should capture much of the influence that the linkage of owner and company exerts via management strategy and style. Management should be more committed and show a more positive attitude. In addition, the linkage should foster long-running business relationships and improve the reputation of the managers and the firm. The existence of trust on the part of the bidder should increase his confidence in realizing the desired transaction outcome. Hence, trust should positively influence the willingness to negotiate on price upsides, offer an up-trade on the indicative bid after being in the management presentation, and lead to increased confidence in the target's management.

Exhibit 2.32 provides an overview of all variables that are included in the study.

3

Valuing Private Companies – the PCD

Chapter 2 focuses on the transaction process and show that acquisitions involving private companies are different from those involving public companies, not only because the shares are not eligible for public trading but especially because the relation between owner and company within independent private firms leads to characteristics of these firms that influence the transaction outcome (the purchase price). This chapter takes a closer look at the listing criterion and shows if and why a missing stock exchange notation leads to valuation and price difference when private companies are acquired compared to public companies. According to empirical evidence provided later, the resulting PCD is a crucial important discount factor for the valuation of a majority business interest in a private firm. Therefore the PCD is especially important in the context of M&A transactions when talking about selling/buying a controlling ownership interest or even the complete firm.

The chapter explains the PCD in the context of other discounts and distinguishes it from the well-known "DLL" (Discount for the Lack of Liquidity) for minority ownership interests and its empirical evidence.

Furthermore, the chapter shows that the PCD differs between market environments and changes over time, therefore it provides empirical evidence for four different markets: Germany, the US, Europe, and the UK for the years 1997 to mid-2011. The focus outside the US tries to overcome application problems non-US analysts have with empirical results from US studies. Given the origin of the author, the German market is described in more detail. For quick reading the reader can focus on the empirical results for the region they are interested in, although some insights on the German market may also be interesting for cross-border application.

The chapter discusses the application of the PCD in the context of different valuation methodologies and standards of value but does not discuss in depth any valuation models. For this, the reader should refer to standard literature available, e.g. by Pratt and other authors.

As the study is not comprehensive and regular updates on the PCD are useful, the chapter describes at the end how the reader can conduct his own study on the PCD, gives tips for handling insufficient data, selection of multiples, modelling the regression equation and other problems one faces when setting up an empirical study.

3.1 LIQUIDITY VS. MARKETABILITY

Empirical literature often differentiates between two terms when talking about liquidity meaning marketability and liquidity. The distinction depends on the base of comparison depending on which respective discount is taken (Pratt and Niculita, 2008). Measurement of a discount for the lack of marketability is related to a non-control event (i.e. the sale of small block of securities on a public market) and therefore marketability denotes the right to sell an asset in an established and efficient capital market (public or private), within a reasonable time, with relatively low transaction costs, and with minimal effect on that security's public market price.

In contrast to that, measurement of a discount for lack of liquidity is related to a control event, i.e. an asset or stock sales or merger and therefore liquidity refers to the ability to readily convert an asset, business, business ownership interest or security into cash without significant loss of principal.

For the purpose of the book, the terms are used interchangeably and define liquidity/marketability as "the ability to convert a business ownership interest to cash quickly, with minimum transaction and administration costs and with a high degree of certainty of realizing the expected amount of net proceeds" (Pratt and Niculita, 2008, p. 417). A discount caused by the lack of liquidity/marketability will be referred to as "DLL" (Discount for the Lack of Liquidity) as the term is widely recognized among business appraisers.

3.2 OVERVIEW OF DISCOUNTS AND PREMIUMS

Discounts and premiums can be applied to different levels of value. The DLL belongs, as well as the discount for the lack of control, to the shareholder level discounts because it reflects characteristics of ownership. In contrast to that, entity level (or company level) discounts apply to the whole entity, for example discounts for key personnel, for pending litigations, or environmental liabilities. These affect the whole company and are unrelated to ownership characteristics. Exhibit 3.1 shows the traditional level of value overview and how the DLL relates to other shareholder level discounts. Only the publicly traded equivalent or stock market value shown in Exhibit 3.1 reflects real liquidity as an owner has the right to sell the share in a timely fashion and receive cash within a few business days. The term marketable minority interest is directly applicable to it although the discussion is ongoing if the publicly traded value may represent a control value (see discussion later).

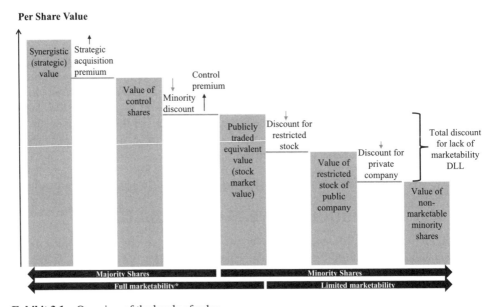

Exhibit 3.1 Overview of the levels of value
*A control share in a private company is also subject to a marketability discount, see Section 3.3 and Exhibit 3.21 in Section 3.8.1.

For shareholder level discounts, it is practical for valuation advisors to use as a starting level of value either the level of control shares or the minority marketable value. This is because empirical data for both levels of value are available, in contrast to a minority non-marketable level. Control over a company is commonly assumed at an ownership level of more than 50% as this level is sufficient to decide most matters of the company. Further thresholds exist, which differ with respect to the rights they trigger and vary across countries. In Germany a 75% of shareholders vote is necessary to remove members of the advisory board or in relation to constitutional amendments. In the US, an 80% holding is required to allow a holding company to file consolidated corporate tax returns with a subsidiary. The different ownership levels with increasing rights imply incremental value attributable to such a position, but in context of the discount discussion, the "classical" 51% threshold is used when talking about control. For the application of discounts, the level of control is considered before marketability because, depending on the degree of control, the size of the DLL is different and also the methodology to quantify the discount.

Solid empirical evidence for the existence of the DLL is only available for minority ownership interests. This is because public market data are available to compare public share prices to restricted share price or share price in private transactions (restricted stock studies and pre-IPO (initial public offerings) studies discussed later). Due to missing benchmarks, such comparison is not possible for majority ownership interests. The only possibility is to compare multiples achieved in majority ownership transactions with private target companies to multiples achieved in majority ownership transactions with public targets. At the control level, the resulting difference in multiples is usually a discount and called the Private Company Discount (PCD). The PCD is not a discount for missing liquidity only, but includes other factors that drive valuation differences between private and public target companies in M&A transactions.[1] As the DLL is not measurable directly, some researchers and practitioners state that it is not possible to classify a controlling ownership interest as marketable or non-marketable. Therefore, the next question to answer would be:

3.3   IS A DISCOUNT FOR THE LACK OF LIQUIDITY FOR A CONTROLLING OWNERSHIP INTERESTS NECESSARY?

How marketable is a controlling interest in a private and also a public company? A controlling interest can be considered as marketable because it is generally possible to sell it but it cannot be regarded as marketable in the sense of a publicly traded minority interest. In the latter case, cash is available within a number of business days whereas it can take months to sell a controlling ownership interest. Some authors are of the opinion that a control ownership interest is never marketable independently whether the controlling interest is held in a publicly traded or a private firm.

They argue with transaction costs and timing to sell and emphasize that is not possible to call a broker and receive cash within three business days. This level of liquidity can only be attached to a marketable minority interest and is not possible with controlling ownership interests, even if the interest is held in a publicly traded stock. Therefore they argue that a marketability

---

[1] Furthermore, the control premium can also be measured at the control level (and only at the control level). Control premiums are observed in the public securities markets with regularity as publicly traded companies are acquired by or merge with other companies. The control premium is measured by the (normal) premium in pricing paid for controlling interests of publicly traded companies relative to their previously unaffected, freely trading minority interest pricing, five days before announcement of the transaction. In contrast, the direct measurement of a minority discount in the marketplace is not possible.

discount for a private controlling interest should not be applied. As a consequence, no discount for lack of liquidity should be applied to a controlling interest in a private firm. The argument seems somehow reasonable but the necessity to also account for a DLL in control ownership situations stems from three different issues faced by a controlling owner who wishes to liquidate a controlling interest:

1. The uncertainty involved in the transaction process, which relates mainly to the time until the completion of the transaction and the actual sales price to be realized.
2. The costs associated with the selling process (e.g. legal costs, auditors' fees, brokerage and transaction costs). These costs include those for accountants associated with preparing and receiving necessary audits for financial statements. In addition, legal documentation needs to be prepared, e.g. the SPA, third parties advising the transaction require substantial payments for their services and, in case an IPO is planned, flotation costs arise for printing prospectuses, stock exchange admissions, as well as costs for the advising bank and bookrunner in the IPO.
3. The inability to hypothecate, meaning to use the stake as collateral for a bank loan.

Furthermore, one cannot deny the empirical evidence on discounts for private companies. In prior years, most studies focused on minority ownership interests and therefore professionals could state that there was no empirical evidence to support a liquidity discount for a controlling interest. During the last few years research on discounts for majority ownership interests has increased significantly and several empirical studies show that private companies are almost always acquired at lower valuation multiples than are otherwise comparable companies.

3.4 DISCOUNTS IN PRAXIS

For a correct application of discounts and premiums, the analyst needs to understand three issues:

1. He needs to understand the standards of value and the level of value. That means, does the value base he uses assume a control or minority value and does it include marketability characteristics or not? In this context the analyst also needs to understand which valuation methodologies can be used to arrive at a certain standard of value and how the valuation methodology affects the resulting level of value.
2. He needs to understand the characteristics of the value of the subject interest and why they differ from the characteristics inherent in the base value.
3. He needs to understand the content, context, and results of empirical studies done on discounts for minority ownership interests and majority ownership interests.

Why is this crucial? Obviously, without careful assessment and understanding of the value base and valuation methodologies, the application of discounts becomes a rough guess and subject to errors. Furthermore, in valuation reports, he must be able to state the reasons why a discount (or a premium) is applied and the empirical evidence in deriving the discount.

The following chapters give an overview of the empirical evidence that exists on the DLL for minority ownership interest (Section 3.5) and majority ownership interests (Section 3.6). Then levels of value and standards of value are discussed in Section 3.7 and Section 3.8 shows which valuation methodology leads to which level of value.

3.5   DLL FOR MINORITY INTERESTS

Different streams of research focus on empirical evidence for the DLL for minority interests. As results from bond markets are difficult to apply to equity markets and evidence for the real estate market is relatively weak, most prominent evidence comes from equity markets, separated into analyses of cross-section return differences and controlled differences (see Exhibit 3.2).

3.5.1   Cross-Sectional Differences

Evidence for the DLL, which examines cross-sectional differences between stocks, compares the returns generated by investors who invest in publicly traded companies to those of private equity investors, and then tries to attribute the return differences to liquidity. Private equity and venture capital investors provide capital to private businesses and receive a stake in exchange. However, a stake in a private company is illiquid. This fact can be used to determine the value of liquidity by comparing the returns earned by private equity investors to those of an investment in a publicly traded company. Following this approach, Ljungqvist and Richardson (2003) document excess returns of about 5% to 8% for private equity investors in comparison to the aggregated public equity market. The authors argue that this excess return is potential compensation for holding a 10-year illiquid investment. Das, Jagannathan, and Sarin (2003) analyze more than 50,000 financing rounds in over 23,000 firms and compute the expected exit multiples and gains from the private equity investments of venture capital and buy-out firms. They find that financing in late-stage companies results in private equity discounts of about 11%; for early-stage firms, the discounts are 80%. Since early-stage firms are more illiquid than late-stage companies, they conclude that differences are attributable to liquidity.

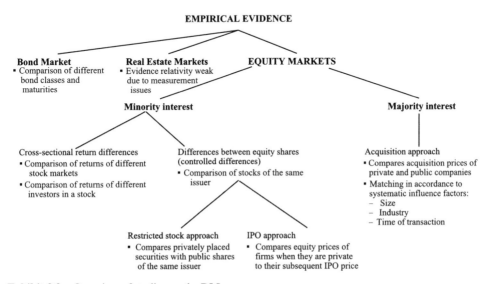

Exhibit 3.2   Overview of studies on the DLL

3.5.2 Controlled Differences

The main drawback of studies which compare cross-sectional differences is that they are potentially biased due to omitted variables and systematic differences between companies which are not controlled for. For example, a venture capitalist demands higher returns in early-stage companies as he undertakes substantial monitoring and mentoring, which requires costly resources. Therefore, if differences in return are used to examine the impact of liquidity, it has to be taken into consideration that these differences can also be caused by other factors.

One approach to addressing this problem is to compare stocks with a different degree of liquidity issued by the same company. Most recognized studies in this context are restricted stock studies and IPO studies. Both compare stocks with a different degree of liquidity issued by the same company. The main advantage of this procedure is that the company-specific characteristics are constant and therefore do not need to be controlled for. Therefore, price differences should mainly be attributable to liquidity.

3.5.3 Restricted Stock Studies

The restricted stock approach compares the prices of restricted or unregistered stocks of publicly quoted firms to the trading prices in public markets on the same day. There are three main reasons why companies whose stocks are publicly traded, have outstanding share with some restrictions: (1) at the time of the IPO not all shares have been registered for trading by the underwriter or registered but restricted from trading during a lockup period, (2) a company issues share that are used as payment in acquisitions, and (3) companies raise capital with private placements of shares to institutional investors without registering.

Registered/restricted stocks are typically placed at a discount. If these stocks only differ in marketability, the discount can be attributed to the lack of liquidity. Some of the most essential studies are presented in the following paragraph; their results can be found in Exhibit 3.3 below.

Study Results

The first restricted stock study was conducted by the US Securities and Exchange Commission (SEC), and it consists of 398 observations from 1966 to 1969. It takes into account the market

Study	Number of transactions	Reporting dates	Median discount	Mean discount
SEC Institutional Investor	398	1966-1969	24%	26%
Gelman	89	1968-1970	33%	33%
Moroney	148	1968-1972	34%	35%
Maher	33	1969-1973	33%	35%
Trout	60	1968-1972	n/a	34%
Stryker/ Pittock (Standard Reseach Consultants)	28	1978-1982	45%	n/a
Willamette Management Association	33	1981-1984	31%	n/a
Silber	69	1981-1988	n/a	34%
Hall/ Polacek Study (FMV Opinions, Inc.)	100+	1979-1992	n/a	23%
Management Planning, Inc.	49	1980-1990	29%	28%
Johnson	72	1991-1995	n/a	20%
Achwald (Columbia Financial Advisors (pre-1997))	23	1996-1997	14%	21%
Aschwald (Columbia Financial Advisors (post-1997))	15	1997-1998	9%	13%
FMV Opinions Database	475	1980-2005	19%	22%
LiquiStat Database	41	2005-2006	32%	31%

In 1990, the SEC issued Rule 144A: instead of registration of restricted stock transactions, qualified institutional investors are allowed to trade unregistered 31% (restricted) securities among themselves

21% Effectively April 1997, the SEC reduces the required holding period for restricted securities from two to one year

Exhibit 3.3   Results of restricted stock studies

in which the unrestricted stock trades. The four categories are: "New York Stock Exchange (NYSE)", "American Stock Exchange (AMEX)", "OTC reporting companies", and "OTC non-reporting companies". It becomes evident that discounts on restricted stocks are the lowest for NYSE-listed stocks and increase for the other three categories. Since the abovementioned groups act as a proxy for market efficiency, the results reveal the impact of market efficiency on discounts. *Ceteris paribus*, investors prefer to hold a restricted stock, which is traded on a more efficient market after the restriction period. Moreover, the data is grouped by annual sales volume as a proxy for size. Firms with the largest sales volumes tend to have the smallest discounts, whereas companies with the smallest sales volumes are subject to the highest discounts. On average, the discount for restricted stocks found by the SEC study was about 26%. However, the average is not meaningful due to the high variance. Subsequent studies, e.g. from Management Planning (reported in Reilly and Schweihs (2000)) and Johnson (1999), also find a relationship between size and discounts. The heavily cited studies from Silber (1991) are consistent with these results. Silber (1991) uses the data of private placements by 69 companies from 1981 until 1988. The result is an average discount of 34% for restricted stocks. The standard deviation is around 24%, with a maximum discount of 84% and a minimum discount about −13%, which in fact means a premium of 13%. The high variance indicates that the average discount has to be handled with care. More importantly, Silber (1991) shows that factors other than liquidity influence the discounts for restricted stocks. Firms with higher revenues, earnings, and market value of equity are associated with lower discounts.

Determining the Appropriate Discounts for the Lack of Marketability with Restricted Stock Studies: Study Selection and Assessment

In the US, registration requirements are regulated by the SEC. In 1990 the SEC amended the registration requirement for restricted stock transactions. Since then, securities that are privately placed with accredited investors (rather than offered to the public at large) do not have to be registered with the SEC. Instead, these shares cannot be resold in the open market for a two-year holding period under the new SEC Rule 144A. Effective from April 1997, the SEC amended the holding period from two years to one year.

The amendments of the SEC have implications for determining the appropriate discounts. For this purpose, appraisers have often quoted restricted stock studies conducted prior to the Rule 144A amendment in 1990. With the changing requirements, the discounts for restricted stock have been declining due to increased liquidity, especially after the shortening of the restricted stock holding periods beginning April 1997. According to Exhibit 3.3, prior to 1990, the discounts ranged from 33–35%; since 1990 the discounts have been lower. The only study available after the change of holding period shows a significantly reduced discount of 13%.

Therefore, for determining the appropriate DLL, studies using data after 1990 are not relevant for privately held stocks because they reflect the increased liquidity and the market for restricted securities. This liquidity increase is not present in privately held securities.

Furthermore, when restrictions are lifted, the share can be traded in an active public market. Every market participant is aware of this. On the contrary, privately-held companies may be effectively restricted for a much longer period of time and it is impossible to predict if these companies will ever become marketable. From this viewpoint, the derived discounts may be too small.

Other drawbacks exist to using restricted stock studies to determine the DLL: the results of restricted stock studies may be distorted by a self-selection bias. Firms which issue restricted stocks are substantially different from companies that do not do so. In addition, investors with whom equity is privately placed may be providing other services to the firm, for which the discount is compensation. From this viewpoint, the discounts reported in Exhibit 3.3 seem to overestimate the appropriate DLL.

To find the amount of discount that truly results from the lack of marketability, Hertzel and Smith (1993) use a comparison of unregistered with registered private placements. This solves the problem that the level of services provided is different between private and public placements.

Following this approach, Hertzel and Smith use a sample of 106 private placements from 1980 until 1987. They report a median discount of 13.26% across private placements. More importantly, the discount for restricted stocks is 13.5% higher than for their unrestricted counterparts. In a sample of 88 private placements from 1990 to 1995, Bajaj, Denis, Ferris, and Sarin (2001) find an incremental effect of marketability which amounts to 7.23%. Since differences in firm characteristics are controlled, this once again indicates that the DLL determined by using restricted stock studies is too high and that the lack of liquidity of these securities is only one of several factors which determine the discounts.

The comparison of registered and unregistered placements mitigates the overestimation.

However, this approach suffers from another shortcoming. Unlike the method of the standard restricted stock approach, different companies are compared with each other. This makes it necessary to control for additional influence factors; especially because empirical evidence reveals differences between restricted and unrestricted stock placements.

To conclude, the changing liquidity of restricted stocks makes data before 1990 more appropriate to estimate the DLL. At first glance, the study results seem to underestimate the DLL, but it should be kept in mind that the validity of the results depends strongly on the accuracy of controlling for extraneous factors like the service level provided by investors within private placements.

3.5.4   Initial Public Offerings (IPOs)

The IPO approach compares the equity prices of firms when they are private to their subsequent IPO prices. Since shares become fungible after an IPO, differences in price can be deemed to be an illiquidity discount.

Study Results

Emory has undertaken a series of 10 IPO studies 1980–2000 and adjusted the results of all studies in 2002. The methodology of all studies remained the same: the private stock transactions had to be carried out five months before a subsequent IPO in a company which was financially healthy (no development stage, no history of operating losses, no bargain offerings under USD 5 per share). In this series of studies, Emory found remarkably consistent discounts over the period of 1985 to 1997, ranging between 41% and 47% (see Exhibit 3.4).

Willamette Management Associates reports median discounts ranging from 28% in 1999 to 73% in 1984. The discount is calculated by comparing the P/E multiples of transactions occurring in the three years prior to the IPO with the public offering P/E multiples. Changes in industry P/E multiples are controlled. The results can be found in Exhibit 3.5. They are quite similar to those of Emory. Emory stopped doing studies after 2000, whereas Willamette Management Associates updated their study for 2001 and 2002. But in 2001 and 2002 there

Exhibit 3.4   A summary of Emory's adjusted IPO studies

Study number	Sample period	Number of transactions	Median discount	Mean discount
1	1980–1981	12	68%	59%
2	1985–1986	19	43%	43%
3	1987–1989	21	43%	38%
4	1989–1990	17	40%	46%
5	1990–1992	30	33%	34%
6	1992–1993	49	43%	45%
7	1994–1995	45	47%	45%
8	1995–1997	84	41%	43%
9	1997–2000 (only dot-com)	51	68%	63%
10	1997–2000	266	52%	50%
All transactions (excl. dot-com)		543	47%	46%

were too few private transactions for the study to be statistically meaningful. Nevertheless, Emory and Willamette Management Associates provide strong evidence on the size of the discount for the lack of marketability.

A more recent study on the DLL is a database of Valuation Advisors (Lack of Marketability Discount Study™) that compares the IPO prices to the pre-IPO common stock price, common stock option, and convertible preferred stock price and contains data on over 3,800 transactions from 1995 to the present with a monthly update. The database is available online from Business Valuation Resources under www.bv.marketdata.com.

Exhibit 3.5   A summary of Willamette Management Associates IPO studies

Sample period	Number of transactions	Median discount	Mean discount	Standard deviation
1975–78	31	34%	53%	59%
1979	17	56%	63%	30%
1980–82	113	48%	57%	30%
1983	214	50%	61%	35%
1984	33	43%	73%	64%
1985	25	41%	43%	44%
1986	74	39%	47%	44%
1987	40	37%	44%	50%
1988	19	42%	52%	30%
1989	19	47%	50%	19%
1990	23	31%	49%	43%
1991	34	24%	32%	38%
1992	75	42%	52%	43%
1993	110	47%	53%	34%
1994	48	32%	42%	50%
1995	66	32%	59%	76%
1996	22	32%	44%	45%
1997	44	28%	35%	47%
1998	21	35%	49%	43%
1999	28	26%	28%	45%
2000	15	18%	32%	59%

Determining the Appropriate Discounts for the Lack of Marketability with IPO Studies: Study Selection and Assessment

In the US, the Internal Revenue Service (IRS) and courts accept restricted stock studies and pre-IPO studies as empirical evidence to quantify the discount for the lack of marketability. In contrast to restricted stock studies after 1990, the pre-IPO studies represent a more current estimation of the DLL. Nevertheless, the use of IPO studies has some shortcomings.

- IPO studies may underestimate the DLL as the lack of liquidity is only temporary. Hence, future marketability is anticipated by the seller of pre-IPO shares. This would imply a higher DLL for shares in private companies, which do not have a foreseeable marketability.
- IPO studies contain a self-selection bias. The data consist of those companies which succeeded in going public. Firms that take into consideration an IPO and discard such plans later are not included in the sample. Possible reasons for this decision can be that they lack the required size, business plan, or investor appeal. From this viewpoint, a higher DLL for shares in private companies would be appropriate.

The transaction results can also be biased due to omitted variables. Transactions prior to the IPO differ from those that take place at the time of the IPO, since pre-IPO investors are likely to be insiders who provide monitoring or mentoring services to the firm, like venture capitalists. Therefore, discounts may reflect compensation for these services rather than compensation for the lack of liquidity, so that the DLL is underestimated. This can also be a reason for the high standard deviation of the discounts shown in Exhibit 3.5 since the level of services provided varies.

To conclude, the use of mean or median discounts in valuation without consideration of the underlying explanatory variables is inappropriate. Decisions of the US tax courts going back to the year 2003 have already rejected the blind application of a standard DLL and have forced business appraisers to explain discounts used in the respective valuation analyses in detail.[2] Therefore, professionals valuing private companies must take into account that their respective company may never go public due to the lack of requisite size, business plan, or investor appeal, and therefore the application of the results derived with the IPO approach need, like the restricted stock approach, a careful look at the level of the single transactions. It is recommended to select those that have characteristics in common with the subject company with respect to size, potential for a public IPO, profitability, information access, and other characteristics that influence the liquidity of the subject company.

3.5.5   Can Empirical Evidence for Minority Stakes be Used for a Controlling Ownership Interest in a Private Company?

It is important to know that study results on the marketability discounts for minority interests like IPO and restricted stock study results should not be applied to controlling stake interests in a private company because:

- Holding a majority stake differs significantly from holding a minority stake; in the case of a majority interest, the investor can adjust the corporate strategy. Hence, the future cash flows are not simply estimated, but optimized. This makes the company *ceteris paribus* more valuable. In addition, a majority owner can launch an IPO, and in doing so make his stake liquid compared to a minority ownership interest in a private firm.

---

[2] See, for example, *Lappo v. Commissioner*, T.C. Memo 2003-258 (2003), or *Peracchio v. Commissioner*, T.C. Memo 2003-280 (2003).

- The reasons for a marketability discount are different. As described above, a majority share usually is not as liquid as a minority share and cost and uncertainty associated with a potential sale exists in contrast to minority stakes.
- The empirical evidence for the DLL for majority ownership interests needs to be provided with a completely different methodology. There is no empirical transaction database from which an appraiser can draw guidance for quantifying the discount as there is for restricted stock or pre-IPO transactions. Furthermore, empirical evidence from the US reveals control premiums of more than 40%. However, the high variance in these control premiums makes it really difficult to assess the value of a majority interest from the value of a minority interest, and vice versa. This has the consequence that practitioners are not able to deduce the necessary adjustments with respect to the ownership level.
- The empirical findings existing for the DLL for majority ownership interests show that the selection of the part of discount that is really attributable to the lack of liquidity is more difficult than in the evidence provided for minority ownership and the adjustments need to include further factors that distinguish private from public companies. The next chapter gives a detailed overview of influence factors on the DLL for controlling ownership.

3.6 THE DLL FOR CONTROL OWNERSHIP SITUATIONS AND THE PCD

The studies mentioned so far implicitly analyze minority ownership interests and make no distinction between the levels of ownership. But as described above, holding a majority interest is different from holding a minority interest and the impact of illiquidity is different for a majority and a minority interest. Therefore, the results of the restricted stock and IPO approaches are only suitable for valuing minority stakes.

In the following section, studies are presented that are explicitly applicable to control ownership situations as they pick up the idea that a possible illiquidity discount can be estimated by the difference between multiples achieved in private company vs. public company transactions where majority ownerships have been acquired. As described earlier, a (control) transaction with private and public targets differs not only with respect to liquidity and its reasoning but also because of other differences between private and public firms. Researchers using the acquisition approach try to account for those differences but cannot block out 100% of them. Therefore they acknowledge that differences in multiples between private and firm transactions are explained by liquidity and other factors and call the resulting difference (the resulting discount) the PCD. A pure DLL as for minority ownership interests (with the restrictions discussed) does not exist for majority ownership interests in private companies.

3.6.1 Acquisition Approach

The acquisition approach benchmarks transaction valuations of private companies and matches them to comparable transactions involving public companies. Comparable means that the companies must (1) operate in the same industry, (2) be close in size, and (3) acquired around the same time. After identifying the matching pairs the idea is to compare valuation in terms of multiples like EV/Sales, EV/EBITDA, EV/EBIT, and P/E. Discounts can be viewed by the difference between the multiples of publicly traded companies and privately held companies and are computed by comparing the multiples using a formula shown in Equation 3.1.

$$PCD = 1 - \left(\frac{Private\ company\ multiple}{Public\ company\ multiple} \right) \qquad (3.1)$$

Often multivariate regressions are used in addition to the univariate analysis to control other factors that might influence multiples and value like payment method, leverage, or market activity. For details on the procedure see Section 3.13. In the following, the results of some prominent studies using the acquisition approach are summarized.

Koeplin, Sarin, and Shapiro (2000)

John Koeplin, Atulya Sarin, and Alan Shapiro examine 192 acquisitions of private companies between 1984 and 1998, excluding financial and regulated firms. For each of the private company acquisitions, Koeplin et al. identify the acquisition of a public company in the same country, the same year, and the same industry. They also account for comparable sales in cases where several public company acquisitions meet the first three criteria. Thus, each private company is matched with a similar public company that was also acquired around the same time. The final sample includes 84 acquisitions of private companies in the US (domestic transactions) and 108 acquisitions of private companies outside the US (foreign transactions). To estimate the discount associated with private companies, Koeplin et al. calculate the ratio of the firm's EV (defined here as the purchase price of the acquisition multiplied by the number of outstanding shares, plus the book value of the liabilities.) to its earnings, sales, and book value. These ratios are then compared to the acquisitions of the private and comparable public companies.

As shown in Exhibit 3.6, they find that private companies are purchased at a substantial discount to comparable public companies, e.g. at 18% at the EV/EBITDA multiple for domestic

Exhibit 3.6   Results of Koeplin et al. (2000)

	Private targets	Public targets	Discount
Domestic transactions	**Median**	**Median**	**Median**
Net sales ($ million)	56.32	91.71	
Assets ($ million)	40.62	60.11	
Enterprice Value/EBIT	8.58	12.37	30.62
Enterprise Value/EBITDA	6.98	8.53	18.14
Enterprise Value/Sales	1.13	1.14	0.79*
Foreign transactions			
Net sales ($ million)	28.22	73.45	
Assets ($ million)	41.13	112.72	
Enterprice Value/EBIT	11.37	12.09	5.96
Enterprise Value/EBITDA	7.1	9.28	23.49
Enterprise Value/Sales	1.35	1.63	17.18*

Descriptive statistics and valuation metrics of 84 (108) private companies acquired in the United States (outside the United States) between 1984–1998. The private company discount is measured as 1-(private company multiple/public company multiple).
*Discounts not significant.

Exhibit 3.7   Results of Kooli et al. (2003)

	Private targets Median multiple	Public targets Median multiple	Median discount
Price/Sales	1.4	1.9	0.17
Price/Earnings	15.3	24.4	0.34
Price/Cash Flow	11.2	15.1	0.20

Median multiples and discounts from 331 transactions with private US companies between 1995 and 2002.

transactions and 24% on foreign transactions. They find greater variation in discounts among foreign transactions and argue that this is probably due to the fact that different countries have different accounting standards, and therefore multiples could vary across countries. Hence, they argue that the market region needs to be taken into account for the computation of discounts. Koeplin, Sarin, and Shapiro conclude that the observed differences between private and public company valuations might be partly attributable to differences in characteristics (e.g. earnings growth) between private and public companies rather than liquidity, and they emphasize that the observed discounts constitute a private company discount (PCD) rather than a discount for pure liquidity (DLL).

Kooli, Kortas, and L'Her (2003)

Maher Kooli, Mohammed Kortas, and Jean-François L'Her pursue an approach similar to Koeplin et al. They analyze 331 transactions with private US companies between 1995 and 2002, which they match to transactions with public companies of the same size and from the same year and industry. They find discounts of 17% to 34% depending on the multiple used (see Exhibit 3.7), again encompassing not only liquidity aspects, but also other differences in characteristics between public and private firms. Kooli et al. show that the multiples are significantly lower for these private firms that are smaller than the average of firms (in terms of assets). In addition, they show that median valuation increases for private targets during active M&A years, such as 1998 and 1999, compared to the years before, as discounts decrease significantly.

Mergerstat Statistics

The concept of benchmarking multiples is also used by *Mergerstat Review*, which publishes a yearly table presenting average price earnings multiples for acquisitions of private companies and those of public companies, showing that the observed multiples for private companies are significantly lower, see Exhibit 3.8.

Officer (2007)

Micah Officer analyzes acquisition discounts for the sample of acquisition attempts for unlisted targets between 1979 and 2003. He calculates acquisition discounts as the percentage difference between acquisition multiples (price to book equity, price to earnings, deal value to EBITDA, or deal value to sales) for an unlisted firm and the average multiple for industry- and size-matched comparable acquisitions of publicly traded targets. He finds average acquisition discounts for private firms (stand-alone and unlisted subsidiaries) of 17% to 30% relative to acquisition

Exhibit 3.8   Results from Mergerstat Review

	Private targets		Public targets		
Year	Median P/E offered	Transaction reporting P/E	Median P/E offered	Transaction reporting P/E	Calculated discount
1996	17.7	31	21.7	288	0.18
1997	17	83	25	389	0.32
1998	16	207	24	362	0.33
1999	18.4	174	21.7	434	0.15
2000	16	130	18	379	0.11
2001	15.3	80	16.7	261	0.08
2002	16.6	83	19.7	161	0.16
2003	19.4	107	21.2	198	0.08
2004	19	108	22.6	188	0.16
2005	16.9	127	24.4	230	0.31
2006	19	65	23.7	294	0.20

Median P/E ratios offered for US companies, Excerpt from Mergerstat Review (factset Mergerstat, LLC). See www.bvmarketdata.com.

multiples for comparable publicly traded targets. Furthermore, he finds that the sales prices for private companies are affected by the liquidity needs of the buyer and that discounts are significantly greater when debt capital is relatively more expensive to obtain. During a period when the spread between the corporate interest yield and the federal function rate is higher than usual (debt financing more difficult than usual), the discounts are high (23% for stand-alone and 34% for an unlisted subsidiary) compared to easy debt financing periods (14% discount for a stand-alone and 25% for an unlisted subsidiary). See Exhibit 3.9.

De Franco, Gavious, Jin, and Richardson (2007)

Gus de Franco, Ilanit Gavious, Justine Jin, and Gordon Richardson compare EV/EBITDA and EV/Sales multiples paid for private firms with multiples paid for public firms. The study encompasses 664 acquisitions of private firms (stock purchase), 274 acquisitions of private

Exhibit 3.9   Results of Officer (2007)

	Private targets	
	Stand-alone	Unlisted subsidiary
Discount EV/ Sales (all acquisitions)	18.15	29.99
Discount P/E (all acquisitions)	22.85	28.90
Dicount EV/ EBITDA (all acquisition)	17.18	26.91
Dicount EV /EBITDA		
– in cash acquisitions	22.46	28.25
– in non-cash & mixed acquisitions	12.43	28.25
– when C&I loan spread > time series median	22.83	34.37
– when C&I loan spread < time series median	13.77	24.51

Median discounts from 417 stand-alone companies and 416 unlisted subsidiaries acquired in the US between 1997 and 2003.

Exhibit 3.10   Results of De Franco et al. (2007)

	Private targets		Public targets	
	Stock purchase	Asset purchase	Stock Purchase	Asset purchase
Assets ($ millions)	8.67	7.24	131.09	n.a.
Sales ($ millions)	15.86	13.82	130.11	n.a.
EV Sales predicted multiple[1]	0.79	0.65	0.99	0.82
Discount (EV/Sales)	20.2%	20.7%	nm	nm
EV/ EBITDA predicted multiple[2]	7.51	6.05	12.46	9.88
Discount (EV/EBITDA)	39.7%	38.8%	nm	nm
Companies with Big4 auditor				
– EV/Sales predicted multiple	0.89	0.72		
– EV/EBITDA predicted multiple	7.92	6.94		
Companies without-Big4 auditor				
– EV/Sales predicted multiple	0.68	0.59		
– EV/EBITDA predicted multiple	7.03	5.32		
Non-Big4 auditor discount				
– EV/Sales	23.6%	18.1%		
– EV/EBITDA	11.2%	23.3%		

Descriptive statistics and valuation metrics of 664 (274) private US companies purchased in stock (assets) acquisitions and 2,225 public U.S. companies acquired between 1994 and 2005. The EV/Sales and EV/EBTDA multiples are estimated via multivariate regression according to:

$$EBITDA/EV = a_0 + a_1 \text{ Private} + a_2 \text{Target Size} + a_3 \text{Sales Growth} + e$$

$$SALES/EV = a_0 + a_1 \text{Private} + a_2 \text{Target Size} + a_3 \text{Sales Growth} + a_4 \text{R\&D} + a_5 \text{Profit Margin} + e$$

To predict the private-firm (public-firm) multiple the "private" indicator variable is set to one (zero). The predicted EV is median EBITDA (or median Sales) multiplied by the predicted multiple. For Big 4 auditor analyses, the regression includes two more variables $a_j \text{Big4} + a_j \text{Big4} \times \text{Private}$.

firms (asset purchase), and 2,225 acquisitions of public firms. To complement the multiples comparison they perform multivariate regression analysis to control for value-influencing factors like size, sales growth, and R&D expenditure. According to Exhibit 3.10, the estimated discounts range from 20% to 40% for stock purchases and from 21% to 39% for asset purchases. De Franco et al. suggest that the discount can be explained by lower earnings quality in private firms. Earnings quality refers to the ability of a company's reported earnings to reflect true and to predict future earnings. They suggest another explanation for the discount that is related to the information quality facing the buyer. Specifically, they present evidence that (not) hiring a Big 4 auditor increases (decreases) the sale proceeds of private firms. They classify the deals according to asset and stock deals and argue that information risk is lower for an assets-only deal, compared to buying shares, because with the former the buyer is not responsible for any unrecorded liabilities. Thus, the costs of doing due diligence are lower for assets-only deals. They find that, although information risk is lower for asset purchases, it is still important to address these risks via a high-quality audit as the resulting discount attributable to non-Big 4 auditors amounts to between 11% and 24%. De Franco et al. criticize prior research that attributes valuation differences solely to the lack of and desire for liquidity and call the discount the PCD to emphasize that the reason for the discount applied to private firms relative to public firms goes beyond simple differences in liquidity.

3.6.2 Which Factors Influence the Measurement of the PCD?

What are the factors that drive differences in multiples between public and private acquisitions? As mentioned before, size, industry, and time are factors that influence multiples. These are called systematic influence factors and have been accounted for in most of the empirical research shown above.

Influence on the PCD – Size Differences

Practitioners apply a size premium to the cost of capital for small companies to account for the higher risk associated with lack of size. The size factor has been examined and included already by many authors who analyzed the DLL. For example, Silber (1991) examines factors that explain differences in discounts across different restricted stocks by relating the size of the discount to observable firm characteristics, including revenues and the size of the restricted stock offering. He shows that the private placement discount increases with the size of the placement. Ang and Kohers (2001) show that with the increasing relative size of the targets compared to their acquirers, a greater potential for synergies together with an increased bargaining power lead to higher premiums being paid in transactions. Nowadays, the Duff & Phelps Risk Premium Report[3] provides comprehensive up-to-date empirical evidence on size premiums for small companies and presents premiums for 25 size-ranked portfolios using eight alternative measures of company size; it is used by many practitioners to estimate the appropriate cost of capital for smaller targets.

Exhibit 3.11 shows that private companies are generally smaller than public targets in terms of revenues and assets.

In Germany, the average assets of private companies amount to approximately EUR 33.2m compared to EUR 93.9m for public companies (the last balance sheet total before the transaction). Independent private companies (Mittelstand companies[4]) are significantly smaller than other private companies, with average assets of EUR 11.5m. A comparison of the relative size of the target vs. the acquirer mirrors the differences in absolute numbers. Relative size in terms of assets is higher for public targets than for private (14.1%) vs. 2.2%.

According to Exhibit 3.11, private North American[5] companies are generally smaller than public companies. The average assets for independent companies are about EUR 50.9m vs. EUR 159.5m for dependent private and EUR 265.5m for public companies. Compared to the market in Germany, private companies in North America bigger. However, relative to their acquirers, they are only slightly bigger than German companies (relative size in terms of assets is higher for public targets than for private (15.2% vs. 4.9 %)).

In the US dependent private companies with absolute assets of EUR 159.5m are relatively smaller compared to their acquirers than independent companies are (compare 4.2% for dependent companies to 5.1% for independent). Maybe it is sometimes easier or more attractive for bigger companies to acquirer a subsidiary from a mother company.

---

[3] The Duff & Phelps Risk Premium Report is based on a series of articles published by Roger Grabowski and David King, culminating with a seminal 1996 article and a subsequent article in 1999 which together served as the Report's foundation. See Roger J. Grabowski and David King, New Evidence on Size Effects and Equity Returns, *Business Valuation Review* (September 1996, revised March 2000), and Roger J. Grabowski and David King, New Evidence on Equity Returns and Company Risk, *Business Valuation Review* (September 1999, revised March 2000). The 2012 Duff & Phelps Risk Premium Report is in the 17th year of publication and available at http://www.duffandphelps.com/expertise/publications/pages/ResearchReportsDetail.aspx?id=70&list=ResearchReports.

[4] A detailed definition of the Mittelstand is given in Section 1.3.

[5] The Zephyr database used revealed transactions for the North American market including Canada and the US. But 95% of the transactions involve US targets, so basically the US market is analyzed.

Exhibit 3.11   Size differences between private and public firms

	Target status		Assets (EUR'000) Median	RelSize (assets) Median
Germany	Public		93,936	14.1%
	Private	independent	11,518	1.6%
		dependent	61,699	2.5%
	Private total		33,224	2.2%
North America	Public		265,465	15.2%
	Private	independent	50,933	5.1%
		dependent	159,482	4.2%
	Private total		81,363	4.9%
Western Europe	Public		91,788	18.4%
	Private	independent	5,295	2.4%
		dependent	27,819	5.4%
	Private total		12,552	3.7%
UK	Public		74,711	22.9%
	Private	independent	5,813	3.1%
		dependent	17,332	4.0%
	Private Total		10,051	3.5%

The sample is based on completed majority-ownership transactions between January 1997 and June 2001 used in the study in Section 3.11. For details on data see Exhibit 69. The sample comprises of those transactions that include figures on asset size. The table shows different financial metrics for the private and public companies in the four regions.
Source: Zephyr database, Bureau von Dijk.

In Western Europe and the UK the former patterns in size differences and relative sizes are repeated; public targets are bigger than private, dependent private companies are bigger than independent also compared to their acquirers.

Given the size differences between company classes and the influence of size on a company's value, one should expect that size would influence the measured discounts and it will be investigated whether there are differences between the single regions.

Influence on the PCD – Industry Differences

Practitioners know that performance differences between companies across different industries exist depending on capital intensity, growth, and other characteristics. There are many examples in recent history where the impressive growth (prospects) of high-tech and service companies has led to (sometimes irrationally) higher valuation compared to e.g. other, stable companies with more decent growth assumptions. Again, researchers like Ang and Kohers (2001) examine industry effects and find for example that companies in some capital intensive and retail industries are valued lower than others, as high fixed costs lead to high operating leverage which is accounted for by a high β in the capital costs used to discount cash flows.

Certain financial characteristics of the different industries are examined and it can be shown that especially the trade and service industries reveal distinctive characteristics compared to others (for the classification of industries see Section 3.13).

Exhibit 3.12 shows that private German companies in the service industry are, with a relative size of 1.7% compared to their acquirers, smaller than private companies in other industries

Exhibit 3.12   Parameters of the trade, the manufacturing, and the service industries

	Target Status	Ratio	All other	Trade	All other	Manufacturing	All other	Service
Germany	Public	Target D/E	1.0x	3.0x	0.6x	1.4x	1.2x	0.5x
		Relative size (assets)	16.0%	5.1%	13.8%	25.9%	12.5%	31.5%
	Private	Target D/E	1.8x	2.0x	1.6x	2.1x	2.2x	1.3x
		Relative size (assets)	2.1%	5.4%	2.1%	2.6%	2.4%	1.7%
North America	Public	Target D/E	0.9x	1.0x	1.0x	0.6x	1.0x	0.6x
		Relative size (assets)	14.8%	92.1%	16.2%	26.3%	14.7%	22.5%
	Private	Target D/E	1.7x	2.0x	1.7x	1.0x	3.0x	0.9x
		Relative size (assets)	4.7%	10.6%	5.0%	6.9%	5.0%	5.1%
Western Europe	Public	Target D/E	1.0x	1.0x	0.8x	1.0x	1.1x	0.7x
		Relative size (assets)	16.1%	133.5%	18.1%	40.4%	21.0%	15.3%
	Private	Target D/E	1.6x	1.9x	1.6x	1.6x	1.8x	1.4x
		Relative size (assets)	3.7%	6.5%	3.3%	6.8%	4.2%	3.7%
UK		Target D/E	0.9x	1.3x	0.9x	1.0x	1.0x	0.8x
		Relative size (assets)	21.8%	44.5%	24.9%	33.2%	21.8%	34.9%
	Private	Target D/E	1.4x	1.8x	1.4x	1.3x	1.5x	1.3x
		Relative size (assets)	3.5%	6.0%	3.5%	4.3%	3.5%	4.1%

The sample is based on completed majority-ownership transactions between January 1997 and June 2011 used in the study in Section 3.11. For details on data see Exhibit 3.35. The sample comprises of those transactions that include figures on leverage and assets. The table shows different financial metrics for the trade, the manufacturing, and the service industries compared in each case to all other industries. The computation is done for private and public companies separately.
Source: Zephyr database, Bureau von Dijk.

(relative size 2.4%). Furthermore, the Debt/Equity (D/E)[6] ratio of the private companies in the service industry is 1.3x lower than the D/E ratio in other industries (2.2x). One can see that private companies in the manufacturing industry are little larger than other private companies compared to their acquirers (relative size 2.6% vs. 2.1%) but are more highly leveraged than all other industries (D/E ratio of 2.1x for the manufacturing industry vs. 1.6x for all other industries). Private trade companies, with a D/E ratio of 2.0x, are more highly leveraged than private companies in other industries (D/E ratio of 1.8x); public trade companies seem to have significantly more debt than companies in other industries (D/E ratio of 3.0x vs. 1.0x).

In North America, there are no size differences between private service companies and other private companies (relative size of service companies of 5.1% vs. 5.0% all other), but they have significantly lower leverage (D/E ratio service companies of 0.9x vs. 3.0x all other). Trade companies seem to be on the one hand relatively bigger than others (relative size of 10.6% vs. 4.7%% all other) but also more highly leveraged than other private companies (D/E ratio of 2.0x for trade companies vs. D/E ratio 1.7x for all other).

In Western Europe, the relative size of private targets compared to their acquirers differs across industries. Furthermore, leverage differences exist. The leverage of private service companies is lower (D/E ratio of 1.4x) than those of other industries (D/E ratio of 1.8x). Private manufacturing companies have an average D/E ratio of 1.6x, which is the median D/E

---

[6] Defined as the total interest bearing debt divided by the shareholders' equity (share capital + retained earnings - treasury stocks, if applicable) using balance sheet (book) values.

ratio across all industries, whereas private trade companies seems to be more highly leveraged than other private firms (D/E ratio of 1.9. vs. D/E ratio of 1.6x for other industries).

In the UK, there are leverage and size differences between all industries especially service and trade. Private service companies have lower leverage and are larger than other private companies (relative size of 4.1% vs. 3.5% all other and D/E ratio of 1.3x vs. 1.5x all other). Private trade companies are more highly leveraged and larger than other private companies (relative size of 6.0% vs. 3.5% all other and D/E ratio of 1.8x vs. 1.4x all other).

In some regions the classification in industries implicitly accounts for distinct financial metrics, such as leverage and size, which can explain valuation differences between companies from different industries. Together with the differences between public and private companies within the industries, matching according the industry criterion may improve the measurement and interpretation of the PCD.

Influence on the PCD – Time

The state of the economy affects activity on the M&A market and the prices paid in transactions. Similar to the IPO market, there are periods with increased market activity when private targets are in high demand from investors. During these "hot" market phases, high bidder competition for private targets strengthens their bargaining power, and the general positive sentiment leads to increased valuation. In addition, a more readily available transaction financing increases prices. A study done by Acharya and Pedersen (2005) shows that not only the asset illiquidity itself matters, but also that an illiquid asset is even more illiquid when the market itself is illiquid (which usually coincides with down markets and economic recessions). Officer (2007) finds confirming results as liquidity discounts increase when a seller's bargaining position weakens if alternative sources of liquidity are unavailable or costly. Facing refinancing constraints, the seller may grant discounts especially when the buyer provides immediate liquidity in cash transactions (see later on payment method).

Stock market ups and downs influence M&A transaction multiples, not necessarily because FMVs change but also because recent transaction multiples are used as price references during negotiations. In a stock market decline, M&A multiples for private companies decrease as well but with a time lag (of six months), which can be explained by the length of an M&A transaction process. The magnitude of the decline may not be as severe as for public multiples, because if M&A prices go down too much, no owner of a private company is willing to sell if he does not need to.

The private equity boom years in 2006 and 2007 in association with the high market liquidity, strong availability of funds, plus low interest rates, led to strong competition for private targets and sellers of private companies faced an unusually liquid market for their firms.

In addition to the systematic influence factors of size, time, and industry, several other aspects need to be accounted for when comparing multiples between private and public companies as they may influence multiple differences:

Influence on the PCD – M&A Profiles and Firm Characteristics

Independent private companies can have different M&A profiles with respect to acquisition strategy and behaviour during the M&A transaction, which influence the transaction outcome. For example, these firms may break out of an unfruitful M&A process without incurring high prestige costs or private owners stop bargaining with certain parties due to private reasons.

In addition, the linkage between the enterprise and the owners of independent private companies influences the market behaviour, the performance of these companies, the choice of legal form, the means of financing, the potential for innovation, and the managerial way to run a business. Especially in cases where the owner(s) of a company are active in management (owner-management), potential principal–agent problems are mitigated, which leads to agency cost efficiencies. Improved leadership through centralized decision-making at lower transaction costs, as well as stakeholder efficiencies through a family atmosphere with employee and customer loyalty and a degree of "freedom" in taking strategic decisions makes family firms valuable. On the other hand, these firms potentially suffer from a number of performance-limiting characteristics such as above average compensation, the pursuit of non-profit maximizing projects, low innovation, and slow adaptation to new circumstances, usually related to maintaining traditionally successful business practices. The linkage between owner and company needs to be taken into account when comparing transaction valuations of independent private and public companies, therefore a split into dependent and independent private companies is a prerequisite to compare like for like multiples.

Influence on the PCD – Accounting and Information Quality

The availability of financial information for private firms is much more limited, both in terms of history and depth, since private firms are often not governed by the strict accounting and reporting standards or requirements to release detailed financial information which publicly traded firms face that have evident exposure to the market. Therefore the problem of information asymmetry is likely to be most severe in the acquisitions of private firms. In addition, historical price information as a value indicator is missing and monitoring through stockholders is not possible. Therefore, higher risk and uncertainty are considered when acquiring private companies even though advisors for both the buyer and seller work to limit the amount of information asymmetry between the parties. As a consequence bidders might lower their offer price to protect themselves against the possibility that they are less than fully informed about the business they are acquiring. A general problem with information asymmetries is that they are difficult to measure, and empirical proxies for asymmetric information are naturally imprecise.

Influence on the PCD – Payment Method

The choice of the payment method has two different implications. Firstly, the desire for liquidity: sellers of unlisted targets accept lower acquisition multiples in return for the provision of liquidity, as cash (in contrast to stocks) provides immediate liquidity.

Officer (2007) finds that sales of unlisted targets are often motivated by liquidity constraints at the parent company. These firms show significantly worse cash characteristics (lower cash balances, lower cash flow, lower net working and other) relative to other firms of similar size in the same industry together with significantly higher leverage. Parents' liquidity constraints are mitigated by the sale of a relatively small (4% of parent assets on average) subsidiary whose sale proceeds can provide significant cash inflow (average sale proceeds of 105% relative to the parent's pre-sale cash balance). Similar results have been shown by other research, e.g. Lang, Poulsen, and Stulz (1995). Parent firms seem to time subsidiaries sales. They divest liquid subsidiaries in industries in which there has been a lot of M&A activity in the recent past and they sell liquid subsidiaries when the costs associated with alternate sources of liquidity are prohibitively high. In this context the term "fire sale" has been established meaning the necessity for sale of an asset quickly to generate liquidity.

In Germany, sales of Mittelstand firms may also be motivated by the high debt level of the Mittelstand that induces a special desire for liquidity especially during tightening refinancing conditions and therefore owners might accept lower transaction valuations in exchange for cash compared to payments in shares.

Secondly, incomplete information: it has been shown that the method of payment can be a proxy for existing information asymmetries between buyer and seller. A bidder with less than complete information about the target's financials and prospects will choose stock as the method of payment in acquisitions. Officer (2007) finds that information asymmetries (as induced by the payment method) contributed approximately one-quarter to the average discounts (17% for stand-alone unlisted targets and 28% for subsidiaries).

With respect to the empirical research, one should be aware that the method of payment may be related to the size of the transaction. According to Exhibit 3.13, cash deals are smaller than non-cash deals. This holds true for public and private companies in all regions except for the UK, where cash deals involving private companies are slightly bigger than non-cash deals involving private companies. Comparing the average deal size of private cash and non-cash transactions, cash transactions in Germany have on average a lower deal size (EUR 22.5m) than non-cash deals (EUR 30.0m), and targets in cash deals are smaller relative to their acquirers than in non-cash deals. Lower synergy potentials and decreased bargaining power may explain the discounts applied to cash deals.

Exhibit 3.13 A comparison of deal sizes across payment method

		Share of cash transactions			Average deal size	
		Target status			Target status	
	Payment	Public	Private	Payment	Public	Private
Germany	Cash	76%	63%	Cash (EUR '000)	88,339	22,500
	Non-Cash	24%	37%	Non-Cash (EUR '000)	247,400	30,000
	Total	185	544	Total	114,529	25,500
North America	Cash	66%	61%	Cash (EUR '000)	199,825	37,997
	Non-Cash	34%	39%	Non-Cash (EUR '000)	266,794	78,011
	Total	4,232	4,021	Total	225,115	59,825
Western Europe	Cash	79%	65%	Cash (EUR '000)	53,528	14,000
	Non-Cash	21%	35%	Non-Cash (EUR '000)	168,859	15,098
	Total	1,598	3,368	Total	67,320	14,479
UK	Cash	76%	67%	Cash (EUR '000)	50,842	14,477
	Non-Cash	24%	33%	Non-Cash (EUR '000)	83,198	13,867
	Total	1,266	3,605	Total	58,584	14,190
All regions	Cash	71%	64%	Cash (EUR '000)	99,435	30,774
	Non-Cash	29%	36%	Non-Cash (EUR '000)	171,423	32,658
	Total	7,281	11,538	Total	117,000	32,422

The sample is based on the data set that comprises completed majority-ownership transactions between January 1997 and July 2011 used in the study in Section 3.11. For details on data see Exhibit 3.35. The sample is comprised of those transactions that include information on the payment method. The table reports the share of transactions that is paid in cash separately for public and private targets (left side). On the right side, the table reports the differences in deal sizes for cash and non-cash deals separately for public and private companies.
Source: Zephyr database, Bureau von Dijk.

Comparing the number of cash and non-cash transactions all companies seem to have a desire for liquid payment. Interestingly, the percentages of share deals are higher for private targets in all regions than for public targets. About 64% of the transactions involving private targets are cash transactions, compared to 76% involving public targets.

This may be related to the fact that deal values differ significantly between public but not between private companies depending on the payment method as cash deals are significantly smaller than non-cash deals for public targets.

In analyzing PCD, practitioners should also focus on differences in the deal size as the proven influence of the method of payment might be blurred by size differences.

Influence on the PCD – Buyer Characteristics

Some academics make the application of the DLL contingent upon the buyer in the transaction. They argue that some buyers, e.g. private equity investors, plan to end their commitment in the acquired company after a certain period of time and plan an exit via an IPO. Therefore, the illiquidity discount attached to a private firm's value should be lower because the value that the buyer can obtain from an IPO will exceed the value that he will receive from selling the target in a private transaction. Furthermore, with an exit after a few years, the illiquidity of the investment is only temporary, an argument used already in the restricted stock and IPO studies. They pointed out that the DLL depends on the restriction period. It is natural to assume that the assessment of a successful exit and therefore the amount of DLL applied depends on the market environment. Therefore the DLL contingent on the buyer's exit possibilities is subject to changes over time. The valuation guidelines published by the European Private Equity and Venture Capital Association (EVCA)[7] clearly state that the applied marketability discounts should be lower, the more certain and closer a possible realization event (exit) is. Furthermore, the discounts should be lower, the greater the influence of the fund over the timing and process of the realization, and the more favourable market conditions for M&A and acquisition activity. Given the recommendations, it is not really surprising that the EVCA recommends a static discount range between 10–30% (in steps of 5%), although it recommends to "consider specific circumstances" and "all relevant factors" in application of the discount.

The liquidity of the buyer also might influence the size of the DLL. Firstly, from a buyer's perspective, if the buyer of a private firm is liquid itself (e.g. publicly traded) the private asset becomes a relatively liquid investment and the DLL should be adjusted accordingly. Refinancing possibilities for the buyer itself influence the pricing of target companies. Tight refinancing possibilities especially for financial buyers who use financial leverage negatively influences prices paid in transactions.

Secondly, from the seller's perspective, the desire for liquidity has already been mentioned and allows owners of private firms to accept higher discounts from bidders with a stock listing on a liquid exchange such as the NYSE or the German DAX (Deutscher Aktienindex).

Influence on the PCD – Leverage Differences

Higher risk associated with leverage is a factor which influences company valuation, and depending on the financing environment, the lack of access to equity via stock offering, and other historical influence factors, family firms in particular are characterized by high debt

---

[7] The "International Private Equity and Venture Capital Valuation Guidelines" (2005) have been developed by the Association Française des Investisseurs en Capital, the British Venture Capital Association, and the EVCA and are available www.ecva.eu.

Exhibit 3.14   Comparison of leverage and equity ratios

	Independent private Germany		Dependent private							
			Germany		North America		Western Europe		UK	
	Median	#	Median	#	Median	#	Median	#	Mcdian	#
Target E/A	0.2	153	0.3	286	0.3	791	0.3	3146	0.3	2120
Target D/E	3.3	170	2.0	305	1.9	772	1.8	3365	1.4	2681

The sample is based on the data set that comprises completed majority-ownership transactions between January 1997 and July 2011 used in the study in Section 3.11. For details on data see Exhibit 3.35. The sample is comprised of those transactions that include information on the leverage and assets. The table reports the Equity/Assets (E/A) ratio (shareholders' equity divided by total assets using balance sheet book values) and the Debt/Equity ratio (D/E) ratio (total interest bearing debt divided by shareholders' equity (share capital + retained earnings – treasury stocks, if applicable) using balance sheet (book) values) separately for independent private companies and dependent private companies.

Source: Zephyr database, Bureau von Dijk.

levels. In Germany, financing of independent private companies (the Mittelstand) was for a long time characterized by a relationship based financing concept, called the house-bank concept where the Mittelstand used bank debt provided by a local bank with long-term relationship to the company as the only source of external financing. For example, according to the Deutscher Sparkassen- und Giroverband (2006), prior to the subprime crisis, only 1% of Mittelstand companies used mezzanine capital; nearly 71% were not familiar with it. Furthermore, the German tax law differs from regulations in other countries as it encourages firms to distribute profits and raise external capital for financing needs.[8] At the same time, in Germany the trade balance is derived from the tax balance, resulting in incentives to understate earnings. As a consequence of the German relationship based financing, a tax law unfavourable to earnings retention and with incentives to understate earnings, the financing behaviour of Mittelstand companies can be characterized, in contrast to Anglo-Saxon companies and other private companies in Germany, by low equity ratios, by trade credit and bank debt as the primary forms of external financing, by strong dependence on internally generated cash flows, as well as by the minor relevance of alternative forms of financing. Therefore, independent private companies in Germany are characterized by much higher debt levels than dependent private and public companies. They tend to have a leverage ratio that is more than 60% higher than that of other private companies in Germany and more than 70% higher than North American companies with a D/E ratio of 1.9x. Details are provided in Exhibit 3.14.

   The D/E ratio of independent private companies amounts to 3.3x in comparison to 2.0x for dependent private companies in Germany, 1.9x for dependent private companies in North America, 1.8x for dependent private companies in Western Europe, and 1.4x in the UK. The E/A ratio for the Mittelstand, at 0.2x, is quite low compared to other private companies in Germany (0.3x), North America (0.3x), Western Europe (0.3x), and the UK (0.3x).

---

[8] Until 2001, the split tax rules for corporations and limited liability partnerships taxed retained profits at a higher rate than distributed profits. In 2001, the German legislature introduced the "Halbeinkünfteverfahren" to encourage the retention of earnings in limited liability companies. Under the "Halbeinkünfteverfahren" all profits are taxed at 25% at the corporate level and, if distributed, shareholders receive half of the dividend tax-free while the other half is subject to personal income tax. For the overwhelming majority of the German Mittelstand, such preferential tax treatment of retained profits does not exist, as the "Halbeinkünfteverfahren" does not apply to proprietorships and partnerships. The "Halbeinkünfteverfahren" was replaced by the "Abgeltungssteuer" as of 1 January 2009. In this system dividends are taxed at a constant rate of 25%.

The recent market developments including the restructuring and consolidation of the German banking industry starting before the subprime crisis and tightening requirements for debt collateralization implied by the Basel Committee on Banking Supervision (Basel II) and upcoming Basel III left independent private companies in Germany cut off from traditional debt financing, forcing corporate restructuring and the seeking of fresh capital. In combination with the latest market turmoil and difficulties in refinancing possibilities for Mittelstand investors, a question can be raised over whether these factors influence independent private companies in Germany more than those in the US, making an application of recent findings on the PCD in the US difficult.

Influence on the PCD – Regional Differences in M&A and Equity Market Environment

Market activity over time influences the discounts as multiples for public and private companies react differently to changes in market environment. Therefore it is intuitive to assume that regional differences in discounts also exist. The PCD measured on the US market for a certain time span is different from the PCD measured in German or Asian markets. Even for snapshot analyses spanning only a few years, differences in market activity and market liquidity will result in in PCDs that vary between market regions.

Exhibit 3.15 reports the medians of the five computed valuation multiples for both classes of private companies and public companies. As shown in the table, across all regions, the median multiples for public companies are higher than those for private companies; average sales multiples for public companies amount to 1.5x, whereas the average for private companies amounts to 1.1x. The average EV multiples (ex EV/Sales) are 12.3x for public and 9.4x for private companies. Furthermore, the P/E multiple is higher for public than for private companies. (16.3x vs. 13.0x). One can see that there are regional differences between multiples and differences between independent and dependent private companies.

Furthermore valuation differences vary across multiples. For example, differences between private and public firms seem to be more pronounced on the EV/EBITDA to the P/E multiple than on the sales multiples. In addition, differences between private and public company multiples in Germany are lower than in Western Europe (except for the P/E multiple, this multiple is excluded from further analyses because of missing observations) and is on average lower than in North America and higher than in the UK. In three regions (Germany, Western Europe, and the UK), independent private companies seems to have slightly lower EV multiples than dependent ones, whereas in North America, dependent private firms reach overall lower valuations.

Interpretation of single multiples is difficult; what is more important to know is that the different levels of multiples need to be recognized when comparing transaction valuations between public and private firms. Without recognition of multiple differences, a discount applied to a subject company that stems from a different market region than the companies used in the empirical study leads to a valuation bias. As a consequence, it is better to use empirical studies done in home markets.

Influence of the PCD – Summary of Factors

Exhibit 3.16 summarizes the factors that drive differences in multiples between public and private firms in acquisitions. They have proven influence on the PCD in empirical studies and need to be accounted for in the application of discounts.

Exhibit 3.15   Median multiples for private and public companies for different regions

		Public	Independent private	Dependent private	All private	Abs. diffference public-private multiple
Germany	P/Sales	1.5x	1.3x	1.0x	1.1x	0.4x
	EV/Sales	1.9x	1.3x	1.3x	1.3x	0.7x
	EV/EBITDA	11.4x	9.2x	10.4x	9.9x	1.5x
	EV/EBIT	13.8x	13.0x	13.9x	13.1x	0.7x
	P/E	15.8x	13.1x	11.3x	12.9x	2.9x
North America	P/Sales	1.8x	2.2x	2.6x	2.4x	−0.6x
	EV/Sales	1.9x	2.5x	1.7x	1.9x	0.0x
	EV/EBITDA	12.0x	13.5x	9.6x	9.8x	2.2x
	EV/EBIT	15.5x	18.3x	12.7x	13.7x	1.8x
	P/E	17.3x	20.1x	19.0x	19.3x	−2.0x
Western Europe	P/Sales	2.1x	1.1x	1.1x	1.1x	1.0x
	EV/Sales	2.4x	1.1x	1.3x	1.2x	1.2x
	EV/EBITDA	10.1x	8.5x	9.9x	9.2x	0.9x
	EV/EBIT	13.7x	10.3x	13.6x	11.9x	1.8x
	P/E	15.7x	13.0x	16.4x	14.5x	1.2x
	P/Sales	1.4x	0.9x	0.8x	0.8x	0.5x
UK	EV/Sales	1.3x	1.2x	1.3x	1.2x	0.1x
	EV/EBITDA	9.9x	9.6x	11.0x	10.4x	−0.4x
	EV/EBIT	13.9x	12.3x	13.9x	13.1x	0.8x
	P/E	17.7x	15.0x	14.6x	14.9x	2.8x
All regions	P/Sales	1.7x			1.1x	0.7x
	EV/Sales	1.3x			1.1x	0.2x
	Average sales multiple	1.5x			1.1x	0.4x
	EV/EBITDA	10.7x			8.5x	2.2x
	EV/EBIT	13.9x			10.3x	3.6x
	Average EV multiple	12.3x			9.4x	2.9x
	P/E	16.3x			13.0x	3.3x

The sample is based on the data set that comprises completed majority-ownership transactions between January 1997 and July 2011 used in the study in Section 3.11. For details on data see Exhibit 3.35. The table reports the median multiples for each class of company.
Source: Zephyr database, Bureau von Dijk.

To analyze the PCD, some of the factors can be accounted for using careful matching, others need to be tested in multivariate regression analyses. After taking care of the main valuation drivers, an appraiser may be able to assess how big the part of the PCD might be that is really attributable to liquidity differences, if he wants to do so. This must not be the case as one can, especially in M&A situation, apply a PCD, tailored to the case but account for "general valuation differences between private and public firms" that lead to a discount when valuing a private company for sale or to buy.

3.6.3   Determining the Appropriate Discounts with the Acquisition Approach: Study Selection and Assessment

An important factor for the application of studies on the PCD is that the companies need to be matched according to systematic influence factors. The comparison of raw acquisition multiples done in the Mergerstat Review is not particularly useful in determining the PCD, as

Exhibit 3.16 Summary of influence factors

Factor	Influence	Dependence on market environment	Existence of regional differences	Relationship to a potential discount and model implementation
Size	Smaller firms are associated with higher risk which decrease valuation. Synergy possibilities are lower which decrease valuation. The smaller the acquired company is (absolute size and relatively to its acquirer), the lower the valuation may be. Compared to public company transactions, this should have an increasing effect on discounts.	No	Yes, company sizes are different across regions.	The bigger the target company the lower the discount. Absolute size and relative size included in the model.
Industry	Performance differences between companies across different industries exist depending on capital intensity, growth and other characteristics. The industry must be accounted for otherwise comparison of multiples between private and public transaction are distorted by differences in industry characteristics.	No		No linear relationship, indicator variable for different industries included in the model.
Time	The state of the economy affects the activity on the M&A market and the prices paid in transactions. Active, liquid M&A markets: high bidder competition for private targets strengthens bargaining power and leads to increased valuation. A more readily available transaction financing increases prices. Market downs: liquidity discounts increase when a seller's bargaining positions weakens if alternative sources of liquidity are unavailable or costly. Facing refinancing constraints, the seller may grant discounts especially when the buyer pays cash. Stock market multiples are used as price references during negotiations. Market-downs: M&A multiples for private companies decrease but with a time lag. The magnitude of the decline may not be as severe as for multiples in transactions with public targets, if M&A prices go down too much, no owner of a private company is willing to sell if he does not need to.	N.m.	Yes, market crises like the subprime crisis hit companies differently given their financing and economic environments.	The better the market environment, the smaller the discounts. Indicator variables for different periods included in the model.

M&A Profile and firm characteristics	Private companies can break up unfruitful M&A processes without public pressure. The linkage between owner and company may influence the outcome of M&A transaction process positively. Value increasing characteristics through agency cost efficiencies, value decreasing characteristics through non-profit maximizing objectives and reluctance to sell to certain investors.	No		No linear relationship, no indicator variable possible, included in "other unknown factors" to sum up everything that cannot be accounted for elsewhere.
Accounting & information quality	The available of financial information for private firms is much more limited, both in terms of history and depth. Bidders might lower their offer price to protect themselves against the possibility that they are less than fully informed about the business they are acquiring. In Germany, the Mittelstand has a widespread aversion to drawing up financial plans, making a commitment in figures, and to publishing financial data.	No	Yes	No linear relationship, no indicator variable possible, included in "other unknown factors" to sum up everything that cannot be accounted for elsewhere.
Leverage	Higher risk associated with leverage influences company valuation. In some countries like Germany, independent private companies are characterized by much higher debt levels than dependent private and public companies because of the debt-based financing concept via house-banks.	Yes, bad re-financing environment, the lacking access to equity via stock can force owners of private companies to sell at lower valuations.	Yes	Higher leverage for private companies leads to increased discounts for private companies that are higher levered than otherTarget's D/E ratio included in the model.
Regional differences in M&A and equity market environment	Market activity over time influences the discounts as multiples for public and private companies do not react synonymous to changes in the market environment. Therefore it is intuitive to assume that also regional differences in discounts exist. Market activity also depends on the competition among investors and behavior of local and foreign investors. In some countries like Germany, a high level of interest from foreign investors has driven the M&A market over recent years and it could be shown that these investors pay more for independent private companies than domestic acquirers, indicating a strong demand for them.	Yes, a foreign investor pays more, applies lower discounts.	Yes, behavior of investors and the composition of investors (foreign, local) changes over time.	No direct relationship, but transactions need to be compared for different markets separately.

(continued)

Exhibit 3.16 (*Continued*)

Factor	Influence	Dependence on market environment	Existence of regional differences	Relationship to a potential discount and model implementation
Payment method	Seller's desire for liquidity: sellers of unlisted targets accept lower acquisition multiples in return for the provision of liquidity. Parent's company's desire for liquidity: Parents liquidity constraints are mitigated with the cash sale of a subsidiary, especially when costs associated with alternate sources of liquidity are prohibitively high (fire sales). Method of payment as proxy for existing information asymmetries between buyer and seller. A bidder with less than complete information about the target choose stock payment in acquisitions as cash payment is associated with higher risk.	Yes, in time of market downs, transaction that provide immediate liquidity should receive lower valuations.	No	No linear relationship, nominal indicator variable included in the model: Cash payment: DLL increases due to seller's desire for liquidity.
Buyer characteristics	Buyer's exit possibility: buyers who plan an exit via an IPO might receive a value that outnumbers other exit routes and decreases a discount applied to a private company target. Buyer liquidity: if the buyer of a private firm is liquid itself (e.g. publicly traded) the private asset becomes a relatively liquid investment and the DLL should be adjusted accordingly. Sellers's likes and dislikes: some sellers of family firms may have a reluctance to sell their firms to a private equity investor, therefore either these sellers are desperate or the private equity investor offers an very good compensations for "raiding" the company. Tight refinancing possibilities especially for financial buyers influences price paid in transactions negatively. The desire for liquidity let sellers of private firms accept higher discounts from bidders with a stock listing on a liquid exchange ("second best" method of payment after cash).	Yes, DLL applied depends on the market environment, if likelihood of future IPO is assed positive, the applied DDL should be lower.	N.m.	No linear relationship, nominal indicator variables included in the model: 1) Private equity investor: DLL decreases due to IPO exit, sellers' likes and dislikes mix with PE influence. 2) Listed acquirer: DLL increases as seller prefers liquid stock compare to non-liquid stocks.

differences in acquisition multiples between public and private firm acquisitions could simply reflect differences in the type of targets. In contrast to the Mergerstat Review, systematic differences are accounted for in early research by Koeplin et al. (2000) and Kooli et al. (2003). They use different enterprise- and equity-related multiples to sales, earnings, and book values. Private and public companies are matched according to criteria which have had a proven influence on the company value in various prior analyses—namely size, industry, and time of the transaction. Since the study of Kooli et al. (2003), other researchers have refined the results on the PCD with a more thorough accounting of systematic valuation differences between private and public companies beyond the standard acknowledgement for size, year, and industry. De Franco et al. (2007) have hypothesized a number of potential reasons for the value differences, including quality of financial information and Big 4 auditor involvement.

Estimates using the acquisition approach lead to the PCD and therefore should only be viewed as an upper boundary for the DLL. Characteristics other than liquidity differences drive differences in the valuation ratios of public and private acquisitions. Studies account for some of the systematic differences in the characteristics of private and public firms and emphasize that the observed discounts are discounts for private companies rather than discounts for the lack of liquidity per se.

Even nowadays, due to the lack of complete analysis of the discounts, their application for valuation professionals is difficult. Some valuation professionals still seem to use lump sum discounts, especially when valuations are not used for court decisions. In a global empirical survey within their client base in 2008 on the use of liquidity discounts, PricewaterhouseCoopers found that respondents use a 15–20% range for the liquidity discount irrespective of the size of the stake, industry, or situation to which it is applied. But the above review shows that professionals need to consider carefully the appropriateness of the liquidity discount applied in each case.

It is recommended to use studies that account for systematic influence factors, to assess other factors that have proven their influence, such as accounting quality, market environment (financing conditions), and method of payment, and to clearly communicate the reasons for the selection of the discount and potential deviations from study results to the situation in question.

3.6.4   Discount for the Lack of Marketability – Summary of Study Results

Exhibit 3.17 summarizes the abovementioned studies and gives an overview of the main findings and limitations.

In the context of recent developments in the financial markets and the increase in management liability, the discount discussion is ongoing. It challenges the magnitude of discounts to be applied in situations to which a discount is reasonably applicable. Two (and for non-US analysts three) general application problems result for both lines of research studying minority and control ownership transactions:

1. **Broad spectrum:** empirical studies on the liquidity discount suggest a wide range of discounts between 20% and 80%. Picking the right study and numbers is tricky and creates pitfalls. Whether the results constitute an upper or lower bound for the DLL is a subject of discussion. For example, IPO studies may underestimate the DLL as the lack of liquidity is only temporary. The same argument holds for results of restricted stock studies. Privately-held companies may be effectively restricted for a much longer period of time than restricted stock. On the other hand, the analysis of private placements may overestimate the DLL as the discounts may serve as compensation for services institutional investors may provide.

Exhibit 3.17 Studies on the illiquidity discount

Ownership interest	Approach	Findings	Limitations
	Analysis of cross sectional differences	Private equity investors demand excess returns between 10–80% compared to aggregate public market	Discounts also attributable to monitoring and mentoring costs occurred to PE
Minority	Restricted stock approach	Median discounts ranging from 13% up to 35% depending on the study year	– From main SEC studies, only older (before 1990) usable – Self selection bias – Restriction lasts for limited period of time – Transaction among insiders – Discounts reflect additional return for increased information costs that occur when restricted stocks are valued
	IPO approach	Median discounts ranging from 28% up to 73%, depending on the IPO year	– Upside biased as only successful firms do an IPO – Lack of liquidity is temporary – Discount for exit probability and for monitoring and mentoring role of private equity investors and buyout firms
Control	Expected exit multiple	Median discounts ranging from 11% up to 80%, depending on the stage of exit	– Discounts reflect services of venture capital and buyout firms
	Acquisition approach	Median discounts ranging from 15% up to 35%, depending on the multiples used and the control group	– Discounts attributable to generic differences between private and public firms

The discounts found with acquisition approaches are thus influenced by other systematic differences that researchers tend to call the discount PCD, not DLL, with the PCD as upper bound for the DLL.

2. **Application to situation in question:** transaction characteristics in research do not perfectly match the subject company's characteristics and transaction; sometimes no good matches can be found. With respect to marketability, the richest evidence comes from the restricted stock and IPO approach, which are only suitable for valuing minority stakes. Major stakes may not need a liquidity discount at all as there is no such thing as a marketable majority interest. Different cases in the US show that it is crucially important to present thorough analysis and explanations for the application of a DLL.[9]

3. **Majority of empirical research only focuses on the US market meaning US target companies with US or non-US acquirers:** Restricted stock and IPO studies are possible in the US because of the depth of the market and the jurisdiction. In other markets things such

---

[9] See for example *Okerlund v. United States*, 53 Fed. Cl. 341 (Fed. Ct. 2002), *motion for new trial denied*, 2003 U.S. Claims LEXIS 42 (Fed. Cl. 2003), *aff'd*, 365 F.3d 1044 (Fed. Cir. 2004).

as restricted stock do not exist or data for IPO analysis are not available. The application of such studies is difficult when differences in company classes and markets between regions exist. These aspects will be discussed in detail in Section 3.9.

3.7 UNDERSTANDING THE STANDARDS OF VALUE

Most prominent standards of value which are relevant before, during, and after an M&A transaction are the FMV and the Investment Value as discussed in Section 2.7. The concept of the FMV is an internationally known and accepted term because the International Financial Reporting Standards (IFRS) use this concept for valuation of property, plant, and equipment in financial reporting. Additionally the FMV is used in the International Accounting Standards (IAS). Because most countries in the world with developed economies comply largely with IAS and comply in financial reporting with the requirements of the IFRS, the concept of the FMV is used globally. For example over 100 countries already require, allow, or are in the process of converting their national accounting standards so as to comply with IFRS. Despite its prominence, the usage and exact definition differs from country to country.

The Investment Value is a standard sought by a real estate appraisal and differs from FMV, which is impersonal and detached. In the context of M&A, the Investment Value is used at different stages and for different purposes. For the evaluation of strategic options and review of business planning the seller or an external advisor may asses the value of its business for a specific investor to prepare potential one-to-one negotiations. To track the development of shareholder value after a transaction, an acquirer may want to implement an integrated planning and valuation tool on the basis of the Investment Value of the target. Exhibit 3.18 and Exhibit 3.19 give an overview of value concepts and usages in the context of sell-side and buy-side M&A with reference to the respective standard setter and regulations in Germany.

In Germany, the standard of the FMV is well established because of the application of the IFRS in financial reporting and the definition of the term corresponds to the one used in the US. In the US, the FMV is the statutory value for all federal tax cases and is used throughout the Internal Revenue Code among other federal statutory laws including bankruptcy. The concept of the FMV is used in the context of M&A as a standard for fairness opinions, solvency opinions for impairment tests, and for evaluation of a potential transaction. In Germany, business valuation that is done by German public auditors needs to fulfil the requirements of the standards of the Institute of Public Auditors in Germany (IDW). The so-called IDW Standards are issued by either the Auditing & Accounting Board (the IDW's main technical committee) or the relevant technical committees such as the Expert Committee for Enterprise Valuation and Business Management. IDW Standard 1 sets out the principles for the performance of business valuations and is generally accepted not only by auditors but also by other valuation experts. In the context of M&A, IDW S1 finds its application because it defines a standard of value called the "objectively-determined corporate value" (Objectively Determined Value). In contrast to the FMV, this concept of value

- focuses on the existing business concept and actions clearly defined as of valuation date;
- is based on the last signed-off business plan and capital structure;
- values the target company stand-alone (including general synergies);
- uses the "German Income Approach" ("Ertragswertverfahren, EWV") as the dominant method (the DCF method is not used, even though it is accepted); and
- uses the market approach only for plausibility purposes.

Exhibit 3.18 M&A: value base and methodologies (sell-side M&A)

Phase	Situation	Deliverable	Rationale	Value concept	Valuation methods	Standards (Germany)
Evaluation of strategic options, review of business planning	• External analysis of business plan • Restructuring possibly necessary • Need of pre-deal reorganization • Risk of insolvency	• Independent Business Review • IDW S6	• Outside-in view • Unbiased analysis of strategic options • Show restructuring ability • Secure financing	• Investment value • Fair Market Value • N.a.	• Scenario analysis • Real options	• None • Best practice • IDW S6
Evaluation of transaction type & structure, recommendation to sell	• Leveraged & distressed situations • Fraud. conveyance • Spin-off, LBO • Regulated situations (corporate law): (de-) merger, shareholder resolution	• Solvency Opinion Analysis • IDW S1	• Affirm ongoing solvency after transaction • Protect decision makers • Valuation under corporate law are reserved for accountants	• Fair Market Value • Objectively Determined Value	• DCF/multiples/ balance sheet, cash flow and capital tests • Income approaches (DCF)/multiples for plausibility check	• Legislation, merger clauses • § 93 AktG/ UMAG • Legislation • IDW S1

Marketing: evaluation of offers, marketing presentation, due diligence	• Information asymmetry in favour of management • Management needs to publish a statement of position acc. WpÜG	• Fairness Opinion	• Show that decision to sell based on adequate information • Ensure knowledge of facts required under the transparency principle	• Fair Market Value	• DCF/multiples/ share price • pre-deal PPA	• DVFA/§ 93 AktG/§ 27 WpÜG/ 2290 NASD/ • IDW S 8
Deal structuring & negotiations: one or more selected buyers, negotiate SP&A elements & closing conditions	• Fraudulent conveyance: intentional/ constructive fraud, transfer of company with intend to defraud creditors	• Solvency Opinion	• Attest solvency to protect decision makers from personal liabilities and need to reverse transaction	• Fair Market Value	• DCF/multiples/ balance sheet, cash flow and capital tests	• Legislation, merger clauses • § 93 AktG/ UMAG

Value concept and methods which are useful before, during, and after an M&A transaction. In the evaluation and preparation of an M&A process, the seller and the buyer calculate their marginal prices at which they are willing to sell (lower boundary) or buy (upper boundary). An independent party may provide a fairness opinion to the decision maker (board) to see if the value of the target company corresponds to the offer price. Situations that are governed by corporate law may adhere to specific value concepts and methodologies like the Objectively Determined Value. From the seller's point of view, the M&A process is divided into four main phases: evaluation of strategic options, evaluation of transaction type, marketing, and negotiations. Different situations may occur for the seller and make distinct financial analyses necessary. The deliverables include different value concepts which again lead to the application of tailored valuation methods. In Germany, legislation and standards exist that prescribe the value concepts and valuation methodologies to be used. WpÜG stands for Wertpapierübernahmegesetz (German Securities Acquisition and Takeover Act), AktG for Aktiengesetz (German Stock Corporation Act), UMAG synonymous for Gesetz zur Unternehmensintegrität und Modernisierung des Anfechtungsrechts (German Code of the corporate integrity and modernization of the right of avoidance bill), DVFA for Deutsche Vereinigung für Finanzanalyse und Asset Management (Society of Investment Professionals in Germany), and NASD for National Association of Securities Dealers.

Exhibit 3.19 M&A: value base and methodologies (buy-side M&A)

Phase	Situation	Deliverable	Rationale	Value concept	Valuation methods	Standards (Germany)
Business planning & DD: BP and target evaluation, site visits & mgmt. interviews	• Pre-acquisition financing • Change of market conditions	• Solvency Opinion	• Eliminate uncertainty towards buyer's ability to comply with financial requirements from financing	• Fair Market Value	• DCF/multiples/balance sheet, cash flow and capital tests	• Legislation, merger clauses • § 93 AktG / UMAG
Deal structuring & negotiations: risk minimization, optimization of financial impact	• Regulated situations (corporate law): squeeze-out of minority shareholders • Significant change of acquirer's risk profile • Provisions in bond indenture or credit agreements	• IDW S1 • Fairness Opinion	• Valuation under corporate law are reserved for accountants • Address covenant that pertains to affiliated party or M&A transaction and requires a FO from independent provider	• Objectively Determined Value • Fair Market Value	• Income approaches (DCF) • Multiples for plausibility check • DCF/multiples/share price	• Legislation • IDW S1 • DVFA/ §93 AktG/2290 NASD/IDW ES

• Development of a realistic integration plan • Integration of general processes, reporting and planning systems	• PPA (IFRS) • Impairment test (IFRS/HGB) • Tax valuation	• Accounting consolidation and transparency • Assessments of impairment needs Creditor protection (HGB) • Create transparency • Support transfer pricing	• Purchase Price and Fair Value • Fair Value less costs to sell, value in use • Fair Value	• DCF and methods for intangible valuation • DCF/multiples und methods for intangible valuation • DCF/multiples/ net asset- and liquidation value	• IDW S 5/IDW RS HFA 16/IFRS 3/IAS 38 • IDW RS HFA 16/ IAS 36/ IDW RS HFA 10 • Tax authorities/ IDW S1/ Jurisdiction/ transfer pricing regulation
• Implementation of tools to monitor synergies & costs	• Post acquisition controlling • Development of an integrated planning and valuation tool	• Track shareholder value development after transaction	• Investor value	• Shareholder value added/ DCF/ Economic Value Added (EVA)	• Best practice

Value concept and methods that are useful before, during, and after an M&A transaction. In the evaluation and preparation of an M&A process, the seller and the buyer calculate their marginal prices at which they are willing to sell (lower boundary) or buy (upper boundary). An independent party may provide a fairness opinion to the decision maker (board) if the value of the target company corresponds to the offer price. Situations that are governed by corporate law may adhere to specific value concepts and methodologies like the Objectively Determined Value. From the bidder's point of view, the M&A process is divided into four main phases: business planning and due diligence, deal structuring and negotiations, (post M&A) integration, and monitoring. Different situations may occur for the bidder and make distinct financial analyses necessary. The deliverables include different value concepts which again lead to the application of tailored valuation methods. In Germany, legislation and standards exist that prescribe the value concepts and valuation methodologies to be used. WpÜG stands for Wertpapierübernahmegesetz (German Securities Acquisition and Takeover Act), AktG for Aktiengesetz (German Stock Corporation Act), UMAG for Gesetz zur Unternehmensintegrität und Modernisierung des Anfechtungsrechts (German Code of the corporate integrity and modernization of the right of avoidance bill), DVFA for Deutsche Vereinigung für Finanzanalyse und Asset Management (Society of Investment Professionals in Germany), and NASD (National Association of Securities Dealers).

The Objectively Determined Value takes the viewpoint of a typical market participant. As a consequence, no real synergies arc included and no discounts and premiums to the value are applied. The Objectively Determined Value standard is mainly used for situations that are regulated by law in Germany and finds its way into the M&A sell-side process in the evaluation phase when a de-merger is planned or when, following a majority transaction, the remaining minority shareholders should be squeezed out. In the evaluation and later stages of the M&A process other standards of the IDW may be applicable in case a restructuring opinion is necessary (IDW Standard 6) or the seller needs a Fairness Opinion (IDW Standard 8). Both standards do not require calculating an Objectively Determined Value. Other concepts of value are used; in case of a Fairness Opinion the FMV. The restructuring opinion does not include a valuation of the subject company but a feasibility study on the restructuring potential and the likelihood of long-term survival of the subject company.

How do the Standards of Value Tie into the Discount Discussion?

The seller of a private company is by definition the controlling owner. That means that a discount for the lack of liquidity should be taken from a control level of value. This value should reflect either what a control owner can expect to receive upon sale on a cash equivalent basis (in a transaction that is paid with cash) leading to a control buy-out value or what he might receive in a potential IPO. These are the value bases from which a potential DLL or PCD can be deducted. Section 3.3 has already mentioned that a discount for controlling ownership interest is justifiable because of transaction, flotation, and accounting and administrative costs a seller needs to bear for the selling process and the preparation of the company for the sale.

The value base needs to be estimated at a certain valuation date. The seller or advisor of the seller or provider of a fairness opinion uses the FMV standard to give an estimate about a potential buy-out price and narrow the lower bound for the selling price to be obtained. For the application of shareholder level discounts it is necessary to know if the FMV (and the Investment Value from the buyer's perspective) lead to a value that represents a control value.

Furthermore the FMV (and the Investment Value) constitutes a cash equivalent value at the valuation date. Therefore potential costs (direct and indirect) associated with the sale need to be deducted to derive the FMV today, which is achieved by application of a discount. With respect to the amount of discount to be deducted, either empirical evidence for the DLL at minority ownership level is available or the PCD at majority ownership interests. The PCD again accounts for more than liquidity differences and is more a "lump-sum" discount for risks that are associated with the sale of private firms.[10]

If the standard of value leads to a control value that requires liquidity, depends on the valuation methodologies used and on the cash flow streams that are included in the valuation.

3.8   UNDERSTANDING THE METHODOLOGIES

Various opinions exist amongst M&A professionals on the application of financial valuation theory on private companies. It is agreed that the principles of valuation remain the same, but there are estimation problems that are unique to private businesses, mostly related to the limited availability of accounting data, financial projections, and the lack of comparable

---

[10] Note at this point that depending on the measurement, the DLL is also not a measure of pure liquidity difference. See discussion of empirical studies on the DLL in Section 3.5.

companies. Two main methodologies prevail in the valuation of private companies in context of M&A and both can lead to different levels of value and liquidity assumptions.[11]

Income Approach

The income approach frames a group of valuation methodologies used by an appraiser for real estate and business valuation. The most prominent methodologies are the DCF approach or the capitalization of earnings or cash flows. Whether the income approach results in a value that reflects control depends on the cash flow or income streams included in the analysis. If the cash flow includes payment streams that are only available for the control owner, the income approach produces a control value. If an individual bidder includes potential synergies, then the income approach produces an Investment Value. Without any control adjustments to the cash flow streams, the resulting value represents a minority ownership value.

Two notes on the discount rate or capitalization rate. Firstly, although data are drawn from public stock markets from minority ownership returns, a differentiation or adjustment to derive control returns in the capitalization rate is impractical and would not yield to significant return adjustments as investors require returns depending on liquidity and systematic risk characteristics. Therefore, despite the minority ownership capitalization rate, it depends on the cash flows as to whether the income approach results in a minority or control value. Secondly, public stock market data generally require full marketability. Without any liquidity adjustments in the cash flows (e.g. potential floatation costs for later IPO) the resulting value derived by the income approach requires liquidity, which could be regarded as normal because M&A valuation specialists usually do not adjust cash flows for the cost of liquidity.

Analysts regard the income approach as the most important valuation approach since it reflects the fundamental value of the subject company. In Germany, standards of value like the Objectively Determined Value require the application of the EWV as the main valuation methodology. This is in contrast to the standards underlying the FMV, where the market and income approaches are equally important.

The main disadvantages in the application of the income approach to private companies are high unsystematic risk, unavailable ready-to-market values, and less reliable cash flow projections. Therefore, relative valuation methods (market approaches) are often used by investment professionals to back up fundamental valuation and to obtain a complete picture of the potential value of the company in question.

Market Approaches

Market approaches are widely used for valuation purposes especially in situations where the results of the income approaches need to be backed up by market date and situation where market transactions (M&A and IPO) are planned. In addition, some investor groups rely more or less heavily on market approaches. For example, venture capitalists heavily use multiples for their investment decisions. Furthermore, some accounting standards like the IDW Standard 1 suggest that multiples can be used to check whether the results of a previously conducted DCF valuation are reasonable.

---

[11] Next to the income approach and the market approach, the net asset approach gains more and more importance for distressed M&A situations. The asset based approach usually derives control values independently if the asset accumulations or the excess earnings method is used.

The underlying assumption using the market approach with multiples is that companies which expect the same future cash flows and face the same risk should be sold at the same prices. Although there are no completely identical companies, it is reasonable to assume that similar companies have similar prices. In most cases, a peer group of comparable companies or transactions can be found. To make the companies of the peer group comparable, multiples adjust differences in scales between firms by expressing their value relative to the firm scale.

Deriving multiples from publicly trading companies with similar characteristics as the subject company and application of the comparable transaction multiples to the subject company establishes a marketable minority level of value. Therefore it is appropriate to apply a control premium on the valuation done with comparable companies to derive a control value. However there are ongoing debates among valuation professionals, whether publicly traded minority interests represent a minority or a control value. All the discussion is animated in times where public market values exceed what any rational buyer would pay. But it is more appropriate to assume that public market values are meaningless when there are widely out of line with intrinsic values instead of claiming that publicly traded minority interests represent a control value. However, one point of the discussions is particularly interesting and would change the traditional level of value chart in Exhibit 3.1; that is the existence of liquidity (a publicly traded minority interest) tends to outweigh worries about the lack of control as long as the company is well managed. This would imply that a freely traded minority share with very high liquidity and little or no power would be worth more than a 100% control value with low or moderate liquidity and nearly total power. The debate is ongoing and no final recommendations have been concluded. The advice for valuation analysts at this point in time would be to be cautious when applying a control premium to a public market value to derive a control value, especially in markets with stock valuations that significantly exceed intrinsic values. A few words on the empirical evidence for control premiums: Mergerstat Review provides US data with yearly control premium statistics with median and mean premiums in the range of 30–40%. But, the variability of the results is large and premiums are affected by market conditions, form of consideration (cash vs. stock), and transaction terms. In particular, acquisition motives of the two main buyer groups (strategic, financial) are not accounted for, therefore the empirical measured control premiums may include more than pure control but synergistic premiums. Further problems arise as negative premiums are excluded from the median and mean calculations, so that these are too high whereas the variability of results is understated.

Deriving multiples from comparable transactions and application of the comparable valuation multiples to the subject company usually establishes a control level of value because most transaction data are derived from majority ownership transfers. If an analyst wants to evaluate a 100% ownership, it makes sense to look for transactions of 100% stakes. It is recommendable to look into transactions in detail to assess potential synergetic control premiums that are paid in addition to pure control values. As it is not easy to assess the amount of such premiums, positive outliers can be removed from the transaction universe together with the use of median multiples.

Whether majority transactions presuppose liquidity depends on the kind of company that has been acquired and other factors. A control transaction with a private firm would be the best comparable value in terms of liquidity as it is not necessary to deduct a discount. Unfortunately, the data situation is bad and transaction multiples are very rare. Therefore most information is available for control transactions with a public target, which assume higher liquidity than those with private targets (see Exhibit 3.21). It has been shown already that a transaction with a public company is more liquid but transaction multiples depend on different factors. Even when the analyst finds a transaction with similar target and transaction characteristics (size, time, industry), it is not possible to find a 100% match as too many other factors exert an influence. One should conclude that for control transactions with public targets the application of the PCD is indeed theoretically justified and empirically proven, but one cannot deduct a pure discount for the lack of liquidity as the empirical evidence for control transactions is missing.[12]

3.8.1 Summary

In praxis, valuation analysts use different methods (mostly income and market approaches), deriving a range of value for each of the approaches. For the situation in question he wants to compute the FMV, the Investment Value, or other standards of value. To derive these, he needs to make sure that the methods used derive at the right level of value. Assume that the analyst wants to value a 100% stake in a private company for a sale or an acquisition. He needs to assure that the valuation methods he uses derive control values. Before he/she selects a value or value range as the base value of the respective company with the approaches, he needs to check (1) what characteristics in terms of liquidity the value resulting from the single approaches has, and (2) how much discount he wants to apply for what reasoning. After application of an appropriate discount, he computes his base value (either a single value or, more commonly, a value range) by selecting a value range from the results of the single valuation approaches. These results can either be single value or value ranges. "Selecting from" usually means that the analyst takes the midpoint result of the single ranges that he computed with the different valuation approaches.

When looking at Exhibit 3.20 one can see that the traditional level of value overview and the respective discounts and premiums do not really help an analyst who wants to compute a control value in a private company. It is possible to derive a non-marketable minority ownership in a private company by application of a marketability discount to a publicly traded value. According to Exhibit 3.20 it is also possible to derive the value of a control share in a publicly traded company by application of a control premium to the stock market value of a minority share (this procedure is problematic due to biases in the evidence for control premiums). But it is not possible to derive the value of a control ownership in a private company using information in this chart.

Looking at control value shown in Exhibit 3.20, one can ask if this value suggests a control value in a publicly traded company. By looking at the methodology, one can see that the control value is either derived indirectly by application of a control premium to the publicly traded equivalent value or directly using either control cash flows with the income approach or the market approach using majority transactions with public targets. Therefore, one can conclude that the control value shown in Exhibit 3.20 is a control value in a publicly traded company.

Furthermore, the computation methodologies shown in Exhibit 3.20 to derive the control value suggest that the control value is a value that require a level of liquidity that is comparable to that of a publicly traded value. But is this true? No—it has already been shown that a

---

[12] Note again even the empirical evidence for the DLL for minority ownership transactions includes more than pure liquidity differences (see Section 3.6).

Indirect value computation   **Direct value computation**

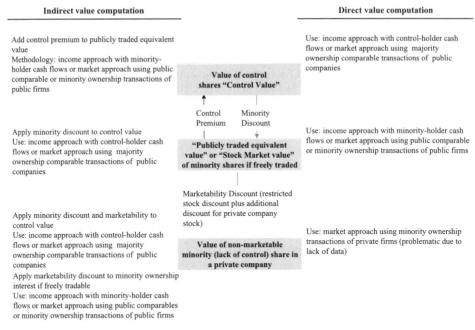

Add control premium to publicly traded equivalent value
Methodology: income approach with minority-holder cash flows or market approach using public comparable or minority ownership transactions of public firms

Apply minority discount to control value
Use: income approach with control-holder cash flows or market approach using majority ownership comparable transactions of public companies

Apply minority discount and marketability to control value
Use: income approach with control-holder cash flows or market approach using majority ownership comparable transactions of public companies
Apply marketability discount to minority ownership interest if freely tradable
Use: income approach with minority-holder cash flows or market approach using public comparables or minority ownership transactions of public firms

Use: income approach with control-holder cash flows or market approach using majority ownership comparable transactions of public companies

Use: income approach with minority-holder cash flows or market approach using public comparable or minority ownership transactions of public firms

Use: market approach using minority ownership transactions of private firms (problematic due to lack of data)

Exhibit 3.20   Level of value and associated discounts

majority ownership interest is not as liquid as a minority ownership interest. Why is this? In the context of selling a control ownership textbooks usually talk about transaction costs and the uncertainty of the selling process. Cash is not available within three to four business days, especially with legislations where the bidding company needs to submit an official, binding offer to all shareholders. These offers are often strictly regulated and force the bidding company to prepare accounting information and financial prospects and other preparations. These costs and these difficulties are not accounted for in the traditional view in Exhibit 3.20. The marketability discount referred to in the overview is especially dedicated to minority ownership interests; the empirical evidence is summarized under the term DLL. In addition, the empirical evidence for a possible marketability discount for majority ownerships in private companies is not included in the chart. To solve this dilemma, the overview in Exhibit 3.21 focuses on the liquidity and control dimension of value.

One can see that a control interest in a publicly traded firm (No. 2 in Exhibit 3.21) is never as liquid as a minority ownership interest (No. 4 in Exhibit 3.21) and a non-marketable control share in a private company (No. 1 in Exhibit 3.21) is more liquid than a non-marketable minority share in a private company (No. 3 in Exhibit 3.21), therefore the marketability discount for minority interests is not the same as for majority ownership interests. Furthermore one can only apply the classical empirical evidence for the marketability discount (DLL) when going from the full liquidity of the publicly equivalent value (No. 4 in Exhibit 3.21 to the liquidity of a minority interest in a private company (No. 3 in Exhibit 3.21). Theoretically there is a way from the publicly traded equivalent value (No. 4 in Exhibit 3.21) to the value of a control ownership in a private company (No. 1 in Exhibit 3.21) via a control premium and the respective marketability discount for majority interests. This way is troublesome: on the one

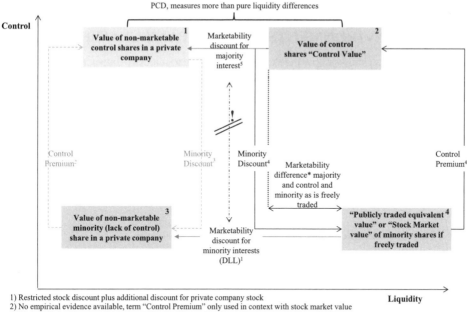

1) Restricted stock discount plus additional discount for private company stock
2) No empirical evidence available, term "Control Premium" only used in context with stock market value
3) No empirical evidence available, term "Minority Discount" only used in context with Control Value
4) Empirical evidence available
5) No empirical evidence available, empirical studies focus on measurement of the PCD, part of the discount is attributable to liquidity
   differences between a Control Value and a non-marketable control share in a private company.

Exhibit 3.21   Liquidity and control as two dimensions of value

hand one needs to apply the control premium first which leads to some bias already at this point, on the other hand, the evidence for a pure marketability discount for majority ownership interests is not available. In addition, the application of a control premium on the value of a non-marketable minority interest (No. 3 in Exhibit 3.21) to derive at the non-marketable control interest (No. 2 in Exhibit 3.21) (and vice versa with the minority discount) is not feasible for two reasons. First, to derive at the value of a non-marketable minority interest (No. 3 in Exhibit 3.21), a marketability discount (DLL) has already been deducted which should not be used when the (ultimate) goal is to value a non-marketable control value in a private company. The value of a non-marketable minority interest (No. 3 in Exhibit 3.21) is not directly calculable as minority ownership transactions with private firms with sufficient transaction data are not observable. Secondly (and more simply), the evidence for the control premium and the minority discount refers to value differences between publicly traded ownership interests (Nos 2 and 4 in Exhibit 3.21) and is therefore not applicable for private company valuation. Theoretically the best way to compute the value of a non-marketable control interest in a private firm (No. 1 in Exhibit 3.21) is to compute and use empirical evidence on the marketability discount for majority ownership interests to derive the value of control interest in a private firm. This pure marketability evidence does not exist, but rather evidence for the PCD that accounts for more than liquidity differences. With the PCD and a thorough analysis of the PCD and its influencing factors, an analyst can assess the influence of the marketability on the value of the non-marketable control interest in a private firm more precisely.

3.9   APPLICATION PROBLEMS RESULTING FROM SYSTEMATIC DIFFERENCE BETWEEN MARKET ENVIRONMENTS AND COMPANY CLASSES

The previous chapter showed how the PCD can be applied to majority transactions: the standard of value was introduced and how methodologies to derive such need to be taken into account. The magnitude of such has been shown and existing empirical evidence summarized. Furthermore explanations for the PCD and factors that influence differences in transaction multiples between private and public firms have been shown. The upcoming sections aim to show which issues arise for professionals outside the US who want to use empirical research done on the US market for the PCD. Next to differences in accounting standards which can be overcome by the choice of transaction multiples, the geographical and economic disparity between countries limits the applicability of studies from the US market area to non-US markets.

3.9.1   Economic Market Environment

Studies done outside the home country of an analyst who wants to value a local company may be not applicable to the special market environment and company characteristics prevailing in his home country. In Germany, for example, independent private companies are smaller than US firms and compared to their acquirers, smaller than the respective private firms in the US. As valuation multiples increasing with increasing relative size of the targets compared to their acquirers, the PCD found in the U.S. studies may be too small for an application in Germany and other countries.

Furthermore, market liquidity and activity on the M&A markets influence the PCD and depend, in addition to general economic conditions and investor sentiment, also on the behaviour of local and foreign investors which can be different across market regions. In Germany, a high level of interest from foreign investors has driven the M&A market over recent years and it could be shown that these investors pay more for private companies than domestic acquirers, indicating a strong demand for them (see Exhibit 3.39). According to Exhibit 3.22, between 1997 and June 2011 around 69% of deals with private targets were cross-border deals in Germany vs. around 16% in North America and 26% in Western Europe as a whole; 48% of public companies were acquired by foreign investors in Germany compared to 19% of public companies in North America and 40% of Western European public companies.

Next to the size differences between the markets (huge domestic market in North America vs. small domestic markets in Germany and Western Europe), the attractiveness of the German and other Western European markets has been increased for foreign investors by the Eastern enlargement of the European Union and continuing globalization. The opening up of the market and the impounded buying power has revived the European market and Germany itself as the largest national economy. In particular Germany represents an optimal platform to supply the whole European market. Furthermore, foreign investors are interested in well-known German brands, in innovative technologies, and in the appreciation of their own brands with the label "made in Germany". Often American, European, and Asian investors are willing to pay significantly more than a comparable local buyer, thereby influencing the size of the PCD measured if controlled for this factor. As foreign investors are not as present in other markets (like the US) as in Germany, the PCD in Germany not controlling for the investor's region may underestimate the observed discount.

Exhibit 3.22   Fractions of domestic and cross-border transactions

	Region							
	Germany		North America		Western Europe		UK	
Target public status	Cross-border share	Transactions	Cross-border share	Transactions	Cross border share	Transactions	Cross-border share	Transactions
Public	47.8%	232	18.6%	4,413	39.3%	1,866	32.8%	1,330
Independent private	73.7%	327	15.5%	3,408	25.5%	2,819	16.9%	2,436
Dependent private	65.6%	500	18.0%	1,883	26.5%	3,495	23.8%	2,780
Total private	68.8%	827	16.4%	5,291	26.0%	6,314	20.6%	5,216
Grand total	64.2%	1,059	18.6%	10,713	29.8%	8,756	22.7%	7,137

The sample consists of completed majority-ownership transactions between January 1997 and June 2007 used in the study in Section 3.11. For details on data see Exhibit 3.35. For each region and separated for public, independent private, and dependent private companies, the table reports the percentage of companies that have been acquired by firms with headquarters outside of the targets' home country.
Source: Zephyr database, Bureau von Dijk.

3.9.2   Market Environment – Time

A main problem with respect to the application of existing DLL studies is that they are often outdated and the time span used is often too short to capture different market cycles. Research has already indicated that the state of the economy affects the activity on the M&A market and the prices paid in transactions. For example, in periods of decreased market activity, private targets suffer from a lower liquidity leading to a higher PCD. Most studies do not capture changes in the market environment after 2007. Since mid-2007, the subprime crisis has influenced the M&A, stock, and credit markets all over the world but with different consequences for the single markets with respect to transaction valuations, transaction activity, as well as equity and debt financing. In Germany, for example, this period constitutes a particularly critical time especially for independent private (Mittelstand) companies. Financing conditions for the Mittelstand have worsened in the course of the subprime crisis, not only because banks have suffered financial losses, but also because the regulatory conditions for the banking environment have been tightened (Basel II and Basel III). Furthermore, the use of alternative forms of financing, e.g. via mezzanine products, is nowadays more difficult for the Mittelstand as the mezzanine market with its EUR 5–6 billion volume was disrupted by the subprime crisis. A further consolidation and restructuring within the banking sector, risk-adequate credit pricing, and a lack of financing alternatives shaped the future development of the lending business and increased the pressure on independent private firms to seek an equity investor for their companies. According to Exhibit 3.23, owners of independent private companies were able to sell their firms before the subprime crisis even when the company's financial condition was tight. The median D/E ratio for companies sold between 2004 and June 2007 was 3.7x compared to 2.1x for dependent companies in Germany, 2.4x for dependent private North American companies, and 1.4x for dependent private companies in Western Europe and the UK.

Exhibit 3.23   Development of leverage ratios

			before 2001	2001–2003	2004–Jun 07	Pre Subprime (1997–Jul 07)	Subprime (Aug 07-Mar 09)	Post Subprime (Apr 09-Jun 11)	1997–June 11
Germany	Target D/E	independent private	3.1x	3.4x	3.7x	3.6x	2.8x	1.8x	3.3x
		dependent private	2.2x	2.8x	2.1x	2.6x	1.7x	1.3x	2.0x
North America	Target D/E	independent private	2.1x	2.5x	2.1x	2.1x	1.8x	1.6x	2.1x
		dependent private	2.3x	2.9x	2.4x	2.5x	1.6x	1.7x	1.9x
Western Europe	Target D/E	independent private	1.9x	1.5x	1.6x	1.6x	1.6x	1.2x	1.5x
		dependent private	1.7x	1.5x	1.4x	1.8x	1.4x	1.3x	1.8x
UK	Target D/E	independent private	1.5x	1.4x	1.5x	1.5x	1.2x	1.3x	1.4x
		dependent private	1.8x	1.4x	1.4x	1.4x	1.4x	1.2x	1.4x

The sample consists of completed majority-ownership transactions between January 1997 and June 2007 used in the study in Section 3.11. For details on data see Exhibit 3.35. Only those transactions are shown for which information on leverage is available. For each region and separated for independent private and dependent private companies, the table reports the development of the targets' D/E ratios over the different time periods.
Source: Zephyr database, Bureau von Dijk.

During the subprime crisis leverage ratios of independent private companies sold decreased (from D/E ratio of 3.7x to 2.8x) indicating that highly leveraged companies had no chance to be sold at all during this period and increasing pressure on the seller of independent private companies. This pressure in combination with worsening debt financing conditions and the decreased liquidity in the M&A markets may have led the owners of independent private companies to accept lower transaction valuations in exchange for cash. Exhibit 3.24 shows the development of multiples over the different market periods in Germany and investigates whether the development of multiples differs between the independent private companies, dependent private companies, and public companies.

Comparing the first three periods, one can see that despite the slowdown of markets between 2001 and 2003, multiples for all three company classes increased constantly; differences exist in the magnitude of increase: whereas multiples (ex P/E) of independent private companies increased by on average 100%, multiples of public companies improve by nearly 110% and those of dependent private only by around 75%.

Comparing the period before the subprime crisis (2004–June 2007) to that of the subprime crisis itself (August 2007–March 2009), one can see that sales multiples for independent private companies decreased nearly 30% and valuation on EV/EBITDA and EV/EBIT by around 27%. At the same time, multiples for public targets increased on average by around 10%. Valuations for dependent private companies did not change on average, but developed differently for the sales and EV/EBITDA and EV/EBIT multiple. Valuations for independent

Exhibit 3.24   Median multiples in Germany across periods

Independent private companies

Multiple	before 2001	2001– 2003	2004– Jul 07	Subprime Aug 07-Mar 09	Post subprime Apr 09-Jun 11
EV/Sales	0.7x	0.7x	1.7x	1.2x	1.3x
EV/EBITDA	5.6x	9.5x	9.9x	8.0x	8.5x
EV/EBIT	6.3x	9.9x	13.7x	9.2x	15.6x
P/E	n.m.	n.m.	n.m.	n.m.	n.m.

Public companies

Multiple	before 2001	2001– 2003	2004– Jul 07	Subprime Aug 07-Mar 09	Post subprime Apr 09-Jun 11
EV/Sales	0.8x	2.0x	2.0x	2.2x	2.4x
EV/EBITDA	6.5x	10.2x	12.4x	14.0x	17.9x
EV/EBIT	7.5x	13.4x	16.1x	16.2x	19.8x
P/E	19.7x	n.m.	14.6x	19.1x	13.7x

Dependent private companies

Multiple	before 2001	2001– 2003	2004– Jul 07	Subprime Aug 07-Mar 09	Post subprime Apr 09-Jun 11
EV/Sales	0.8x	0.9x	1.3x	1.0x	1.6x
EV/EBITDA	5.6x	8.3x	9.3x	11.1x	12.6x
EV/EBIT	6.8x	13.0x	12.6x	12.6x	16.3x
P/E	n.m	n.m	15.3x	n.m	n.m

The sample for the period before the subprime crisis consists of completed majority-ownership transactions between January 1997 and June 2011 used in the study in Section 3.11. For details on data see Exhibit 3.35. 327 transactions include acquired independent private companies, 500 transactions include dependent private companies and 232 transactions include public targets. "n.m." indicates that the number of observable transactions for this multiple/period combination is less than 20. The P/E multiple is therefore excluded from further analyses.
Source: Zephyr database, Bureau von Dijk.

private companies seem to have suffered most during the bad market environment between August 2007 and March 2009 even though the highly leveraged firms have not been sold on the M&A market at all. Later chapters will show how the discounts developed when companies are matched correctly.

Post the subprime crisis all three company classes in Germany seem to have experienced a recovery in transaction multiples. Altogether one can see that multiples react to overall market conditions but the development is not always as expected and might be biased through hidden influence factors or problems with respect to sample size. Therefore, development of multiples only gives a very imprecise indication of how discounts might behave over time; the correct matching of companies is necessary to be able to interpret the influence of market conditions more precisely.

Our analysis of periods in Section 3.12 shows that the selection of periods and the clustering of transaction years into five periods cannot account for the development of every multiple in each region; in particular the time pattern during/post subprime seems not to be as pronounced as would be desirable. In regions like Western Europe, the pattern is more obvious perhaps due to better data availability.

3.9.3   Firm Characteristics

Independent private firms, especially the Mittelstand in Germany, seem to have a widespread aversion to drawing up financial plans, making a commitment in figures, and to publishing financial data. In Germany, although there exists according to §325ff and §364a to §364c of the German Commercial Code (HGB) a legal requirement for capital companies, including GmbH and GmbH & Co KG and certain partnerships to publish some financial data (annual accounts), only approximately 50% of companies follow this order due to weak enforcement. Since January 2007, only small penalties of between EUR 2,500 to EUR 25,000 have been enforced. Only 7% of the 40 companies used in the analysis in Chapter 2 of the book have financial planning data readily available. The vast majority create financial plans only in the context of the disposal process.

Many owners of independent private firms have problems in finding a qualified successor within the family. Owners are often heirless and therefore someone external is brought in to run the company after their retirement. According to the IfM, about 110,000 small and medium-sized companies need(ed) to solve the succession problem between 2010 and 2014; around 20% are sold to outside investors because there is no appropriate family member to take over the company, and of those, 44% are sold to strategic investors or private equity firms. The necessity to secure the company's survival via an exit may increase the selling pressure on independent private companies, leading to an unfavourable timing decision. During difficult market conditions, as in the subprime crisis, succession problems may induce some additional disposal pressure that leads to an unfavourable timing decision and lower valuations.

Furthermore, there exists a widespread myth especially in Germany that owners of independent private firms show a reluctance to sell their firms to a private equity investor. These are called "Heuschrecken" (lit. "locusts" but a synonym for corporate raiders), a dangerous species of investors that tries to sneak into a company and sell off the firm maximizing their own wealth regardless of the interests of employees, customers, and other stakeholders. It is assumed that many families worry about the loss of their company's heritage and identity. This negative image persists especially in Germany, in contrast to other markets like North America where market participants tend to be much more open to investors from the PE scene.

A detailed analysis of time periods is shown in Exhibit 3.25. One can see that the vast majority of independent private companies are sold to strategic investors, but private equity investors are increasingly interested in these companies. The share of independent private companies sold to private equity investors increases from 12.1% before the subprime crisis to 24.5% during the subprime crisis. A possible explanation might be that the subprime crisis forced the private equity industry to finance a higher share of a transaction with equity. Before the subprime crisis, around 30% equity was sufficient to obtain debt financing for a leveraged buy-out (LBO) transaction. In the course of the crisis, the figure changed to 40–50%. An increased equity portion and tight refinancing conditions mean that active private equity investors need to focus on smaller transactions. For example, according to the Zephyr database,[13] no private equity investor announced any deal with a transaction above USD 250m in Germany in Q4/2007. In addition, deal volumes of private equity investors decreased by approximately 60% in 2008 compared to the first six months of 2007, whereas the number of transactions only decreased by approximately 22%.

---

[13] For details on the Zephyr database, please refer to Section 3.13.6.

Exhibit 3.25 A comparison of time periods

				Period		
Target	Parameter	before 2011	2001–2003	2004-June 07	Pre subprime (1997-Jul 07)	Subprime (Aug 07-Mar 09)	Postsubprime (Apr 09-Jun11)
Independent private	Number of deals	51	74	123	248	53	26
	Deals per year	13	25	35	24	30	12
	Share sold to private equity investors	23.5%	13.5%	6.6%	12.1%	24.5%	38.5%
	Median D/E ratio	3.1	3.4	3.7	3.6	2.8	1.8
Dependent private	Number of deals	47	99	213	359	83	58
	Deals per year	12	33	61	34	47	27
	Share sold to private equity investors	8.5%	13.1%	10.8%	11.2%	11.1%	7.0%
	Median D/E ratio	2.2	2.8	2.1	2.6	1.7	1.3

The sample for the period before the subprime crisis consists of completed majority-ownership transactions between January 1997 and June 2011 used in the study in Section 3.11. For details on data see Exhibit 3.35. For computation of the D/E ratio, only those transactions are shown for which information on leverage is available. The table reports the median leverage and percentage of companies sold to private equity investors. It compares the development over the five different time periods for the independent and dependent private companies separately.
Source: Zephyr database, Bureau von Dijk.

With an increasing share sold to private equity investors, one can ask if the selling pressure, the lack of alternative financing, and severe succession problems make owners of independent private companies sell to private equity. According to Exhibit 3.25 the leverage of independent private companies has no clear relationship to the percentage of companies sold to private equity investors. In the last two periods before the subprime crisis, the median D/E ratio increased from 3.4x (period 2001–2003) to 3.7x (period 2004–06/2007) whereas the share sold to private equity firms decreased from 13.5% to 6.6%. But during the subprime crisis, the D/E ratio of independent private targets decreased (compare the D/E ratio of 3.7x to 2.8x despite the strongly rising share of independent private companies sold to P/E (from 6.6% to 24.5%). From this point of view, there seems to be no additional selling pressure on independent private companies to desperately sell their highly leveraged companies to private equity investors trying to make a good bargain. One may conclude that private equity investors actively seek independent private companies and turn away from mega deals to lower target values. It will be shown later, if and how the transaction valuations for independent private companies by private equity investors have increased, for example due to a certain investing pressure and the stronger focus on the Mittelstand. After the crisis, the share of independent private companies sold to private equity investors changes to 38.5% with leverage remaining at 1.8x.

Given the differences described in the market environments across regions, the different development of multiples over time, and because those factors that drive systematic differences between firms – such as leverage, information availability, or financing possibilities – are not the same in all economic regions, one must conclude that the application of US research for non-US company valuations is problematic. The consideration of regional differences seems to improve the accuracy of the research and the applicability of results in company valuations. Furthermore, the changes in market environments over time influence the M&A activity and valuations. Therefore, the following sections present the results of a study that uses the acquisition approach and analyzes the valuation of private companies in majority ownership M&A transactions over the period from January 1997 to June 2011 and compares the transaction valuations of the private companies to publicly traded target companies. The analysis encompasses several regions including: Western Europe (excluding Germany), Germany, United Kingdom (UK), and North America (NA) and attempts to analyze regional differences with a focus on the German market and on the North American market as the world's biggest market.

The study seeks to answer the following questions: what are the actual magnitudes of PCDs for different companies and how do the PCDs develop over time? Are discounts different with respect to regions and do the idiosyncrasies of independent private firms influence transaction multiples? Is it therefore necessary to differentiate between independent and dependent private companies in PCD studies? What are the explanatory factors for the PCD?

Thus, the study

- splits private companies into two classes (independent and dependent), and analyzes them separately;
- looks for the existence of valuation differences between the independent private and dependent private companies and publicly traded firms;
- focuses on factors that influence the PCD and the determination of the magnitude of the PCD depending on the factors;
- looks at factors beyond those already incorporated in existing studies that are especially related to the idiosyncrasies of private companies and local market environment in North America and Germany;

- shows that the application of results found in US studies to private firm valuation outside the US and especially to the German Mittelstand is limited, and comes up with actual numbers for the PCDs in different regions;
- analyzes how the subprime crisis influences the M&A market, especially in Germany, and
- analyzes the development of multiples over time and especially during the subprime crisis and compares the deterioration of multiples between the independent and dependent private companies, and public companies.

The next Section 3.10 starts with a description of some market developments and shows how M&A activity and valuations have been influenced by the recent changes. Thereafter the results of the study are presented in Section 3.11 and Section 3.12 and tips for conducting one's own research on the PCD are given in Section 3.13.

3.10 DEVELOPMENT OF THE MARKET ENVIRONMENT

Time is an important factor when analyzing M&A transactions and multiples. Exhibit 3.26 shows M&A transaction volumes across different regions. Until December 2000, M&A markets were relatively active reaching high levels at the end of 2000. The M&A markets slowed down sharply beginning in 2001 and further decreased during 2002 and 2003. From the beginning of 2004 M&A volumes increased and reached a record level in the second half of 2007.

In the course of the subprime crisis, a dramatic decrease in volumes began. The development of the stock market indices starting mid-2007 (see Exhibit 3.30) shaped M&A activity and had a very notable effect on economic conditions and several market participants. The subprime crisis has led, for example, to significant losses for banks and pension and hedge funds due

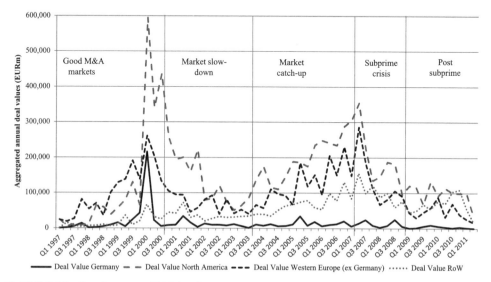

Exhibit 3.26 Development of M&A volumes
Source: Zephyr database, Bureau von Dijk.

to mortgage asset devaluation and significant write downs.[14] After mortgage bonds lost about 60% to 80% of their value in 2007, the leveraged finance and high-yield debt markets experienced a notable slowdown in issuance levels in high-yield and leveraged loans.[15] Uncertain market conditions have led to a significant widening of yield spreads all over the world. Furthermore, after the announcement of significant write downs by major lenders, the leveraged finance markets have come to a near standstill, making it nearly impossible to finance an LBO and impeding general M&A activity. In addition, tighter lending standards and a general rise in risk aversion have led to banks making more frequent use of 'material adverse change' clauses in their financing contracts to withdraw agreed acquisition financing.

According to the Zephyr database, global M&A volumes decreased by more than 35% in the first half of 2008 compared to the first six months of 2007. The European core markets Germany and France in particular experienced an even stronger downturn in M&A volumes in the first half of 2008 (−58.4% and −61.1%) compared to the market in North America (−40.9%), as the subprime crisis hit the European markets later than the US. After a very bad first quarter in 2008, with a volume decrease of 78% to USD 6bn, the German M&A market showed improving tendencies in the second quarter and some professionals estimated that the slowdown in M&A activity for 2008, as a consequence of the subprime crisis, would be smaller than predicted. Since mega mergers were rare, this would be mainly attributable to lower volume transactions. According to the Zephyr database, from the first half of 2007 to the first half of 2008, transactions with a deal volume below USD 250m decreased by 39%; whereas for the same period, transactions with deal volumes above USD 250m decreased by around 71%. The dramatic decline in M&A volumes continued until the first quarter of 2009. From then, a slight recovery rings in the period post subprime crisis, starting in countries like Germany where extensive governmental support programmes were launched. For example, in 2008 the German Minister of Economics and the Minister of Finance jointly announced that the total government backed bailout amounted to EUR 7.2bn for the IKB. The German IKB was the first European bank to declare financial trouble due to the subprime disaster, as it had heavily invested (around EUR 13bn) in US subprime loans with one of its funds. Furthermore, the government decided to scrap the premium of EUR 5,000 to promote the sale of new cars beginning in 2009, a measure that was extremely successful in encouraging consumer sentiment. Comparable rescue packages were also introduced in other countries in Western Europe like France, Spain, and Austria and quickly improved the general market climate.

During the subprime crisis, not only did M&A volumes change but also the activity of certain groups of market participants. Exhibit 3.25 has already shown that private equity investors change their focus from mega merger to smaller transaction with private companies. Furthermore, Exhibit 3.22 showed that the mix of foreign and domestic investors differs from region to region. In the course of the subprime crisis, the composition may have changed as well with consequences for transaction multiples. Exhibit 3.27 shows that the percentage of foreign investors in Germany is increasing. The percentage of foreign investors that announced acquisitions in Germany increased to 55% in the middle of the subprime crisis Q1/2008 compared to 50% in the year before. Foreign acquirers mainly came from European countries

---

[14] According to Bloomberg as of 12 August 2008, Financial institutions had recognized subprime-related losses and write downs exceeding USD 600bn. In Germany, the biggest write downs so far had to be borne by Deutsche Industriebank (USD 15.3bn), Deutsche Bank (USD 10.8bn), and BayernLB (USD 6.4bn), see http://www.bloomberg.com/apps/news.

[15] According to Standard & Poor's Leveraged Commentary & Data (LCD), North American high-yield issuance was down 47% until August 2008, falling to USD 55.2bn from USD 103.3bn in 2007. According to Thomson Reuters, the number of US junk debt offerings was down 64% to USD 35bn in 2008.

Exhibit 3.27   Target regions of transactions announced by non-German investors

	Germany	Europe	Russia	North America	Asia	South America	Middle East	Africa	Total
Pre subprime (Q1/2007)	49.6%	27.6%	0.4%	8.8%	1.3%	0.9%	0.0%	0.4%	228
Middle of subprime (Q1/2008)	54.9%	23.3%	0.0%	5.2%	3.6%	0.0%	2.6%	0.0%	183
Number of transactions	219	108	1	30	10	2	5	1	411

The sample consists of all the acquisitions in Germany announced by companies headquartered outside Germany. The column "Europe" excludes Germany. The table details the regions of the investors which sought acquisitions in Germany in the first quarter of 2008 compared to the first quarter of 2007.
Source: Zephyr database, Bureau von Dijk.

and market participants expected an increasing demand for German targets from Asia and the Arab world.

On the other hand, German investors increasingly announced domestic transactions.

According to Exhibit 3.28, the share increased from around 55% in Q1/2007 to 59% in Q1/2008. German investors do not seem to have used the weak USD to buy cheaply in North America. The share decreased around by 3 percentage points. In addition, selected acquisitions in Asia and Middle East were planned. Altogether, it seems reasonable to assume that in the course of the subprime crisis in countries like Germany, private firms represented an attractive target for different sorts of investors such as private equity investors or foreign acquirers.

The size differences which exist between public and private companies were discussed in Section 3.6.2. According to Exhibit 3.11, the average assets of independent private companies amount to approximately EUR 11.5m compared to EUR 93.9m for public companies. The question can be raised as to whether the market environment influences the size of companies acquired. Exhibit 3.29 gives an overview of some of the company parameters after the beginning of the subprime crisis and shows that in Germany independent private companies are smaller than other private companies and relatively small in comparison to their

Exhibit 3.28   Target regions of transactions announced by German investors

	Germany	Europe	Russia	North America	Asia	South America	Middle East	Africa	Total
Pre subprime (Q1/2007)	55.1%	31.0%	1.6%	6.1%	3.7%	0.8%	0.4%	1.2%	245
Middle of subprime (Q1/2008)	59.1%	30.1%	1.8%	3.6%	4.0%	0.4%	1.1%	0.0%	276
Number of transactions	298	159	9	25	20	3	4	3	521

The sample consists of all the acquisitions announced by companies headquartered in Germany. The column "Europe" excludes Germany. The table details the regions in which German investors sought acquisitions in the first quarter of 2008, compared to the first quarter of 2007.
Source: Zephyr database, Bureau von Dijk.

Exhibit 3.29 Size differences over time

Target status		Aug 07- Mar 09 Subprime — Assets (EUR '000) Median	Apr 09-Jul 11 Post subprime — Relative size (assets) Median	Aug 07- Mar 09 Subprime — Relative size (assets) Median	2004-Jul 07 (Pre subprime) — Relative size (assets) Median
Germany	Private independent private	4,741	4.7%	1.6%	0.2%
	dependent private	50,286	3.5%	2.7%	2.8%
	Private total	16,420	4.4%	2.1%	1.6%
	Public	73,613	35.6%	11.7%	13.9%
North America	Private independent private	15,015	4.0%	4.4%	4.2%
	dependent private	79,751	4.0%	4.2%	4.1%
	Private total	26,045	3.9%	4.3%	4.1%
	Public	275,284	17.4%	12.5%	13.4%
Western Europe	Private independent private	4,987	2.5%	2.3%	2.5%
	dependent private	23,570	6.4%	5.5%	4.8%
	Private total	11,136	4.2%	3.6%	3.8%
	Public	86,741	33.3%	13.7%	19.5%
UK	Private independent private	5,462	3.7%	2.9%	3.4%
	dependent private	14,981	3.3%	4.2%	4.0%
	Private total	8,978	3.5%	0.3%	3.7%
	Public	88,180	16.9%	30.8%	23.7%

The sample consists of completed majority-ownership transactions between January 1997 and June 2011 used in the study in Section 3.11. For details on data see Exhibit 3.35. The table consists of only those transactions where companies provide information on turnover or assets. The table reports the absolute numbers of the assets of the target companies, and the relative size of the target companies compared to their acquirers. Bold figures denote significance at a min. 10% level.
Source: Zephyr database, Bureau von Dijk.

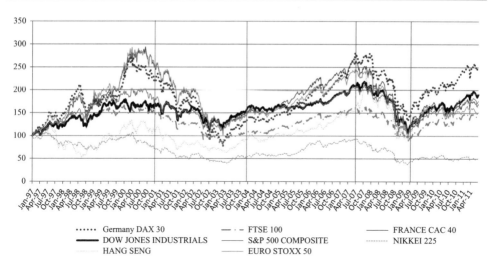

Germany DAX 30	FTSE 100	FRANCE CAC 40
DOW JONES INDUSTRIALS	S&P 500 COMPOSITE	NIKKEI 225
HANG SENG	EURO STOXX 50	

Exhibit 3.30   Development of major indices
Development of major indices (price indices); 1 January 1997 = 100
Source: Zephyr database, Bureau von Dijk.

acquirers. Compared to the pre-subprime period, their relative size increased but remains, at 1.6%, relatively low. Since the subprime crisis, independent private companies seem to profit from the circumstance that the acquisition of a smaller company is easier to finance and therefore attractive to even smaller investors – the relative size increased to 4.7% Transactions with deal sizes below EUR 100m in particular have not experienced as many cutbacks in terms of number and volume as bigger transactions.

Concerning the other regions, there is no clear pattern concerning the development of size over time. From the pre-subprime to the subprime period, all private companies in North America increased slightly in relation to their acquirers, post subprime they decreased. In Western Europe independent private companies decreased from the pre-subprime to the subprime period, post subprime they remain at their starting level. Only dependent private companies increased from 4.8% pre-subprime to 5.5% during the subprime crisis to 6.4% post subprime. In the UK, independent private firms decreased and dependent private companies increased comparing pre-subprime with the subprime crisis. Thereafter, both classes of private companies develop in the opposite direction.

Looking at the stock market development during this period in Exhibit 3.30, one can see that M&A activity develops concurrently with the stock market development. Until the end of 2000, stock markets in all Western regions developed very positively. The market downturns from January 2001 hit stock markets globally but markets like North America showed more robustness. Stock markets recovered mid-2003 and reached peaks mid-2007 or beginning 2008. After the record highs, the main indices fell around 20% until the end of August 2007. High daily losses and increasing volatility characterized the indices all over the world. On 21 January 2008 the DAX, for example, lost more than 7%, and two days later again around 5%. Similar drops occurred in virtually every market in the world. The Nikkei, for example, lost around 6% on 22 January 2008, and the DJ Industrial lost 6% from 7–11 November 2007 and has experienced more than 20 days of daily drops over 2% since July 2007. The crisis caused panic amongst market participants and everyone was nervous, from bank executives, regulators and central bankers to ordinary investors who had taken their money out of risky

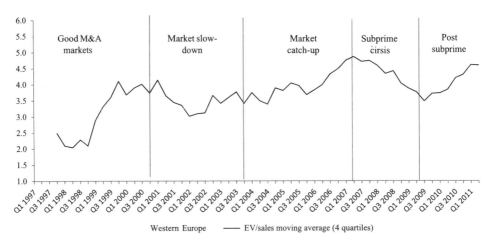

Exhibit 3.31 Development of average EV/Sales multiple in Western Europe
Moving average of average EV/Sales multiples for all completed transactions in Western Europe.
Source: Zephyr database, Bureau von Dijk.

mortgage bonds and equities and put it into commodities as "stores of value". Market recovery started at the end of the first quarter of 2009 after enormous governmental programmes and rescue packages all over the world came into effect.

Exhibit 3.31 shows the development of the EV/Sales multiples in Western Europe. One can see that transaction multiples develop over time; valuations between 2001 and 2003 were lower than in the two years before and in the following market catch-up. The subprime period shows a downgrade of around 35% from the peak end 2006 to the low Q2/2009. After the subprime crisis, multiples came back with a lag of some months; the lag could also be observed in the period 2004–06/2007. Exhibit 3.31 does not distinguish between private and public transactions, usually multiples for private transactions lag around six months behind stock market development and the development of multiples for public targets.

3.11 PCD STUDY

3.11.1 Short Note on Methodology

The objective of this study is to find empirical evidence for discounts attached to private companies in different market environments over time and attribute the discounts to the lack of liquidity and other influence factors. This study uses the acquisition approach, which is explicitly applicable to control situations and compares transaction multiples from private to respective multiples achieved in comparable transactions with public targets by computing a ratio shown in Equation 3.1 in Section 3.6. A matching technique is used to compare valuations of private and public companies, as described in Section 3.13.3.

A two-step procedure is used consisting of a univariate analysis with cross-tabs in a first step and multivariate cross-sectional regressions in a second step. The three systematic factors of size, time of transaction, and industry are accounted for. Furthermore, other controlling factors like payment method, the acquirer's origin, or leverage are included based on prior empirical findings.

For the three systematic influence factors, clusters are built to consolidate data, which is useful as it accounts for the possible limited availability of transactions for some value of the influence factors and allows one to include controlling factors beyond size, transaction time, and industry in the subsequent regressions. Nine size classes (6–14) as shown in Exhibit 3.51 are computed.

Furthermore, five periods (1–5) are taken into account as shown in Exhibit 3.52 and five industry groups (SIC codes 30XX–39XX; 40XX–49XX; 50XX–59XX; 60XX–67Xx; 70XX–79XX) according to Exhibit 3.55. As the study seeks to show whether dependent and independent private companies are valued differently, the universe of private companies is split into dependent and independent and their valuations are compared separately against public companies. For the cross-sectional analysis using multivariate regressions as specified in Equation 3.3 in Section 3.13 the model is computed for ratios on one multiple m (EV/EBITDA) and for two regression samples z involving only German companies (sample 1, sample 2). In addition, two regressions with North American companies (sample 3, sample 4), two with Western European companies (sample 5, sample 6), and two with UK companies (sample 7, sample 8) are computed.

This leads to eight samples z in Exhibit 3.32.

Exhibit 3.32 Overview of samples

Target	Sample	Reference portfolio	Dependent variable	Mutliple used	Number of cases j
German independent	1	Public companies in Germany	Discounts on independent private companies in Germany	EV/EBITDA	143
German dependent	2	Public companies in Germany	Discounts on dependent private companies in Germany	EV/EBITDA	216
North America independent	3	Public companies in North America	Discounts on independent private companies in North America	EV/EBITDA	409
North America dependent	4	Public companies in North America	Discounts on dependent private companies in North America	EV/EBITDA	252
Western Europe independent	5	Public companies in Western Europe	Discounts on independent private companies in Western Europe	EV/EBITDA	1,707
Western Europe dependent	6	Public companies in Western Europe	Discounts on dependent private companies in Western Europe	EV/EBITDA	1,852
UK indpendent	7	Public companies in the UK	Discounts on independent private companies in the UK	EV/EBITDA	1,606
UK dependent	8	Public companies in the UK	Discounts on dependent private companies in the UK	EV/EBITDA	1,750

The sample consists of completed majority-ownership transactions between January 1997 and June 2011, where information for at least one transaction multiple is available as shown in Exhibit 3.36. The number of cases j is derived after matching the private company multiples to the respective public company multiples and computing the discounts. Some cases (transactions) are lost with the matching procedure as shown in Exhibit 3.36.
Source: Zephyr database, Bureau von Dijk.

Exhibit 3.33   Independent variables in cross-sectional regression

Variable	Value	Description
Size	Nominal	'1' if target company has more turnover than the average turnover in it's respective size class
Period 1, Period 2, Period 3, Period 4, Period 5	Nominal	'1' if time of transaction is in respective period (Period 1 − until 12/2000, Period 2 = between 01/2001 and 12/2003 Period 3 = between 01/2004 and 07/2007, Period 4 = between 08/2004 and 03/2009, Period 5 = between 04/2009 and 06/2011
Indu 30, Indu 40, Indu 50, Indu 60, Indu 70	Nominal	'1' if target is in respective industry group (Indu 30 = manufacturing, Indu 40 = transportation, Indu 50 = trade, Indu 60 = finance, Indu 70 = service)
RelSize[1]	Continuous	Relative size in terms of assets (target size/ median size of acquirer in reference portfolio)
Cash payment	Nominal	'1' if payment is made in cash
Cross-border deal	Nominal	'1' if target and acquirer country are not identical
Listed acquirer	Nominal	'1' if acquirer is listed on stock exchange (no OTC)
Private equity investor	Nominal	'1' if acquirer is investor organized in funds providing equity capital (private equity house, venture capitalist, mezzanine buyer)
Target D/E[2]	Continuous	Target's Debt/Equity ratio
Owner-managed[3]	Continuous	'1' if target is owner-managed

1) For the analysis in Appendix C combined with the service industry.
2) For the analysis in Appendix C combined with the trade industry.
3) Only included in the analysis in Appendix C.

The cross-sectional regressions encompass a set of factors which are summarized in Exhibit 3.33. In the regression equation (Equation 3.3 in Section 3.13) the factors are included as a set of independent variables in the vector F_k and take into account systematic influence factors on discounts, mirroring characteristics of the respective market environments and companies. The variables in vector F_k will be tested for inclusion/exclusion by the regression procedure based on the significance of the variables in each step.

3.11.2   The Data Sets

For each region, one data set is created with transaction details including financials of the target and acquirer. An important criterion for including a transaction in the data set is the availability of at least some information on the deal value (either equity value or EV) and target financials like revenues or EBITDA. For the analysis, only completed deals are included and only those transactions where a controlling stake of minimum 50% has been acquired. Exhibit 3.34 provides an overview of the data sets with comprehensive financial information for the four regions of interest.

The Zephyr database (see Section 3.13) reveals 1,059 transactions with German targets and detailed financial information on at least one of the multiples of interest, 827 transactions involving private targets, and 232 transactions involving public targets. Concerning the North

Exhibit 3.34   Number of multiples before data preparation

Target country	Target status		Number of transaction with ratios				Number of transactions
			EV/Sales	EV/EBITDA	EV/EBIT	P/E	
Germany	Private	independent	256	159	151	82	327
		dependent	375	243	228	109	500
	Public		285	190	176	142	232
	Total		916	592	555	333	1,059
North America	Private	independent	722	430	302	117	3,408
		dependent	370	280	87	140	1,883
	Public		3,559	2,341	2,082	893	4,413
	Total		4,651	3,051	2,471	1,150	9,704
Western Europe	Private	independent	2,665	2,013	1,947	185	2,819
		dependent	3,150	2,192	2,057	225	3,495
	Public		1,722	876	838	409	1,866
	Total		7,537	5,081	4,842	819	8,180
UK	Private	independent	2,378	1,798	1,754	152	2,436
		dependent	2,679	1,931	1,852	162	2,780
	Public		1,268	856	782	260	1,330
	Total		6,325	4,585	4,388	574	6,546

The data set includes all majority-ownership transactions between January 1997 and June 2011 in Germany, North America, Western Europe, and the UK where information for at least one transaction multiple is available. The table reports the available multiples before any data preparation (see Section 3.13).
Source: Zephyr database, Bureau von Dijk.

American and Western European targets, the database includes 9,704 transactions involving North American companies, of which 5,291 private companies, as well as 8,180 transactions with Western European targets involving 6,314 private companies. For the UK the database reveals 6,546 transactions, 5,216 transactions involving private targets and 1,330 transactions involving public targets.

To use the transactions shown in Exhibit 3.34, extensive data preparation and information enrichment is necessary. Therefore, different variables and different financial ratios for the target and the acquirer with respect to the influence factors are computed (see Section 3.13). Valuation multiples are re-computed manually with the financial information given in the data sets and controlled for outliers and implausible values.

The final data sets are described in Exhibit 3.35. Due to the low number of reasonable P/E multiples in Germany and in North America, the P/E multiple is excluded from the further analysis of discounts.

The matching procedure shown in Section 3.13 attempts to find for each private transaction a matching transaction with a public company target of the same size, period, and industry group. With the release of one of the matching criteria *Size class*, *Period*, or *Industry group*, it is possible to match nearly all of the cases (see Exhibit 3.36).

3.11.3   Results

This section is divided into two parts. The first part contains the univariate analyses that benchmark multiples and elaborate on discounts separated for the different samples. It encompasses the four regions and attempts to point out valuation differences between dependent and independent and public companies. Furthermore, it compares valuation differences across

Exhibit 3.35   The final data sets

Target Country	Target Status		Number of available multiples after preperation:			Number of Transactions
			EV/Sales	EV/EBITDA	EV/EBIT	
Germany	Private	independent	242	145	134	327
		dependent	349	216	189	500
	Public		254	163	147	232
	Total		845	524	470	1,059
	Private	independent	690	409	252	3,408
North America		dependent	336	252	62	1,883
	Public		3,364	2,165	1,745	4,413
	Total		4,390	2,826	2,059	10,713
	Private	independent	2,508	1,707	1,551	2,819
Western Europe		dependent	2,852	1,852	1,599	3,495
	Public		1,409	690	626	1,866
	Total		6,769	4,249	3,776	8,756
	Private	independent	2,297	1,606	1,480	2,436
UK		dependent	2,575	1,750	1,524	1,883
	Public		1,185	788	680	1,330
	Total		6,057	4,144	3,684	7,137

The data set includes all majority-ownership transactions between January 1997 and June 2011 in Germany, North America, Western Europe, and the UK where information for at least one transaction multiple is available. The table reports the available multiples after data preparation according to Section 3.13).
Source: Zephyr database, Bureau von Dijk.

regions. The second part includes cross-sectional regressions in a multivariate framework to highlight the valuation differences and reveal different factors influencing the valuations of private companies compared to their public counterparts.

Univariate Analyses

Exhibit 3.37 reports the results for the private companies.

Independent private companies (Mittelstand companies) in Germany are highly discounted, depending on the multiple, between 19.0% and 41.5% compared to public companies. The dependent private companies are also discounted (between 16.2% and 30.7%) but not nearly as high as independent private companies. One can see that in particular the discounts on the EV/Sales multiple are much higher for independent private companies than for dependent private companies. The results found in the German sample differ from the discounts found in the other samples.

In North America, the entire group of private companies is discounted compared to North American public companies at 29.4% on average (simple unweighted average across multiples). Discounts seem to be more pronounced on the EV/EBITDA and EV/EBIT multiple than the sales multiple.

It does not seem to be very clear if discounts also need to be differentiated between independent and dependent private companies: independent private companies are discounted at 27.3% on average compared to dependent private companies with an average discount of

Exhibit 3.36 Percentage of cases after matching

Target	Sample	Reference portfolio		EV/Sales	EV/EBITDA	EV/EBIT
German independent	1	Public companies in Germany	Lost with matching (%)	0%	2%	2%
			Available ratios	242	143	132
German dependent	2	Public companies in Germany	Lost with matching (%)	0%	0%	0%
			Available ratios	349	216	189
North America independent	3	Public companies in North America	Lost with matching (%)	0%	0%	0%
			Available ratios	690	409	252
North America dependent	4	Public companies in North America	Lost with matching (%)	0%	0%	1%
			Available ratios	336	252	61
Western Europe independent	5	Public companies in Western Europe	Lost with matching (%)	0%	0%	0%
			Available ratios	2,508	1,707	1,551
Western Europe dependent	6	Public companies in Western Europe	Lost with matching (%)	0%	0%	0%
			Available ratios	2,852	1,852	1,599
UK independent	7	Public companies in the UK	Lost with matching (%)	0%	0%	0%
			Available ratios	2,297	1,606	1,480
UK dependent	8	Public companies in the UK	Lost with matching (%)	0%	0%	0%
			Available ratios	2,575	1,750	1,524

The information shown is based on the data set that comprises completed majority-ownership transactions between January 1997 and June 2011, where information for at least one transaction multiple is available as shown in Exhibit 3.35. The available cases depend on the multiples. The tables report the percentage of cases lost for each multiple when computing the ratio according to Equation 3.1 (detail in Equation 3.2 in Section 3.13), and thereby match the private company transactions with the comparable (public) reference portfolios.

Source: Zephyr database, Bureau von Dijk.

Exhibit 3.37   Median discounts

	Sample	Target	Median discount on multiple		
			EV/Sales	EV/EBITDA	EV/EBIT
Germany	1	independent private	41.5%	27.4%	19.0%
	2	dependent private	30.7%	18.2%	16.2%
	–	all private	31.5%	19.9%	16.9%
North America	3	independent private	24.7%	27.1%	30.0%
	4	dependent private	26.8%	32.1%	31.4%
	–	all private	26.1%	31.4%	30.8%
Western Europe	5	independent private	54.3%	37.6%	16.2%
	6	dependent private	40.3%	21.4%	14.1%
	–	all private	48.2%	29.8%	14.7%
UK	7	independent private	37.2%	12.2%	22.5%
	8	dependent private	8.8%	7.0%	6.1%
	–	all private	24.9%	7.9%	13.5%

The sample consists of completed majority-ownership transactions between January 1997 and June 2011, where information for at least one transaction multiple is available as shown in Exhibit 3.35. For each transaction multiple, the table reports the ratios computed according to Equation 3.1 (detail in Equation 3.2 in Section 3.13). Samples 1–8 denote different categories of private targets compared to the reference portfolio of public companies in Germany, North America, Western Europe, and the UK.
Source: Zephyr database, Bureau von Dijk.

30.1%. This might become clearer when the development of discounts over time or industry patterns is investigated.

In Western Europe and the UK one can see that independent private companies are more discounted than dependent private companies. Dependent private companies are discounted at 25.3% and 7.3% on average in Western Europe and the UK, respectively (compared to average discounts of 36.0% and 24.0% for independent private companies). In both regions, discounts vary with multiples and are most pronounced on the *Sales* multiple. The overall level of discounts compared to Germany seems higher in Western Europe and lower in the UK.

Altogether, one can conclude the following:

- Private companies are discounted compared to public companies with discounts varying across multiples.
- With exception of North America, independent private companies are more heavily discounted than dependent companies. If an analyst wants to apply a discount, he should therefore distinguish between independent private and dependent private companies. It is a mistake to apply discounts found for the North American market to other regions.
- Typical practices which regard all private companies as one group are wrong due to differences between the private firms.
- It is not appropriate for practitioners to use the prevalent lump-sum of around 30%.
- The magnitude of discounts/premiums depends on the multiple used.

A detailed analysis of the development of discounts over time is given in Exhibit 3.38.

The M&A market between 2001 until 2003 was characterized overall by unfavourable market conditions and lower M&A activity which influenced the valuation of all companies. Theory dictates that discounts for private companies are especially high in the context of

Exhibit 3.38 Median discounts across periods

	Multiple	before 2011	2001–2003	2004–Jul 07	Subprime (Aug 07–Mar 09)	Post subprime (Apr 09–Jun 11)
Germany						
Sample 1: independent private vs. public companies	EV/Sales	32.2%	52.8%	42.8%	47.7%	38.5%
	EV/EBITDA	15.0%	22.5%	29.4%	29.6%	19.8%
	EV/EBIT	15.3%	20.0%	22.1%	27.4%	12.4%
Sample 2: dependent private vs. public companies	EV/Sales	23.8%	38.0%	26.9%	30.8%	23.9%
	EV/EBITDA	10.5%	17.9%	9.4%	22.1%	16.8%
	EV/EBIT	10.7%	18.2%	8.4%	18.8%	14.2%
All private vs. public companies	EV/Sales	28.1%	40.4%	35.0%	41.2%	30.2%
	EV/EBITDA	12.9%	20.2%	20.4%	25.6%	14.6%
	EV/EBIT	11.0%	19.1%	15.5%	22.8%	13.0%
North America						
Sample 3: independent private vs. public companies	EV/Sales	18.9%	27.3%	25.6%	28.2%	24.2%
	EV/EBITDA	24.9%	32.0%	21.1%	32.6%	25.7%
	EV/EBIT	20.9%	30.3%	19.9%	32.1%	21.7%
Sample 4: dependent private vs. public companies	EV/Sales	20.7%	32.7%	28.2%	36.4%	30.2%
	EV/EBITDA	27.1%	35.5%	22.6%	42.1%	32.1%
	EV/EBIT	22.8%	33.0%	20.5%	39.5%	26.0%
All private vs. public companies	EV/Sales	19.9%	25.0%	27.0%	33.9%	26.4%
	EV/EBITDA	26.2%	33.7%	23.0%	37.0%	27.4%
	EV/EBIT	21.3%	31.7%	20.6%	36.5%	23.6%

(continued)

Exhibit 3.38 *(Continued)*

		Multiple	before 2011	2001–2003	2004–Jul 07	Subprime (Aug 07–Mar 09)	Post subprime (Apr 09–Jun 11)
Western Europe	Sample 5: independent private vs. public companies	EV/Sales	44.1%	51.5%	44.2%	55.0%	46.7%
		EV/EBITDA	21.3%	32.4%	28.9%	34.8%	35.2%
		EV/EBIT	9.4%	11.6%	28.2%	29.2%	17.3%
	Sample 6: dependent private vs. public companies	EV/Sales	41.3%	45.6%	20.8%	44.1%	33.5%
		EV/EBITDA	20.5%	26.4%	22.0%	24.7%	18.9%
		EV/EBIT	3.7%	1.3%	13.4%	16.1%	21.7%
	All private vs. public companies	EV/Sales	42.9%	43.6%	32.7%	52.0%	38.9%
		EV/EBITDA	21.1%	29.4%	26.7%	29.4%	27.5%
		EV/EBIT	4.5%	8.3%	21.2%	22.4%	19.1%
UK	Sample 7: independent private vs. public companies	EV/Sales	35.8%	36.3%	26.5%	42.9%	44.6%
		EV/EBITDA	15.6%	18.6%	13.8%	17.6%	11.4%
		EV/EBIT	12.5%	16.9%	11.6%	22.2%	24.1%
	Sample 8: dependent private vs. public companies	EV/Sales	6.2%	7.4%	7.0%	18.4%	24.0%
		EV/EBITDA	9.5%	14.6%	7.4%	6.6%	1.4%
		EV/EBIT	2.0%	−8.1%	15.5%	8.3%	11.2%
	All private vs. public companies	EV/Sales	21.1%	16.9%	16.8%	32.2%	33.3%
		EV/EBITDA	12.7%	16.6%	11.1%	12.0%	6.5%
		EV/EBIT	5.3%	5.7%	13.8%	15.1%	17.3%

The sample consists of completed majority-ownership transactions between January 1997 and June 2011, where information for at least one transaction multiple is available as shown in Exhibit 3.35. For each transaction multiple, the table reports the ratios computed according to Equation 3.1 (detail in Equation 3.2 in Section 3.2 in Section 3.13) across the five different time periods as specified in Section 3.13.
Source: Zephyr database, Bureau von Dijk.

lower market liquidity, which can be observed in Germany when all the private companies in Germany are considered. Average discount on all three multiples between 2001 and 2003 amounts to 26.6% which is much higher than in the period before 2001where average discounts amounted to around 17.3%. Despite improving market conditions discounts did not decrease significantly for all private companies between 2004 and July 2007: the average stays around 23.7%.

If one regards independent private companies and dependent private companies separately, it can be seen that independent private companies are discounted more than dependent private companies during 2001–2003 (an average discount of 31.8% vs. 24.7%) and that the independent private companies are on average discounted around 31.5% in the active M&A market 2004–July 2007. This rather unexpected development is perhaps caused by the increase in leverage ratios of independent private companies sold. (D/E ratio increased from 3.4x to 3.7x, see Exhibit 3.25.)

On the other hand, valuation for dependent private companies developed more favourably, in the period 2004–July 2007 with an average discount of 14.9% compared to 24.7% in the period before. Discounts for dependent subsidiaries appear to be lower in total than those for independent private companies. In the first three periods they show an expected pattern and increase during the market slowdown in the second period; valuations recovered in the third period during the market catch-up.

During the subprime crisis the great uncertainty seems to have paralyzed all sorts of market participants and M&A activity declined dramatically. The times were characterized by negative headlines about evil, greedy banks, and buyers, so potential buyers were careful about paying too high premiums even for attractive targets or putting money on the table at all.

Although the M&A market environment is developing unfavourably, the discounts for independent private companies do not increase during the subprime crisis that much (average discount of 34.9%), comparable to the average discounts during the market slowdown of 2001–2003. The theory says that discounts for private companies are especially high in the context of lower market liquidity, which cannot be observed here for independent private companies in Germany.

When looking at leverage ratios, one can see that these are relatively low compared to the period before, so during the subprime crisis only relatively healthy independent private companies could have been sold successfully compared to the period before: the average D/E level decreased from 3.7x to 2.8x. This development perhaps contributed to the stability of discounts as very highly leveraged companies had no change of being sold on M&A markets.

With respect to dependent private companies, the subprime crisis led to a deterioration of valuation compared to public counterparts and increases in discounts could be observed (average discount of 23.9% compared to 14.9% in the period before).

Exhibit 3.22 and Exhibit 3.28 have shown that domestic acquirers increasingly focus on German targets and that foreign acquirers show constant interest in independent private companies in Germany. This demand might influence the valuation of all private companies positively, leading to decreased discounts. According to Exhibit 3.39, foreign investors seem to pay more for independent private companies than domestic acquirers. But transactions with foreign investors are not more valuable for dependent private companies.

Despite a worsening M&A environment with falling transaction multiples in Germany during the subprime crisis, the desire of foreign investors to invest in German companies and increased bidder competition seems to make investors abstain from applying higher discounts on targets out of the German Mittelstand.

Exhibit 3.39   Valuation depending on the origin of the acquirer

Independent private	Eta	Eta^2	Foreign investor	Domestic investor	F-value	Significance
EV/Sales	9.1%	0.8%	2.3x	0.8x	1.86	55%
EV/EBITDA	45.2%	20.4%	10.7x	6.7x	7.39	1%
EV/EBIT	41.9%	17.6%	15.6x	12.6x	7.95	0%

Dependent private	Eta	Eta^2	Foreign investor	Domestic investor	F-value	Significance
EV/Sales	28.5%	8.1%	1.6x	1.6x	1.24	27%
EV/EBITDA	27.2%	7.4%	13.1x	7.4x	0.68	42%
EV/EBIT	19.2%	3.7%	16.3x	18.7x	0.13	72%

The sample is based on transactions during the subprime crisis and the number of transactions included depends on the multiple used. Separated for independent private and other private companies, the table reports the dependency of multiples on the origin (headquarters) of the acquirer using contingency tables and ANOVA. The second and the third column report the Eta and Eta^2 as association ratios between the valuation multiples and the two categories of the acquirer's origin. The F-values display the results of the ANOVA with the respective significance levels reported in the last column. For the EV/EBITDA and EV/EBIT multiples, one can see that the Eta^2 in column 3 shows a significant percentage of variance in the multiples explained by the acquirer's origin, and therefore the existence of a relation between the origin of an acquirer and the achieved transaction values. This relation exists for independent private companies but not for dependent private companies. For independent private companies, 20.4% of the variation in the EV/EBITDA multiple can be explained with knowledge of the acquirers' origins and 17.6% of the variation of the EV/EBIT multiple with knowledge of the acquirers' origins. The sales multiple shows with an Eta^2 coefficient of 9.1% no relation to the acquirer's region. The results of the F-test in columns 6 and 7 support significant differences between mean valuation (on EV/EBITDA and EV/EBIT ratio) depending on the acquirer's origin.
Source: Zephyr database, Bureau von Dijk.

The subprime crisis ended with a tenuous recovery that began in the spring of 2009 with discounts for independent private companies that developed as expected and experienced a strong decrease (average discount of 23.6%).

For dependent private companies, the recovery post subprime was not as strong as for independent private companies (average discount of 18.3%) so in the most recent period, valuation differences still exist between the independent private and dependent private firms in Germany, but compared to the pre-subprime period, differences in discounts are smaller.

A time pattern of discounts in the other three regions can be observed as well. In North America, the time pattern shows pronounced discounts during the market slowdown between 2001 and 2003. Discounts amount on average to 30.1% compared to the period before (22.5%) and thereafter (23.5%). Looking at dependent and independent private companies separately, until July 2007, there are only small differences between those two company classes. Independent companies have been discounted on average by 21.5% (before 2001), 29.9% (2001–2003), and 22.2% (2004–July 2007) compared to independent private companies (23.5%, 33.7%, and 23.8% for the respective periods). From that point (during the subprime crisis), discounts for dependent private companies increased significantly more than those for independent private companies (39.3% for dependent vs. 31.0% for independent private companies during the subprime crisis) and stayed at a higher level post subprime crisis (29.4% vs. 23.9%).

In Western Europe, the time pattern is more as expected and the level of discounts is generally a little higher than in Germany. Discounts for private companies increase during market downturns (2001–2003 and the subprime crisis). Private company discounts amount on average to 27.1% in the period from 2001–2003. Discounts show a great variation across multiples and range between 8.3% on the EV/EBIT multiple to 43.6% on the EV/Sales multiple (period from 2001–2003). In the course of the subprime crisis, multiples decline for all companies in Western Europe (see Exhibit 3.31). Discounts for private companies increase from on average 26.9% (2004–July 2007) to 34.6% during the subprime crisis, which is even higher than the average between 2001 and 2003. Comparing the two company classes, one can see that discounts are higher for independent private firms across all periods and the time pattern is more pronounced for independent than for dependent private companies.

In the UK, private companies are not more heavily discounted across periods than their counterparts in Western Europe and Germany but the difference between dependent and independent private companies is more pronounced than for example in Western Europe. In the UK, independent private companies are on average discounted 21.3% before 2001, 23.9% between 2001 and 2003, 17.3% between 2004 and July 2007, 27.6% between August 2007 and March 2009 (subprime), and 26.7% between April 2009 and June 2011. Discounts for independent private companies amount to 5.9% before 2001, 4.6% between 2001 and 2003, 10.0% between 2004 and July 2007, 11.1% between August 2007 and March 2009 (subprime), and 12.2% between April 2009 and June 2011. Whereas independent private companies show some kind of expected time pattern (except post subprime), dependent private companies do not show a clear pattern, also because of discrepancies between multiples.

Comparing different regions and looking at the time profile of discounts, one needs to recognize that discounts vary with market conditions but also depend on company classes, sometimes on the multiple used, and differ across regions. In some cases they show unexpected patterns that cannot be explained given the limits of the univariate analyses.

Exhibit 3.40 shows a further analysis of discounts for the different industries. The valuation of companies is influenced by the industry a company operates in because different industries are characterized by distinct operational metrics when it comes to margins or balance sheet ratios, e.g. the debt level associated with the higher risk that has to be borne by the investor differs.

In Germany discounts can be observed across all industries, but those for the service and finance industry are on average lower compared to other industries. Finance and service companies are discounted by 18.5% and 14.3% respectively whereas average discounts for the manufacturing, transportation, and trade industries amount to 34.3%, 25.7.1%, and 35.7%. One could already see in Exhibit 3.12 that service companies in particular have lower leverage than the rest of the private companies and higher leverage in the manufacturing industry. Except for the trade industry, average discounts for Mittelstand companies across all industries are higher than those for dependent private companies.

In North America, private trade and manufacturing deals are much more heavily discounted (with average discounts of about 37.2% and 34.4%) than private firms in other sectors, whereas discounts for service companies are lower (average discount about 13.0%). According to Exhibit 3.12, manufacturing companies don't show metrics that can explain the high level of discounts; only service companies are significantly less highly leveraged than the rest of private companies; trade companies' leverage is little higher than in the other industries (D/E ratio of 2.0x vs. 1.7x).

Like in Germany discounts can be observed across all industries in Western Europe, and those for the service and finance industry are on average lower compared to other industries. Finance and service companies are discounted by 21.0% and 18.0% respectively, whereas average discounts for manufacturing and transportation amount to 37.8% and 31.4%. Trade

Exhibit 3.40 Median discounts across industries

	Multiple	Manufacturing	Transportation	Trade	Finance	Services
Germany						
Sample 1: Independent private vs. public companies	EV/Sales	64.2%	36.5%	51.4%	31.1%	24.9%
	EV/EBITDA	42.5%	24.2%	34.0%	20.6%	16.5%
	EV/EBIT	29.5%	16.8%	23.6%	14.9%	13.3%
Sample 2: dependent private vs. public companies	EV/Sales	32.4%	30.4%	51.5%	23.1%	18.4%
	EV/EBITDA	19.2%	18.0%	30.5%	13.6%	10.9%
	EV/EBIT	16.2%	14.6%	27.2%	12.7%	11.4%
All private vs. public companies	EV/Sales	48.8%	36.8%	50.5%	25.7%	19.5%
	EV/EBITDA	31.1%	23.2%	31.6%	16.4%	12.3%
	EV/EBIT	23.1%	17.2%	24.9%	13.3%	11.5%
North America						
Sample 3: independent private vs. public companies	EV/Sales	31.4%	30.7%	34.9%	17.3%	14.8%
	EV/EBITDA	28.9%	28.7%	30.0%	24.4%	16.8%
	EV/EBIT	31.5%	28.4%	25.3%	29.6%	17.9%
Sample 4: dependent private vs. public companies	EV/Sales	32.2%	26.6%	33.7%	17.1%	10.2%
	EV/EBITDA	40.4%	31.8%	42.3%	25.4%	13.2%
	EV/EBIT	38.8%	28.0%	36.5%	24.9%	12.9%
All private vs. public companies	EV/Sales	32.2%	28.0%	37.7%	16.3%	11.3%
	EV/EBITDA	35.5%	29.6%	39.8%	23.9%	13.5%
	EV/EBIT	35.6%	27.6%	34.0%	26.4%	14.3%

Western Europe	Sample 5: independent private vs. public companies	EV/Sales	70.9%	68.1%	71.3%	34.3%	37.1%
		EV/EBITDA	36.1%	27.4%	36.9%	24.6%	14.6%
		EV/EBIT	20.9%	15.1%	25.1%	12.2%	14.7%
	Sample 6: dependent private vs. public companies	EV/Sales	53.8%	45.6%	67.8%	25.7%	23.9%
		EV/EBITDA	25.6%	17.9%	19.4%	21.9%	21.2%
		EV/EBIT	23.4%	12.4%	14.1%	13.6%	2.2%
	All private vs. public companies	EV/Sales	63.0%	55.7%	68.2%	29.4%	29.9%
		EV/EBITDA	29.4%	26.1%	34.4%	20.9%	16.1%
		EV/EBIT	21.0%	12.4%	19.0%	12.6%	8.0%
UK	Sample 7: independent private vs. public companies	EV/Sales	37.8%	29.8%	53.5%	37.4%	18.0%
		EV/EBITDA	24.7%	19.0%	31.7%	7.6%	9.4%
		EV/EBIT	29.2%	15.2%	25.5%	13.9%	6.8%
	Sample 8: dependent private vs. public companies	EV/Sales	17.3%	16.4%	20.9%	−2.7%	−9.3%
		EV/EBITDA	11.0%	17.6%	23.1%	1.5%	−16.8%
		EV/EBIT	11.8%	10.5%	9.6%	6.8%	−3.1%
	All private vs. public companies	EV/Sales	27.8%	22.6%	41.0%	19.1%	13.3%
		EV/EBITDA	14.3%	16.4%	24.1%	1.5%	−0.4%
		EV/EBIT	20.7%	12.6%	19.3%	11.4%	8.6%

The sample consists of completed majority-ownership transactions between January 1997 and June 2011, where information for at least one transaction multiple is available as shown in Exhibit 3.35. For each transaction multiple, the table reports the ratios computed according to Equation 3.1 (detail in Equation 3.2 in Section 3.13) across the industry groups as specified in Section 3.13.

Source: Zephyr database, Bureau von Dijk.

companies seems to be discounted most with average discounts of 40.5%. The comparison of relative size and leverage of these industries to others in Exhibit 3.12 shows differences especially for the service and trade industry.

Exhibit 3.37 demonstrated that the level of discounts is higher in Western Europe than in Germany and that dependent private companies are less heavily discounted than independent private companies, a pattern that can also be found looking at the different industries.

In the UK, the level of average discounts for private service companies (7.2%) and finance companies (10.7%) is lower. Manufacturing companies are discounted by on average 20.9%, transportation by on average 17.2%, and trade companies higher than others by on average 28.1%. Interestingly, dependent service companies receive premium valuations compared to their public counterparts, for independent private companies no premiums are achieved but the average discount is, at 11.4%, significantly lower compared to the highest average discount of 36.9% in the trade industry.

Regression Results – Germany

The first set of regressions refers to companies in Germany and analyzes two different samples: independent private (Mittelstand) companies compared to public companies (sample one) and independent private companies compared to public companies (sample two). Discount regressions are conducted with the EV/EBITDA multiple because, compared to the EV/Sales multiple, the discounts show higher significance and a more consistent profile. In addition, a greater number of cases is available than for the EV/EBIT multiple. According to Exhibit 3.36 143 cases are available compared to 132 for the EV/EBIT multiple.

The stepwise regression accounts for possible correlations between independent variables. The results are summarized in Exhibit 3.41 and Exhibit 3.43. Exhibit 3.41compares independent private companies to public companies in Germany and shows a discount of 21.4%.

The measured discounts decrease the larger a company is relative to its acquirer. In line with the results in Section 3.11.3, the influence of the time factor is significant. Although

Exhibit 3.41   Multivariate regression: Independent private companies vs. public German companies (sample one)

Dependent variable: Discount EV/EBITDA	Coefficient	T-Value	Significance
(Constant)	0.214	3.543	1%
RelSize (assets)	−0.121	−2.552	5%
Period 3 (2004-Jul 07)	0.194	3.940	1%
Period 5 (Apr 07-Jun 11)	−0.115	−1.988	5%
Indu 50 (trade industry group)	0.146	3.401	1%
Indu 70 (service industry group)	−0.220	−3.719	1%
Cash payment	0.124	1.681	10%
Cross-border deal (foreign investor)	−0.197	−4.139	1%
Listed acquirer	0.103	1.8162	10%
R^2	8.6%		

The sample is based on completed majority-ownership transactions between January 1997 and June 2011 in Germany, and consists of 143 transactions including independent private companies as shown in the EV/EBITDA column of Exhibit 3.36. The table reports the results of the stepwise linear regression computed according to Equation 3.3 in Section 3.13. As the dependent variable, the ratio computed according to Equation 3.2 in Section 3.13 on the EV/EBITDA multiple is used. The set of independent variables is described in Exhibit 3.33.
Source: Zephyr database, Bureau von Dijk.

the influence of the market slowdown between 2001 and 2003 (*Period 2*) is not significant, independent private companies are more heavily discounted even when the market conditions between 2004 and July 2007 (*Period 3*) imply lower discounts, at least with respect to liquidity. The different periods were analyzed already in more detail and an increase in the D/E ratio of the target firms from 3.4x between 2001 and 2003 (*Period 2*) to 3.7x in *Period 3* was found (see Exhibit 3.25). This might imply that at that time the independent private companies were subject to increased disposal pressure induced by the German (banking) environment and the requirements of Basel II. The subprime crisis (*Period 4*) seems to have no significant influence on the discounts applied to independent private companies, somehow explainable by lack of transaction data for that period. Furthermore, an increased share of private equity investors focusing on independent private companies could be observed; whereas before the subprime crisis 12% of independent private companies were sold to private equity investors, the share reached 24.5% during the subprime crisis. One can only speculate what this might imply. On the one hand, there are arguments that those acquirers which plan an exit via IPO in the long run do not account for the lower liquidity of private targets and do apply lower illiquidity discounts. On the other hand, there exists the predominate prejudice that independent private companies show a reluctance to sell to a "corporate raider" and do so only when they are in urgent need (financial distress or succession problems). Indications for distress in the form of higher D/E ratios in that period cannot be found (to the contrary, independent private companies before the subprime crisis were characterized by high debt levels which indicated an increased disposal pressure on owners of independent private companies), nor any prove for the reluctance to sell to private equity investors. Instead, there seems to be increased interest from foreign investors in independent private companies during the subprime crisis. Despite the bad market environment, there might have been some sort of competitor for the pearls among German companies, supported by the result that foreign investors seem to pay more for independent private companies than other (domestic) acquirers. According to Exhibit 3.41 the influence of this factor (*Cross-border deal*) is significant at the 1% level and could decrease a discount by 20%.

The results in Exhibit 3.41 confirm the results of Exhibit 3.40; independent private companies in the trade industry are more discounted, and independent private companies in the service industry are less discounted than independent private companies in other industries. Exhibit 3.12 shows that both industries influence the D/E ratio. This factor drops out of the regression and relying on these results, practitioners would apply a higher discount for trade companies and premiums for service companies irrespective of the leverage. Despite the statistical correctness of this approach, leverage differences should always be taken into account irrespective of the industry. With respect of the low R^2 of the regression, the results should give the practitioner some guidelines with respect to influence factors, but cannot claim to be a complete explanation of the PCD.

In line with the theory, the desire for cash seems to increase discounts as independent private companies sold for cash are given higher discounts than other independent private companies, indicating a desire for liquidity that leads some private targets to accept lower prices in exchange for liquidity. The comparison of the percentage of cash deals pre-subprime and during the crisis shows that these numbers do not change significantly. Before the subprime crisis, around 71% of deals with independent private companies were cash deals; during the crisis this percentage changed to 72.2%. However, Exhibit 3.13 already showed that cash deals are smaller than non-cash deals, indicating also lower synergy potential or higher risk associated with smaller targets that might increase applied discounts.

Exhibit 3.42   Relative target size compared to listed and non-listed acquirers

Acquirer status		Public targets	Independent private targets	Dependent private targets
Non-listed acquirer	Relative size	3.4%	2.9%	5.0%
Listed acquirer	Relative size	14.3%	0.8%	2.4%
All	Relative size	14.1%	1.6%	2.5%

The sample is based on completed majority-ownership transactions between January 1997 and June 2011 as shown in Exhibit 3.35 (for public) and Exhibit 3.36 (for private), but consists only of those transactions that also provide information on target assets (221 public, 135 independent private companies, and 194 dependent private companies). The table reports the relative size of the target companies to their acquirers, which are either publicly listed stock corporations or private companies.
Source: Zephyr database, Bureau von Dijk.

The results in Exhibit 3.41 show that listed acquirers seem to increase discounts of independent private targets. According to theory, the DLL should be less relevant for listed acquirers because through the buyer's own liquidity, the investment in private assets become relatively liquid as well. On the other hand, the desire for liquidity can make private targets accept higher discounts as liquid stocks are the second best payment method after cash. Therefore the influence of the factor is difficult to interpret. In addition, Exhibit 3.42 shows that independent private targets with listed acquirers are smaller than other independent private companies relative to their acquirers, which makes interpretation even trickier. For practical use, it is not recommended to increase the discount applied in company valuation when listed acquirers are on the bidder's list. Although the stepwise regression takes the correlation between both factors into account, the low R^2 again does not justify the assignment of the underlying factors to the discounts without careful consideration.

With respect to the regression of the independent private (Mittelstand) companies in Germany, one can conclude that:

- These companies are discounted by approximately 21% compared to public German companies.
- Bigger companies are discounted less.
- Market liquidity influences the discount but also disposal pressure and bidder competition.
- Industry differences exist, but leverage differences must be taken into account.
- Cash payment increases the discount, a desire for liquidity seems to exist, but size differences need to be taken into account.
- Despite statistical relevance, the influence of the buyer's liquidity (*Listed acquirer*) is hard to interpret.
- Foreign investors pay more for independent private companies.
- The application of a lump-sum discount is inappropriate.
- The application of results of US studies is not appropriate.

Exhibit 3.43 reveals the results of the regression for the median discount for dependent private companies to public companies and shows a median of 14.7% on the EV/EBITDA ratio.

The results for the stepwise regression show that the discount seems to be smaller for firms of above average size and for firms which are relatively large compared to their acquirer.

Exhibit 3.43 Multivariate regression: dependent private German companies vs. public Germany companies (sample two)

Dependent variable: Discount EV/EBITDA	Coefficient	T-Value	Significance
(Constant)	0.147	3.238	1%
Size	−0.189	−1.738	10%
RelSize	−0.070	−1.922	10%
Period 2 (2001–2003)	0.221	2.372	5%
Period 3 (2004-Jul 07)	−0.204	−2.011	5%
Period 4 (Aug 07-Mar 09)	0.273	2.928	1%
Indu 50 (trade industry group)	0.105	2.552	5%
Cash payment	0.159	1.999	5%
Listed acquirer	0.188	1.761	10%
R^2	8.5%		

The sample is based on completed majority-ownership transactions between January 1997 and June 2011 in Germany, and consists of 216 transactions including dependent private companies as shown in the EV/EBITDA column of Exhibit 3.36. The table reports the results of the stepwise linear regression computed according to Equation 3.3 in Section 3.13. As the dependent variable, the ratio computed according to Equation 3.2 in Section 3.13 on the EV/EBITDA multiple is used. The set of independent variables is described in Exhibit 3.33.
Source: Zephyr database, Bureau von Dijk.

According to Exhibit 3.43, the market environment has some influence on the magnitude of the discount. An increased discount in *Period 2* and *Period 4* and a decreased discount in *Period 3* seem to confirm that private firms achieve higher valuation in active markets and lower valuation during market downturns subject to changing market sentiment and liquidity.

Looking at the periods more closely, the leverage between 2001 and 2003 (*Period 2*) increased: according to Exhibit 3.25 the D/E ratio increased from 2.2x before 2001 (*Period 1*) to 2.8x in *Period 2* and decreased again in *Period 3* (D/E ratio of 2.1). Therefore again maybe some kind of disposal pressure influenced discounts applied over time. In contrast to the results for the independent private companies, dependent private companies do not receive increased attention from private equity investors during the subprime crisis (according to Exhibit 3.25, their share is relatively low compared to independent private targets) and a statistically significant influence of foreign investors in the regression could not be found. They do not pay premiums for dependent subsidiaries anyway (see Exhibit 3.39).

Like independent private companies, trade companies are discounted more heavily than companies in other industries. Leverage differences may be the main driver of the discounts in the trade industry. Again, practitioners should account for the underlying risk profile and leverage of a company.

Just as for independent private companies, the payment in cash seems to increase discounts caused by differences in deal size or increased liquidity desired.

The variable *Private equity investor* has again no influence on the observed discounts in this model, although theory argues that the target's assets might be regarded as relatively liquid when private equity investors plan their exits via IPO some years after acquisition.

The variable *Listed acquirer* reveals influence again, leading to an increase in discounts, again hard to interpret. One can only see that dependent subsidiaries which are acquired by listed companies are smaller relative to their acquirers (relative size 2.4%, see Exhibit 3.42) compared to when non-listed acquirers buy dependent subsidiaries (relative size of 5.0%).

With respect to the regression of dependent private companies in Germany, one can conclude that:

- Dependent private companies are discounted by approximately 15% compared to public German companies.
- Bigger companies are discounted less.
- The market liquidity influences the discounts and the pattern is more in line with the results of other empirical research from the US; discounts in a positive (negative) market environment are lower (higher).
- Industry differences exist, but leverage differences must be taken into account.
- Potential reasons behind the variation of discounts (premiums) by industry can be the payment method or the listing of an acquirer and are the same as for the independent private companies.
- Discounts increase when the purchase price is paid cash; a desire for liquidity seems to exist.
- Despite statistical relevance, the influence of the buyer's liquidity (*Listed acquirer*) is hard to interpret.
- The application of lump-sum discounts is inappropriate.
- The application of results of US studies is not appropriate.

Regression Results – North America

For North America, two cross-sectional regressions are computed, separately for independent and dependent private. The results of the regression for independent private companies are reported in Exhibit 3.44 which reveals seven explanatory variables that are statistically significant. The intercept shows a median discount of 22%.

Discounts are less for companies of above average size, but there is no influence on the relative size of the target company compared to its acquirers. The market environment influences discounts on independent private companies. The negative environment from 2001 to 2003

Exhibit 3.44 Multivariate regression: independent private North American companies vs. public North American companies (sample three)

Dependent variable: Discount EV/EBITDA	Coefficient	T-Value	Significance
(Constant)	0.220	4.438	1%
Size	−0.148	−2.824	1%
Period 2 (2001–2003)	0.127	2.396	5%
Period 3 (2004-Jul 07)	−0.097	−2.232	5%
Indu 50 (trade industry group)	0.160	2.057	5%
Indu 70 (service industry group)	−0.277	−2.585	1%
Cash payment	0.212	1.756	10%
Cross-border	0.126	2.125	5%
R^2	8.5%		

The sample is based on completed majority-ownership transactions between January 1997 and June 2011 in North America and consists of 409 transactions as shown in the EV/EBITDA column of Exhibit 3.36. The table reports the results of the stepwise linear regression computed according Equation 3.3 in Section 3.13. As the dependent variable, the ratio computed according to Equation 3.2 in Section 3.13 on the EV/EBITDA multiple is used. The set of dependent variables is described in Exhibit 3.33.
Source: Zephyr database, Bureau von Dijk.

(*Period 2*) increased the discounts; in the active M&A markets between January 2004 and June 2007 (*Period 3*) the discounts decreased. The influence of the subprime crisis (*Period 4*) is not significant. It has been shown already that the discounts for independent private companies in Germany during the subprime crisis did not change significantly and that an increased bidder competition for independent private targets in that period took place. Not only German investors were increasingly buying into the German industry but also investor groups such as private equity were increasingly interested in independent private companies. The lacking influence of *Period 4* in North America cannot be explained by foreign investors competing for independent private companies. In the North American market most transactions are domestic. Only 16% of the acquirers come from outside North America. The few foreign buyers even seem to pay less for North American targets and apply higher discounts: from Exhibit 3.44 one can see that the influence of foreign investors is negative here.

As seen in Section 3.11.3, the discounts are especially high in the trade industry and low in the service industry. Again, both industries influence the observed D/E ratios. When applying higher/lower discounts for trade/service companies, it is recommended for practitioners to account for leverage differences.

The method of payment influences discounts significantly given its implication for liquidity, but the analysis shows that cash deals are significantly smaller than non-cash deals (see Exhibit 3.13).

Again, the adjusted R^2 of the regression is, at 8.5%, quite low. This suggests that there is a substantial amount of unexplained variability in the discount.

With respect to the regression of independent private companies in North America, one can conclude that:

- Independent private companies are discounted by approximately 22% compared to public North American companies.
- Bigger companies are discounted less.
- The market liquidity influences the discounts; discounts in a positive (negative) market environment are lower (higher).
- Industry differences exist, but leverage differences must be taken into account.
- Cash payment increases discounts; a desire for liquidity seems to exist.
- The application of lump-sum discounts is inappropriate.
- The results differ from the German sample.

Exhibit 3.45 shows the results of the regression for the median discounts for dependent private companies to public companies and reports a median discount on the EV/EBITDA ratio of 26.6%.

Discounts are less for companies of above average size, but there is no influence on the relative size of the target company compared to its acquirers. The market environment influences discounts on dependent private companies. The negative environment from 2001 to 2003 (*Period 2*) increased the discounts; in the active M&A markets between 2004 and June 2007 (*Period 3*) the discounts decreased. In contrast to independent companies, discounts for dependent companies in North America increased during the subprime crisis (*Period 4*). As in the case of independent companies in North American, one cannot find any interest from foreign investors, moreover their influence in the regression is not significant.

For dependent private companies, discounts are especially high in the trade industry, no lower discounts for service companies being observable.

Exhibit 3.45 Multivariate regression: dependent private North American companies vs. public North American companies (sample four)

Dependent variable: Discount EV/EBITDA	Coefficient	T-Value	Significance
(Constant)	0.266	3.769	1%
Size	−0.135	−3.162	1%
Period 2 (2001–2003)	0.142	2.186	5%
Period 3 (2004-Jul 07)	−0.128	−2.081	5%
Period 4 (Aug 07-Mar 09)	0.127	2.053	5%
Indu 50 (trade industry group)	0.178	2.490	5%
Cash payment	0.146	1.701	10%
Listed acquirer	−0.084	−1.836	10%
R^2		8.2%	

The sample is based on completed majority-ownership transactions between January 1997 and June 2011 in North America and consists of 252 transactions as shown in the EV/EBITDA column of Exhibit 3.36. The table reports the results of the stepwise linear regression computed according Equation 3.3 in Section 3.13. As the dependent variable, the ratio computed according to Equation 3.2 in Section 3.13 on the EV/EBITDA multiple is used. The set of dependent variables is described in Exhibit 3.33.
Source: Zephyr database, Bureau von Dijk.

As for independent companies, the method of payment influences the discounts significantly. Furthermore, listed acquirers seem to apply lower discounts for dependent subsidiaries. The explanation of its influence is two-fold. Listing might increase the liquidity of the acquired assets, so application of lower discounts is appropriate; on the other hand, listed stocks are nearly as desirable as cash when a seller needs liquid payment.

Again, the adjusted R^2 of the regression is quite low, at 8.2%. This suggests that there is a substantial amount of unexplained variability in the discounts.

With respect to the regression of dependent private companies in North America, one can conclude that:

- Dependent private companies are discounted by approximately 27% compared to public North American companies.
- Bigger companies are discounted less.
- The market liquidity influences discounts; discounts in a positive (negative) market environment are lower (higher).
- Industry differences exist, but leverage differences must be taken into account.
- Cash payment increase discounts; desire for liquidity seems to exist.
- The application of lump-sum discounts is inappropriate.
- The results differ from the German sample.

Regression Results – Western Europe

The results of the regression of median discounts for independent private companies in Western Europe are reported in Exhibit 3.46.

The constant shows a median discount of 28.8% and the list of influence variables looks quite familiar. Target size is again important (relative to its acquirer) and unfavourable market environments increase discounts. Higher discounts can be observed in the trade industry group, and lower discounts are applied when service companies are acquired. Cash payment

Exhibit 3.46   Multivariate regression: independent private vs. public companies in Western Europe (sample five)

Dependent: Discount EV/EBITDA	Coefficient	T-Value	Significance
(Constant)	0.288	3.488	1%
RelSize	−0.101	−2.240	5%
Period 2 (2001–2003)	0.109	2.625	1%
Period 4 (Aug 07-Mar 09)	0.197	2.488	5%
Indu 50 (trade industry group)	0.090	3.876	1%
Indu 70 (service industry group)	−0.130	−2.441	5%
Cash payment	0.060	2.079	5%
Cross-border	−0.083	−2.081	5%
R^2	6.3%		

The sample is based on completed majority-ownership transactions between January 1997 and June 2011 in Western Europe and consists of 1,707 transactions as shown in the EV/EBITDA column of Exhibit 3.36. The table reports the results of the stepwise linear regression computed according to Equation 3.3 in Section 3.13. As the dependent variable, the ratio computed according to Equation 3.2 in Section 3.13 on the EV/EBITDA multiple is used. The set of dependent variables is described in Exhibit 3.33.
Source: Zephyr database, Bureau von Dijk.

increases discounts without revealing any relation to deal size (according to Exhibit 3.13 average cash and non-cash deals are about EUR 14m) and in acquisitions with foreign buyers lower discounts are applied.

Exhibit 3.47 shows the results for dependent private companies.

Dependent private companies in Western Europe are on average generally less discounted than independent ones (17.0% vs. 28.8%). Absolute instead of relative size seems to influence discounts; why this is the case, cannot be explained here. Exhibit 3.11 shows that dependent private firms in Western Europe are bigger than independent ones (EUR 27.8m assets vs. EUR

Exhibit 3.47   Multivariate regression: dependent private vs. public companies in Western Europe (sample six)

Dependent: Discount EV/EBITDA	Coefficient	T-Value	Significance
(Constant)	0.170	3.407	1%
Size	−0.079	−2.413	5%
Period 2 (2001–2003)	0.028	1.700	10%
Period 5 (Apr 09-Jun11)	−0.060	−2.253	5%
Indu 30 (manufacturing industry group)	0.063	1.901	10%
Indu 50 (trade industry group)	0.099	3.183	1%
Cash payment	0.094	3.265	1%
Listed acquirer	0.087	5.192	1%
Cross-border	−0.149	−3.746	1%
Target D/E	0.049	2.954	1%
R^2	18.9%		

The sample is based on completed majority-ownership transactions between January 1997 and June 2011 in Western Europe and consists of 1,852 transactions as shown in the EV/EBITDA column of Exhibit 3.36. The table reports the results of the stepwise linear regression computed according to Equation 3.3 in Section 3.13. As the dependent variable, the ratio computed according to Equation 3.2 in Section 3.13 on the EV/EBITDA multiple is used. The set of dependent variables is described in Exhibit 3.33.
Source: Zephyr database, Bureau von Dijk.

5.3m assets) and also bigger relative to their acquirers than independent ones (5.4% vs. 2.4%). How these differences exactly affect regression results is only speculative.

In contrast to independent private companies, improving market conditions after April 2009 (*Period 5*) seem to positively influence discounts attached to dependent private companies. Again, trade companies are discounted more than other industries, but larger discounts also seem to be attached to transactions with manufacturing companies.

Cash payment increases discounts without any obvious differences across deal sizes. Foreign investors also seem to apply lower discounts on dependent targets. In contrast to the regression results for independent firms, the variables *Listed acquirer* and *Target D/E* influence the measured discount. Compared to independent private firms, median leverage for dependent companies seems to be higher (D/E ratio of 1.8x compared to 1.5x for independent firms in Exhibit 3.23). Maybe acquirers react more sensitively to leverage when a certain debt level is reached as the inherent risk in the target increases.

With respect to the regression of independent and dependent private companies in Western Europe, one can conclude that:

- Independent private companies are discounted by approximately 29% compared to public Western European companies.
- Dependent private companies are discounted by approximately 17% compared to public Western European companies.
- Bigger companies are discounted less.
- Market liquidity influences discounts; discounts in a positive (negative) market environment are lower (higher).
- Industry differences exist.
- Cash payment increase discounts, desire for liquidity seems to exist.
- The application of lump-sum discounts is inappropriate; different discounts and influence factors for independent and dependent firms exist.

Regression Results UK

Exhibit 3.48 shows the results of the regression of median discounts for independent private companies in the UK.

The constant reveals a relatively low median discount of 9.5%, a result that is not surprising; Exhibit 3.37 indicated already that discounts attached to transactions with private UK companies are lower compared to other regions. Again, size, time, and industry influence the magnitude of discounts applied.

The absolute and the relative size of a target company are important; unfavourable market environments increase discounts more favourably lead to a decrease in discounts. Higher discounts can be observed in the manufacturing industry group, and again, lower discounts are applied when service companies are acquired. Cash payment increases discounts without revealing any relation to deal size. According to Exhibit 3.13 average cash deals are even slightly bigger (average deal size EUR 14.5m) than non-cash deals (average deal size about EUR 13.9m). In this regression, the variable *Private equity investor* influences the discount applied to independent private targets; a decrease in discounts for this class of investors may be related to liquidity preferences and characteristics of private equity firms as explained in Section 3.6.2.

Exhibit 3.49 shows the results for dependent private companies.

Exhibit 3.48   Multivariate regression: independent private vs. public companies in the UK (sample seven)

Dependent: Discount EV/EBITDA	Coefficient	T-Value	Significance
(Constant)	0.095	3.430	1%
Size	−0.084	−1.815	10%
RelSize	−0.033	−1.758	10%
Period 2 (2001–2003)	0.184	2.759	1%
Period 3 (2004-Jul 07)	−0.110	−1.693	10%
Indu 50 (trade industry group)	0.120	1.847	10%
Indu 70 (service industry group)	−0.238	−2.155	5%
Cash payment	0.117	2.039	5%
Private equity investor	−0.206	−2.395	5%
R^2	21.7%		

The sample is based on completed majority-ownership transactions between January 1997 and June 2011 in Western Europe and consists of 1,606 transactions as shown in the EV/EBITDA column of Exhibit 3.36. The table reports the results of the stepwise linear regression computed according to Equation 3.3 in Section 3.13. As the dependent variable, the ratio computed according to Equation 3.2 in Section 3.13 on the EV/EBITDA multiple is used. The set of dependent variables is described in Exhibit 3.33.
Source: Zephyr database, Bureau von Dijk.

Dependent private companies in the UK are discounted by only 5.7% on average, a result that is in line with the low discount for independent companies in Exhibit 3.48 and those shown in Exhibit 3.37. Absolute and relative size seem to influence discounts, as do market conditions. During the market downturn between 2001–2003 (*Period 2*) discounts for transactions with dependent private companies increased; in the period after the subprime crisis (*Period 5*), discounts for dependent private companies decreased. Again, trade and service companies are discounted more or less heavily when sold and cash deals are discounted more without any obvious relation to size differences. In contrast to the regression results for independent

Exhibit 3.49   Multivariate regression: dependent private vs. public companies in the UK (sample eight)

Dependent: Discount EV/EBITDA	Coefficient	T-Value	Significance
(Constant)	0.057	3.745	1%
Size	−0.096	−2.223	5%
RelSize	−0.068	−2.341	5%
Period 2 (2001–2003)	0.148	2.687	1%
Period 5 (Aug 07-Jun 11)	−0.140	−2.941	1%
Indu 50 (trade industry group)	0.133	2.272	5%
Indu 70 (service industry group)	−0.155	−2.517	5%
Cash payment	0.114	1.990	5%
Cross-border deal	−0.136	−2.299	5%
R^2	22.0%		

The sample is based on completed majority-ownership transactions between January 1997 and June 2011 in Western Europe and consists of 1,750 transactions as shown in the EV/EBITDA column of Exhibit 3.36. The table reports the results of the stepwise linear regression computed according to Equation 3.3 in Section 3.13. As the dependent variable, the ratio computed according to Equation 3.2 in Section 3.13 on the EV/EBITDA multiple is used. The set of dependent variables is described in Exhibit 3.33.
Source: Zephyr database, Bureau von Dijk.

private companies, foreign investors seem to apply lower discounts when acquiring dependent subsidiaries, whereas private equity investors do not influence the discount applied.

3.12 SUMMARY OF FINDINGS

Section 3.11 talked about discounts, whereas Sections 3.5 and 3.6 earlier introduced the DLL and the PCD. So, what exactly has been measured in this study?

Referring back to Exhibit 3.21, it has been shown that a discount due to the lack of liquidity for a majority ownership interest in a private company is in general smaller than for a private minority ownership interest, mainly because a control share in a publicly traded company is always less marketable than a minority share. In addition, the value of a non-marketable control share in a private company is more liquid than the value of a non-marketable minority share in a private company. Therefore the value difference between those two investments (majority shareholding in a public company (control value) vs. a majority shareholding in a private company (value of a non-marketable control share)) that is related to liquidity should be lower than the DLL for minority ownership interests (the value difference between the stock market value of a minority interest (publicly traded equivalent value) and the value of a non-marketable minority share in a private company).

But looking for empirical data that quantify the liquidity differences between a control share in a publicly traded company (control value) and the value of a non-marketable control share in private company, it is necessary to compare transaction multiples paid for those companies. The measured difference between the multiples, the discount, is called the PCD, as not only liquidity aspects but also other factors affect this difference. Some of them are quantifiable, such as size and industry, but others are still not quantifiable, such as differences in firm characteristics, selling behaviour, or accounting information quality. These factors are summarized as a "private factor" that describes the general difference between public and private companies.

So is it possible to compute a "pure" DLL for majority ownership interests in private companies? Not so far with the available data. For now the only possibility is to try to analyze/ examine how certain factors influence the value differences (the discount) and then gauge the size of the discount that is attributable to liquidity differences stripped from other influence factors. Look at the different bars in the diagram in Exhibit 3.50. The complete bar symbolizes the PCD that can be measured when multiples between public and private majority transactions are compared. Different factors contribute to the measured size of the PCD. Some of them are related directly to liquidity and influence how market participants value liquidity differences between public and private companies. For example, the payment method influences the measured PCD and when payment is made in cash, the bar increases (as the influence of the factor increases) and the measured PCD is higher. One cannot exactly know the size of the influence of the single components. In the regressions, cash payment has a beta of 0.06 to 0.21 depending on the sample used.

Is it correct to say that the measured PCD increases by 0.06x "base" PCD when cash payment is made? No, because the low R^2 of the regressions indicates that there are missing factors that cannot be measured with data available in this study. So one can only explain part of the PCD applied to private firms.

The discount measured in the regression is the PCD. The analysis of independent private companies in Germany showed that these companies are discounted more in a period that implied lower discounts. Good M&A markets like the one between 2004 and mid-2007 imply a lower DLL, but other factors interfere/overlay the influence of increased market liquidity,

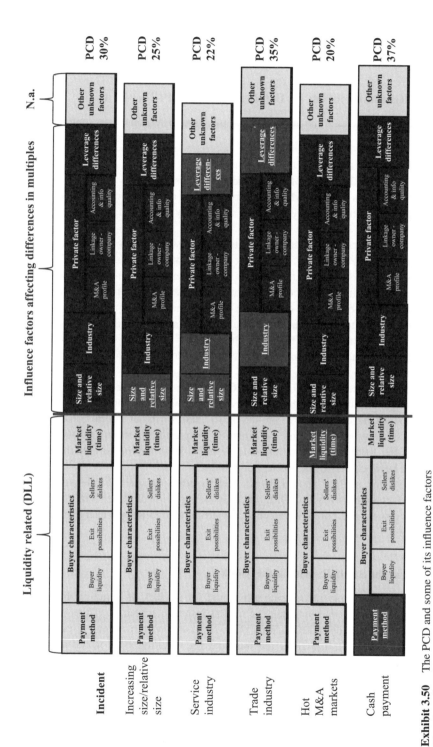

Exhibit 3.50   The PCD and some of its influence factors

The above bars illustrate a hypothetical PCD and its components. Factors include those influence factors described in Exhibit 3.16 without accounting for any regional differences that also might influence the PCD, such as market depth or bidder competition (composition of investor base, e.g. the percentage of foreign and local investors). Given the low R^2 of the regression, the portion of "other unknown factors" is higher in reality and might also interfere with the factors shown in the table above. Fields with underlined text indicate that the influence of these factors changes when the respective incident (shown left) occurs. The resulting magnitude of the PCD is for illustration purposes only and not related to any regression model computed in Section 3.11.

which are all somehow in the PCD basket. A part of them can be named and included in a regression (like leverage differences), others can be named but not included in the regressions (like accounting and information quality), and many can neither be named nor measured (referring again to the low R^2).

3.12.1 General Recommendations for the Application of a PCD or DLL

In this short section, some general remarks for the application of discounts are summarized:

- Generally, one should abstain from the common approach of fixed discounts (irrespective of whether DLL or PCD) as this practice is erroneous.
- The size of the discounts depends on the data and the method used.
- The use of study results on the DLL which focus on minority ownership interests is inappropriate for the application of illiquidity discounts on majority ownership interests in private companies.
- Talking of majority ownership interests, discounts on interests in private firms compared to public companies are called the PCD. The PCD cannot be totally attributed to a lack of liquidity. Analysts need to consider the fundamental differences between independent private firms, dependent private firms, and public companies because the approach to estimating the PCD cannot account for all those differences between the classes.
- For majority ownership interests, the acquisition approach that analyzes differences in transaction multiples suits best to estimate the PCD. The approach using comparable transactions and the matching technique account for some systematic factors which influence transaction multiples of private and public firms.
- It is not appropriate to use static PCDs as the PCD changes over an economic cycle with changing market conditions, availability of financing, and therefore supply and demand.
- If non-US, do not use the size of the PCD found in US studies without careful consideration of the market, company specifics, and the situation in question as company and market characteristics differ from region to region. One should at least use comparable time spans and differentiate between classes of private companies.
- Especially in Germany, analysts should always keep the idiosyncrasies of independent private (Mittelstand) companies in mind. Differences in the valuation of Mittelstand companies relative to other private and public companies are attributable to unique characteristics of these companies.

3.12.2 How to Use the Study Results in this Book

The resulting discounts not only incorporate a discount for the lack of liquidity but include fundamental differences between companies as well as transaction characteristics (e.g. payment method). Therefore, the discount is called PCD. Despite careful matching of companies with respect to size, time of transaction, and industry, the resulting PCD in the univariate analyses are relative lump sum discounts as the influence of other explanatory variables for the PCD is not accounted for. Therefore, the regression analyses aim for a better understanding of potential influence factors on the PCD and include all identified factors in a multivariate setting. Although the potential influence factors and their interdependencies in a statistical setting are accounted for, the resulting constant does not represent a "pure" discount attributable to liquidity. But maybe this constant comes closer to the pure liquidity discount compared to the one computed in the univariate setting before. One needs to be aware that the constant still represents a PCD, driven by the fact that there are explanatory variables missing in the regression.

How should one now use the results of the previous chapter? One should remember that this book talks about the M&A transaction as a valuation purpose and about the problem that more empirical evidence is needed to support a solid argumentation, not only in transaction negations but also for potential litigation and court decisions. Therefore, univariate analysis provides the empirical evidence for the PCD, tailored to regions and company classes. In addition, information is given on how the PCD may change across time periods and industries. The results can be used to apply a more tailored PCD instead of the famous 30% and also provide arguments, e.g. why for a special valuation purpose a higher or lower than median PCD found in Exhibit 3.37 may be be appropriate. Furthermore, as regression results show the influence of additional explanatory factors on the PCD, an analyst may say that for an independent North American company a PCD of 22% is appropriate, but if the transaction is paid in cash, the PCD needs to be higher. Not necessarily by 21.2% (the beta of the variable *Cash payment*) but the analyst has an argument in hand to increase the discounts.[16]

3.12.3   Empirical Results Summary – Germany

The univariate analysis in Exhibit 3.37 supports the application of a PCD of between 19% and 27% to independent private (Mittelstand) companies, when looking at the EV/EBITDA and EV/EBIT multiple. The discount on the sales multiples is higher, but in practice sales multiples are difficult to interpret because they often lack a direct link to a company's earnings and are therefore less frequently used. Data availability for the P/E ratio is too weak; therefore no analysis is done on this multiple.

The PCD is driven by fundamental differences between public and private companies, in case of independent private companies, certain characteristics that are unique to this class of companies (these include, for example, a higher D/E ratio or the interest of foreign investors). Therefore it is necessary on the one hand to separate independent from dependent private companies, and on the other hand to acknowledge that the application of US studies is at least difficult. Given unique characteristics of the German Mittelstand and the market environment, one can even call the analyzed discount the "Mittelstand Discount". Looking at dependent private companies in Exhibit 3.37, lower discounts are applied to them, between 16% and 18% on the EV/EBIT and EV/EBITDA multiple. Without any differentiation, a PCD of between 17% and 20% (on the EV/EBIT and EV/EBITDA multiple) is applied to private companies in Germany.

Our analysis of discounts over time periods shows that the market environment influences the PCD applied but shows also that further time-moving factors influence its development over the periods. For example, in times of active M&A markets (2004–July 2007), the observed Mittelstand Discount increased, while for dependent private German companies the PCD was lower. Analyzing further, it has been shown that in this period highly leveraged independent private (Mittelstand) companies were sold. Maybe these firms cannot time their disposals as they are experiencing an increased disposal pressure through high D/E ratios.

In the course of the subprime crisis between August 2007 and March 2009, independent private companies are still being discounted between 27% and 30% on the EV/EBIT and

---

[16] Note, the regression analysis is not suitable to predict a PCD, e.g. an analyst cannot say that the PCD for a North American company in the service industry paid with cash needs to be 22.0% -27.7% + 21.2% = 15.5%.

EV/EBITDA multiples compared to public companies in Germany; the observed discounts are higher than for dependent private firms, which are discounted by between 19% and 22%.

However, in total, the Mittelstand Discount does not increase significantly during the subprime crisis compared to the period before. It could be demonstrated that foreign investors not only show a lot of interest in the Mittelstand but also pay significantly more for these companies than other investors, and therefore positively influence average valuations of Mittelstand companies. Furthermore, debt levels of companies sold during the subprime crisis decreased significantly from an average D/E level of 3.7x to 2.8x. In contrast to the independent private companies, discounts for dependent private companies more than doubled during the subprime crisis (on the EBITDA and EBIT ratio).

Exhibit 3.40 shows that discounts vary with the industry, but also with different debt levels and size differences. Low-leveraged service companies are discounted less, irrespective of whether the private companies are dependent or independent.

Our multivariate regression in Section 3.11.3 reveals a constant of 21.4% as Mittelstand Discount (Exhibit 3.41).

The size of a company influences the discounts: the higher the relative target size compared to the acquirer, the lower the potential Mittelstand Discount can be. Independent private (Mittelstand) companies in the trade industry group can be discounted more, companies from the service industry less. The Mittelstand Discount after the subprime crisis should be lower; the variable *Period 5* has a negative sign.

Independent private companies seem to have a desire for cash – this payment method increases discounts. Acquisitions planned by foreign investors are discounted less; a sell-side analyst should use this argument to show that acquiring in the Germany market and bidding for "made in Germany" is costly. Transactions with listed acquirers seem to increase discounts; the positive sign of the regression beta is in contrast to the expected influence on liquidity. This aspect has been analyzed already and correlation to the relative size of the target firms was found. As the r elative size is included in the regression results, the influence of listed acquirers remains a mystery; it is recommended to ignore this factor.

Variables which are expected to influence a potential discount like *Private equity investor* which describes buyer characteristics and the D/E ratio do not have the expected influence in the study; they show no significance in the regression analysis. Private equity investors may apply a lower Mittelstand Discount or even apply a higher one because (at least until the subprime crisis) they tend to acquirer distressed firms, but (multi-)correlation with other influence variables excluded the variable from the regression result. Also the Mittelstand is in general more highly leveraged than dependent private companies and public companies sold in the market – the influence of the leverage as an explanatory variable is not significant. Again, this factor correlates with e.g. the time factor; one can see that the variable *Period 3* is included in the regression with a positive sign, increasing the Mittelstand Discount although market conditions imply a negative sign.

The PCD for dependent private companies in Germany amounts to 14.7% according to Exhibit 3.43.

Size and relative size of dependent private companies negatively influence discounts applied; three time periods reveal significant influence. In contrast to independent private companies, liquid and active markets (*Period 3*) decrease the PCD; a higher PCD should be applied when market conditions worsen (*Period 2* and *Period 4*). Correlations to the debt level exist for companies sold between 2001 and 2003 (*Period 2*) and between 2004 and mid-2007 (*Period 3*), so maybe again, not only market conditions but also leverage characteristics of target companies influence the discounts applied. The PCD for trade companies can be higher, while cash deals are discounted more. Again, the variable *Listed acquired* reveals influence, but again interpretation of the positive sign is difficult.

3.12.4   Empirical Results Summary – North America

According to the univariate analysis in Exhibit 3.37, North American private companies are discounted between 26% and 31% depending on the multiple used. Significant differences between independent and dependent private firms only exist for the PCD on the EV/EBITA multiple. EV/Sales and EV/EBIT multiples show discounts of 30% and 31% (independent and dependent companies on the EV/EBIT multiple) and 25% and 27% (independent and dependent companies on the EV/Sales multiple).

The analysis of discounts over time periods in Exhibit 3.38 shows that the market environment influences the PCD. Looking at the recent developments after the beginning of the subprime crisis, a distinction between independent and dependent private companies could make sense. Whereas discounts for independent companies increased from 21% to 31% (on the EV/EBITDA multiple), the PCD for dependent companies increased from 23% to 42%. In the market upside after the subprime crisis, independent private companies are discounted by 26% compared to a PCD of 32% for dependent companies.

Exhibit 3.40 shows that both independent and dependent trade and manufacturing companies are much more discounted than firms in other sectors, whereas discounts for service companies are lower (average discount about 13.0%). The result for service companies is perhaps driven by a significantly lower leverage compared to other companies. Manufacturing companies show neither leverage nor significant size difference compared to firms in other industries.

Cross-sectional regression in Exhibit 3.44 reveals a PCD of 22% for independent private companies in North America. It shows that the PCD varies depending on the characteristics of the firms and the transaction itself. For example, the PCD decreases for independent private companies that are bigger than the average of companies. During the active M&A market between 2004 and July 2007, the observed discount for independent private companies is lower, whereas in more difficult markets between 2001 and 2003, the PCD increased. Discounts vary with industry; trade companies are discounted more, the service industry less. Cash payment increases the PCD, but it is related to company size as shown in Exhibit 3.13.

The PCD for dependent private companies amounts to 27% according to Exhibit 3.45. Discounts are less for companies of above average size.

The negative market environment from 2001 to 2003 increased the PCD; in the active M&A market environment between January 2004 and June 2007 the PCD decreased. In contrast to independent companies, discounts for dependent companies in North America increased during the subprime crisis. In contrast to Germany, interest from foreign investors cannot be found; moreover their influence in the regression is not significant. The PCD is especially high in the trade industry; no lower discounts are applicable for service companies. The method of payment influences the PCD significantly. Furthermore, listed acquirers seem to apply lower discounts for dependent subsidiaries.

3.12.5   Empirical Results Summary – Western Europe

According to Exhibit 3.37, the PCD for independent private companies in Western Europe varies from 16% (EV/EBIT multiple) to 54% (EV/Sales multiple). The big difference is hard to interpret but discounts on the EV/Sales multiple are less meaningful due to the characteristics of the multiple itself.

The EV/EBITDA multiple reveals a PCD of 38%. Dependent private companies are less heavily discounted: between 14% (on the EV/EBIT multiple), 21% (on the EV/EBITDA multiple), and 40% (on the EV/Sales multiple).

The development of the PCD over time in Exhibit 3.38 shows that the PCD for independent private companies increases during market downturns (2001–2003 and the subprime crisis): before 2001, the PCD amounts to 21% (EV/EBITDA multiple), then increases to 32% between 2001 and 2003, declines to 29% (2004–July 2007), and increases again to 35% during the subprime crisis. Thereafter, the PCD stayed at 35%.

Compared to independent private companies, the PCD is lower for independent private firms across all periods: before 2001, the PCD amounts to 21% (EV/EBITDA multiple), than increases to 27% between 2001 and 2003, declines to 22% (2004–July 2007), and then increases to 25% during the subprime crisis. Thereafter, the PCD decreased to 19%.

In Western Europe, the PCDs for service and finance industry are lower compared to other industries. Independent finance and service companies are discounted by 25% and 15% on the EV/EBITDA multiple whereas the PCD for the manufacturing and transportation industry amounts to 36% and 27%. Trade companies are discounted most with a PCD of 37%.

The multivariate regression in Exhibit 3.46 shows an average PCD of 29% for independent private companies. The PCD for relatively big companies can be smaller; the unfavourable market environments between 2001 and 2003 and during the subprime crisis increased the PCD. The PCD is higher for companies in the trade industry and lower when service companies are acquired. Cash payment increases the PCD. A lower PCD is applied in cross-border transactions.

For dependent private companies, the average PCD amounts to 17% in Exhibit 3.47; the PCD is lower for companies with above average size. The PCD increased during the unfavourable market environment between 2001 and 2003. In contrast to independent private companies, a lower PCD is applied during the improving market conditions after April 2009. Again, the PCD for trade companies is higher than for other industries; furthermore, a higher discount is attached to transactions with manufacturing companies. Cash payment increases the PCD without any obvious differences across deal sizes. Cross-border transactions are discounted less heavily.

In the regression, the variables *Listed acquirer* and *Target D/E* influence the measured PCD when dependent private companies, with a D/E ratio of 1.6x are generally less highly leveraged than independent ones (D/E ratio of 1.8x according to Exhibit 3.23).

3.12.6 Empirical Results Summary – UK

The univariate analysis in Exhibit 3.37 supports the application of a PCD between 12% and 23% to independent private companies in the UK when looking at the EV/EBITDA and EV/EBIT multiple, whereby dependent private companies are discounted only at 7% (EV/EBITDA multiple) and 6% (EV/EBIT multiple).

Compared to Germany the overall level of discounts in the UK seems lower. Furthermore, dependent private companies are discounted less that independent ones.

Our analysis of discounts over time periods shows that the market environment influences the PCD applied (measured on the EV/EBITDA multiple) for independent companies with an expected pattern over time. They are discounted at 16% before 2001, 19% between 2001 and 2003, 14% between 2004 and July 2007, 18% between August 2007 and March 2009 (subprime), and 11% between April 2009 and June 2011. In contrast to independent private companies, dependent private companies show no clear pattern over time: the PCD amounts to 10% before 2001, 15% between 2001 and 2003, 7% between 2004 and July 2007, 7% between August 2007 and March 2009 (subprime), and 1% between April 2009 and June 2011. If one tries to investigate factors that could possibly be attributable to this development, one can find constant (decreasing) debt levels for dependent private companies during (after) the subprime crisis in Exhibit 3.23. To what extent changing debt levels influence the development of the PCD is not clear – an analyst needs to be aware of the diverse implications of a changing market environment.

The PCD varies with industry membership. The PCD (measured on the EV/EBITDA multiple) for independent UK companies in the finance and service companies is, at 8% and 9%, lower than the average PCD of 19%. The PCD for trade companies is the highest, at 32%. Dependent private companies in the service industry receive premium valuations with a negative PCD of 17%. Exhibit 3.12 showed that private service companies have lower leverage and are bigger than other private companies (relative size of 4.1% vs. 3.5% all other and a D/E ratio of 1.3x vs. 1.5x all other). Furthermore, private trade companies are more highly leveraged and bigger than other private companies (relative size of 6.0% vs. 3.5% all other and a D/E ratio of 1.8x vs. 1.4x all other).

According to the multivariate regression in Exhibit 3.48, the PCD for independent private companies in the UK amounts to 10%, a number that is lower compared to other regions. The PCD decreases with increasing target absolute and relative size. The unfavourable market environment between 2001 and 2003 increased the PCD, the favourable one between 2004 and mid-2007 led to a decrease in discounts. A higher PCD can be applied for companies in the trade industry group, and a lower PCD for companies in the service industry. Cash payment increases the PCD without revealing any relationship to deal size in Exhibit 3.13. Average cash deals are even slightly bigger (average deal size EUR 14.5m) than non-cash deals (average deal size EUR 13.8m). Targets acquired by private equity investors have lower discounts, perhaps due to liquidity preferences and characteristics of private equity as explained in Section 3.6.2.

According to the regression in Exhibit 3.49, dependent private companies in the UK are discounted only by 6% on average. Again, absolute and relative size influence the PCD as expected. During the market downturn between 2001 and 2003 the PCD for transactions with dependent private companies increased, in the period after the subprime crisis, the PCD for dependent private companies decreased. Again, trade and service companies have higher/lower discounts when sold and cash deals are discounted more. In contrast to the regression results for independent private companies, foreign investors seem to apply a lower PCD when acquiring dependent subsidiaries, whereas private equity investors do not influence the PCD applied.

3.13 CONDUCTING A PCD STUDY

To apply a PCD, it is recommended to use empirical data from a market environment that mirrors the conditions of the subject company, is reasonably up-to-date, and uses a time span that accounts for changes in market developments. If such empirical data are not available, one can consider conducting one's own study on the PCD. In the following, the design from the previous study is described and the steps from raw data through explorative data analysis to regression modelling and result interpretation are demonstrated.

3.13.1   How to Proceed?

The acquisition approach generally follows a two-step procedure. The first step consists of an explorative analysis that benchmarks multiples of private and public companies using cross-tabs. While benchmarking multiples, one can control for the influence of systematic influence factors identified before (e.g. size, transaction year, and industry, but also others, if desired) by matching private and public companies accordingly. For each acquisition of a private firm, one should attempt to find a matching portfolio which includes public company deals in the same year, from the same industry, and of a comparable size. Matching portfolios are built by creating clusters of transactions according to the influence factors. This construction of matching portfolios is a key feature of the acquisition approach and one should examine the data very carefully using explorative analyses to cluster the transactions. Because the cross-tab analysis cannot encompass all the factors that determine observed differences between public and private company multiples, one needs to estimate multivariate cross-sectional regressions as the second step. After thorough clustering and preparatory steps for the regression one can (a) include more influence factors than pure size, year, and industry in the cross-sectional regressions, and (b) include those factors specially tailored to value independent private companies. Next to the careful construction of matching portfolios and the thorough selection of influence factors, an in-depth data gathering and preparation process are additional elements that characterize good empirical research. For all the analyses described in the following, the advanced statistical software package of SPSS Inc.[17] is used.

3.13.2   Which Multiples to Choose

The acquisition approach is based on the benchmarking of multiples. So, one should use multiples which are on the one hand computable, given the financial information provided in the databases, and on the other hand commonly used by investment bankers or analysts. In the study, the book value multiples were not used. Given the unrealistic assumption that the cash return on the book value of assets is constant, these are not very common for transaction valuations.

Three EV multiples were computed, relating the EV to sales (EV/Sales), to earnings before interest, taxes, depreciation, and amortization (EV/EBITDA), and to earnings before interest and taxes (EV/EBIT). Since Sales, EBITDA, and EBIT are distributed between all types of investors in the company (common shareholders, preferred shareholders, and creditors), they reflect the fundamental value of the whole company.

The main advantage is that an enterprise multiple is not affected by the capital structure, since the EBITDA and EBIT are not influenced by interest expenses. Hence, the valuation is not biased by different capital structures between companies. Moreover, the net income which is used for equity multiples includes the yield on shares and other non-operating profits. In general, the risk of these items differs from the operating risk of the company. Therefore, the risk of the company is blurred by these items. Furthermore, the EBITDA and EBIT are often positive when net income is negative, which is favourable in practice. However, one caveat must be issued regarding the EBITDA and EBIT. They include non-cash revenues due to the accrual accounting principle. Because of this, both measures only provide a proxy of company cash flows available for debt and interest payment. As the EBIT is computed

---

[17] For more information, see www.spss.com.

net of depreciation, it is an appropriate surrogate for free cash flow if capital expenditures approximate depreciation. On the other hand, the EBITDA would be appropriate if future capital expenditures are minor.

Because of the advantages of the EBITDA and the EBIT multiple, for the purpose of the previous analyses EV multiples using the EBITDA and the EBIT were computed. Furthermore, the EV/Sales multiple was computed as sales are harder to manipulate, in most cases not subject to accounting discretion and generally more stable than operating earnings. Since sales are always positive, the ratio is often employed for valuation of cyclical, unprofitable and mature companies. Furthermore, sales data is easily available.

In addition to the EV-related multiples, the Price/Earnings (P/E) ratio as equity value multiple was computed. This ratio is widely recognized and used among investors and earnings continue to be the primary driver of Investment Value. Furthermore, the P/E multiple is related empirically to long-run stock returns and P/E multiples that are based on forecast earnings dominate all other multiples in valuation accuracy. On the other hand, the P/E multiple only makes economic sense with positive earnings. In addition, the volatile, transitory portion of earnings makes it difficult to calculate P/E ratios, and management discretion in the choice of accounting methods reduces its comparability. Looking at the number of available multiples and discounts especially in Germany (see e.g. Exhibit 3.34 and Exhibit 3.36), the P/E multiples are excluded from discount analyses in Section 3.11.

The results in Section 3.11 show that using the acquisition approach, different multiples lead to distinct measures of the PCD. Therefore the question arises as to which PCD is the correct one? A satisfactory reply to that question is difficult and can be best argued with the characteristics of the single multiples. Discounts computed with sales multiples are generally weaker than those computed with other multiples: without direct earning implications, the turnover of a target company may be less important than its operating earnings. Therefore the PCD on the EV/ Sales multiple is less meaningful than on the EV/EBITDA and EV/EBIT multiple. The reason why the computed PCD varies across these two multiples may be attributable to the number of available observations, to accounting choices with respect to depreciation, and amortization of mere noise. Given its importance in the context of company valuation, it is recommended to compute the PCD based on the EV/EBITDA multiple.

3.13.3 Matching the Multiples – Computing the Discounts

According to Section 3.6.2, prior research identifies three factors that systematically influence valuation of public and private companies. Therefore, when comparing multiples, one should account at least for these differences by comparing firms of the same size, from the same industry, and transactions that have taken place within the same time frame. Therefore the necessity arises to match the deals according to these criteria. Instead of picking one public transaction that is considered to be similar on the basis of the three criteria and comparing it to one transaction involving a private target, it is recommended to compute a median multiple as the benchmark multiple out of a portfolio of matching public transactions. This increases the likelihood of finding matching pairs of companies. Then compare the multiple in a private transaction with the benchmark multiple from a matching portfolio. One can assume that the universe of public deals in the matching portfolio from which the benchmark multiple is constructed is more rationally priced and less subject to noise than a single, picked transaction. The portfolio of matching public transactions is called the "public reference portfolio", and valuations are compared on the EV/Sales, EV/EBITDA, EV/EBIT and P/E multiple. A ratio comparing the respective private company's multiple with the benchmark multiple out of the public reference portfolio as shown in Equation 3.2 was computed for all multiples m (m = 1 ... 4) for each transaction involving a private target:

$$\text{Ratio}_{m,s,p,i,z} = 1 - \left(\frac{\text{Private company multiple}_{m,s,p,i}}{\text{Public reference portfolio multiple}_{m,s,p,i}} \right) \quad \forall \, z = 1 \dots Z, \quad (3.2)$$

where s, p and i stand for the three systematic influence factors "Size class", "Period" and "Industry group". The variable z stands for the number of samples, if more than one is involved, depending on the concrete set-up of the study. For example, $z = 2$ if one distinguishes independent private companies and dependent private companies, both compared to public companies.

Positive ratios imply discounts; negative ratios imply premiums on the reference portfolio. As mentioned before, these ratios should be analyzed in two different steps. First, do explorative analyses using cross-tables to analyze the median of the ratios for all multiples depending on the target's status and differentiated according to time and industry. Then calculate multivariate cross-sectional regressions.

3.13.4 Detecting Patterns – Data Clustering

To compute the matching portfolios, one should use the influence factors of size, time of the transaction/year, and industry mentioned before. Due to the limited amount of cases (transactions) in some subgroups of the systematic influence factors, it may be useful to recode these variables and build clusters. The data reduction has the significant advantage that one can include additional factors beyond the systematic ones in the cross-sectional regression without reducing the quality of the regressions too much. Data reduction has to be performed carefully to avoid the loss of information. Univariate analysis can be used to examine the variation of multiples across each of the influence factors and to test whether this variation is significant. In order to test the significance of differences, test different statistics, e.g. use non-parametric tests like the Kruskall-Wallis tests; parametric tests can also be used. The following three paragraphs show the procedure on the basis of the analysis for Germany. The other regions, North America, Western Europe, and the UK have been analyzed accordingly.

Clustering – SIZE

To cluster the data according to size, the natural logarithm of target turnover is used to form size classes. This fits in better with the data than the use of quartiles as done by Kooli et al. (2003). Using the natural logarithm of turnover, Exhibit 3.51 gives an overview of the resulting classes. It shows that quartiles would have been too broad, although some categories lack data. While there is variation in the data (for example, the largest fraction of acquisitions of firms is in size class 11), such data are not clustered in any one size class. The data appear to be reasonably well spread out over classes with two limitations: because of the low number of deals in the classes up to class 5 and classes 15 to 19, classes 1 to 6 are summed in class 6, as well as classes greater than 14 in class 14.

The clustering of deals according to the natural logarithm of target turnover results in nine classes and is summarized under the variable *Size class*.

Exhibit 3.51 Distribution of cases across size classes

Number of transactions old classification

Size class	Turnover up to € Mio.	Germany	North America	Western Europe	UK
			Total number of transactions		
<3	<20	4	71	32	98
3	20	6	71	35	57
4	55	8	178	69	116
5	148	18	204	136	249
6	403	23	337	269	454
7	1,097	60	847	477	807
8	2,981	116	1279	832	1244
9	8,103	160	1699	1370	1491
10	22,026	163	1721	1468	1459
11	59,874	188	1521	1163	1189
12	162,755	129	1168	663	794
13	442,413	96	840	337	445
14	1,202,604	53	467	169	200
15	3,269,017	24	187	87	93
16	8,886,111	7	87	27	42
17	24,154,953	3	31	3	10
18	65,659,969	0	5	0	6
19	178,482,301	1	0	0	2
Total		1,059	10,713	7,137	8,756

Number of transactions new classification

Region:	Germany			North America	Western Europe	UK
Total		thereof private	thereof public	Total	Total	Total
59		45	14	861	974	541
60		47	13	847	807	477
116		90	26	1279	1244	832
160		141	19	1699	1491	1370
163		128	35	1721	1459	1468
188		157	31	1521	1189	1163
129		100	29	1168	794	663
96		66	30	840	445	337
88		53	35	777	353	286
1,059		827	232	10,713	8,756	7,137

The data set includes completed majority-ownership transactions between January 1997 and June 2011, where information for at least one transaction multiple is available. The table reports the distribution of transactions across the size classes (computed with the natural logarithm of target turnover) for target companies in Germany, North America, Western Europe, and the UK before and after the clustering of the variable *Size class*.

Source: Zephyr database, Bureau von Dijk.

Clustering – TIME

Prior research has shown already that the time of the transaction influences the size of the discounts and movements in multiples over the periods can be found in Section 3.10. A thorough clustering with respect to the importance of the market environment for discounts is necessary as nobody wants the results of his analyses to be blurred by incomparable matching. To reduce the data dimensions and cluster the transaction with respect to time, the number of deals and the distribution of multiples over time were examined. As the analysis encompasses different regions, the influence of the time factor is controlled as to whether it is in any way comparable across Germany, Western Europe, North America, and the UK. The aim is to summarize the years into a lower number of periods to be used as a cluster variable for further analyses. This leads to a higher number of cases in each period, as well as a lower number of dependent variables in the cross-sectional regression. Exhibit 3.52 shows the distribution of multiples after grouping the years into different periods. For the first three periods, the time pattern of multiples is relatively clear and consistent over the different regions: before 2001 these were relatively high; they came down in 2001 and stayed at a relatively low level until 2003, after which they increased until July 2007. This pattern is better observable in

Exhibit 3.52   Median multiples across periods

Germany	before 2001	2001–2003	2004-Jul 07	Subprime Aug 07-Mar 09	Post subprime Apr 09-Jun 11
EV/Sales	0.8x	0.9x	1.3x	1.7x	1.3x
EV/EBITDA	8.7x	8.5x	10.4x	12.4x	12.5x
EV/EBIT	10.1x	13.0x	14.0x	13.0x	14.2x
P/E	18.7x	14.0x	15.7x	15.6x	13.5x
North America					
EV/Sales	1.5x	1.3x	1.9x	1.7x	1.9x
EV/EBITDA	12.3x	8.5x	11.8x	11.4x	11.5x
EV/EBIT	15.4x	12.5x	16.4x	16.3x	14.7x
P/E	20.5x	16.5x	21.1x	19.5x	19.9x
Western Europe					
EV/Sales	1.2x	1.3x	1.7x	1.6x	1.7x
EV/EBITDA	9.5x	8.2x	9.5x	9.4x	9.4x
EV/EBIT	13.5x	11.1x	12.7x	12.1x	12.2x
P/E	18.4x	16.7x	16.3x	15.3x	15.4x
UK					
EV/Sales	1.1x	1.0x	1.4x	1.3x	1.4x
EV/EBITDA	9.8x	8.7x	10.9x	10.9x	11.1x
EV/EBIT	12.8x	12.1x	14.3x	14.1x	14.1x
P/E	15.8x	15.0x	15.4x	15.6x	15.7x

The sample consists of completed majority-ownership transactions between January 1997 and June 2007 where information for at least one transaction multiple is available as shown in Exhibit 3.35. The table reports the distribution of multiples after assigning the transactions to different periods.
Source: Zephyr database, Bureau von Dijk.

North America, Western Europe, and the UK. In Germany, only the EV/EBITDA and the P/E multiple developed as expected from the period before 2001 to the market slowdown between 2001 and 2003.

During the subprime crisis, one can observe variations across multiples and regions; average multiples went down around 5% in North America and in Western Europe. In the UK, multiples remained relatively constant, only the EV/EBIT multiples came down by 1%. In Germany, valuation for all companies on the EV/Sales and the EV/EBITDA multiple increased, whereas the valuation on EBIT multiples came down by 7%.

For the time after the subprime crisis one can observe an overall increase in multiples in North America and Western Europe and slight improvements in the UK. In Germany, valuation on the EV/EBIT and EV/EBIT multiples improved, the valuation on the EV/Sales multiples decreased by more than 20% and on the P/E multiple decreased by around 14%; the latter may be explainable by the limited number of observations.

Overall, it is not easy to cluster the transactions into periods given the development of multiples in the different market regions. In particular, the market conditions during the subprime crisis/post subprime are not exactly mirrored in the development of multiples. This can also be attributable to the fact that the overall amount of data is richer in the periods before, the limited number of observations in the last periods compared to those before may skew some of the results. Nevertheless, some pattern in the data can be found and given the findings in Section 3.10, the years are split into a smaller number of periods to facilitate further analysis. Furthermore, without building the clusters, there is a lack of multiples during some years. Therefore the variable *Period* is built by clustering the years into five periods as follows: until 12/2000 ("good" M&A years) as "Period 1", between January 2001 and December 2003 ("market slowdown") as "Period 2", between January 2004 and July 2007 ("market catch-up") as "Period 3", between August 2004 and March 2009 ("subprime crisis") as "Period 4", and after April 2009 until June 2011 as "Period 5" ("post subprime").

Clustering – INDUSTRY

To classify the transactions with respect to industry, one might use the first two digits of the four-digit Standard Industrial Classification (SIC) system (see Exhibit 3.53). The SIC system is widely used in empirical research and practice, and it allows a better comparison of the results to other (US) studies which have been conducted on private firms. Furthermore, with respect

Exhibit 3.53   An overview of SIC classes

SIC Code	Industry group according SIC code	SIC Code	Industry group according SIC code
(01XX-09XX)	Agriculture, forestry, and fishing	(50XX-51XX)	Wholesale trade
(10XX-14XX)	Mining	(52XX-59XX)	Retail trade
(15XX-17XX)	Construction	(60XX-67XX)	Finance, insurance and real estate
(20XX-29XX)	Manufacturing	(70XX-79XX)	Services
(30XX-39XX)	Manufacturing	(80XX-98XX)	Social services
(40XX-49XX)	Transportation, communication & utilities	(91XX-99XX)	Public administration

Exhibit 3.54 Numbers of deals in the different industry groups

SIC group	Target industry group	Germany	North America	Western Europe	UK
30XX-39XX[1]	Manufacturing	486	3,990	3,226	2,135
40XX-49XX[2]	Transportation, communication and utilities	89	723	979	634
50XX-59XX	Wholesale and retail trade	87	791	916	953
60XX-67XX[3]	Finance, insurance and real estate	94	1,143	817	770
70XX-79XX	Services	268	3,399	2,489	2,527
N.A.	Not available	35	667	329	118
	Total	1,059	10,713	8,756	7,137

1) incl. construction (15XX-17XX) and mining (10XX-14XX)
2) excl. regulated public utilities (44XX and 49XX)
3) excl. financial institutions (60XX-62XX)
The data set includes the completed majority-ownership transactions between January 1997 and June 2011, where information for at least one transaction multiple is available as shown in Exhibit 3.35. The table reports the distribution of transactions across the industry groups after clustering the cases into the variable *Industry group*.
Source: Zephyr database, Bureau von Dijk.

to the limited number of transactions in Germany, it fits the data better than the narrower six-digit North American Industry Classification System (NAICS).

Although the classification is based on the relatively broad SIC groups, there is only a relatively small number of transactions in the construction (15XX–17XX) and mining (10XX–14XX) industries in Germany. In addition, only a handful of transactions are available in the retail trade industry in Germany. As a result, all deals not within the construction (SIC 15XX–17XX) and the mining industry groups (SIC 10XX–14XX) are classified within the manufacturing industry group (SIC 30XX–39XX). In addition, the wholesale trade (SIC 50XX–51XX) and retail trade (SIC 52XX–59XX) are combined into a trade industry group (SIC 50XX).[18] Financial institutions (SIC 60XX–62XX) and regulated public utilities (SIC 44XX and 49XX) and public administration (91XX–99XX) are excluded from the study because these organizations are not comparable to the rest of the companies involved. For example, the liquidity of the banks' assets may lead to a DLL that is smaller than for "traditional" private companies. Furthermore, valuation multiples on EBITDA and sales are not meaningful for banks. Public utilities such as electricity, gas, and water rarely face any competition and therefore they are often monopolies leading to a distortion of multiples. Excluding these industries improves the quality of the study results. In Western Europe and North America there are more data available for example in the agricultural (91XX–09XX), the construction (15XX–17XX), and the mining (10XX–14XX) industries. To make analysis comparable across regions, the industry classification was matched to the German data. This procedure also makes regression analyses easier as it limits the number of independent variables.

Exhibit 3.54 provides an overview of the number of transactions in each industry group across the samples.

---

[18] This is also done in the other samples.

Exhibit 3.55   Multiples across different industry groups

Germany	Manufacturing	Transportation	Trade	Finance	Services	Average
EV/Sales	1.1x	1.8x	1.5x	3.4x	3.7x	2.3x
EV/EBITDA	10.1x	10.3x	8.9x	16.6x	13.0x	11.8x
EV/EBIT	13.8x	19.2x	9.1x	18.9x	14.7x	15.1x
P/E	14.5x	10.5x	9.3x	19.5x	21.3x	15.0x
						0

North America	Manufacturing	Transportation	Trade	Finance	Services	Average
EV/Sales	1.9x	1.9x	0.6x	4.2x	4.1x	2.5x
EV/EBITDA	10.2x	9.5x	9.2x	13.7x	15.0x	11.5x
EV/EBIT	14.6x	14.8x	14.3x	19.9x	19.0x	16.5x
P/E	19.2x	17.4x	19.0x	18.1x	21.0x	18.9x

Western Europe	Manufacturing	Transportation	Trade	Finance	Services	Average
EV/Sales	1.1x	1.7x	1.7x	2.4x	3.5x	2.1x
EV/EBITDA	8.7x	10.4x	8.9x	13.4x	9.4x	10.2x
EV/EBIT	12.2x	14.4x	10.6x	14.6x	11.9x	12.7x
P/E	15.5x	21.7x	16.6x	11.5x	15.8x	16.2x

UK	Manufacturing	Transportation	Trade	Finance	Services	Average
EV/Sales	1.0x	1.5x	0.7x	2.1x	2.6x	1.6x
EV/EBITDA	9.0x	10.1x	9.1x	12.6x	11.3x	10.4x
EV/EBIT	12.0x	12.4x	11.9x	14.3x	15.7x	13.3x
P/E	13.9x	14.1x	13.8x	15.1x	20.2x	15.4x

The sample consists of completed majority-ownership transactions between January 1997 and June 2011, where information for at least one transaction multiple is available as shown in Exhibit 3.35. The table reports the distribution of multiples after assigning the transactions to industry groups shown in Exhibit 3.54. The "transportation, communication and utilities" industry group is renamed "transportation", the wholesale and retail trade" industry group is renamed "trade", and the "finance, insurance and real estate" industry group is renamed "finance". The average is computed as a simple unweighted average across industry groups.
Source: Zephyr database, Bureau von Dijk.

To examine whether the use of the SIC code and the reclassification of some deals leads to a loss of information, it is useful to compute the distribution of the multiples across the industry groups in Exhibit 3.55.

One can see that the multiples in the finance industry as well as in the service industry are higher on average in all regions. Furthermore, companies in the trade industry seem to be sold on average at lower transaction multiples and manufacturing companies are traded at lower multiples than transportation companies. Differences between industry groups are more pronounced than those across the periods analyzed in Exhibit 3.52. Given the above pattern for the different industry groups, the cluster variable *Industry group* with the five classes "manufacturing", "transportation", "trade", "service", and "finance" was created.

Detecting Patterns – Data Clustering Summary

As a result of the clustering procedure three cluster variables – *Size class*, *Period*, and *Industry group* – are obtained and used in the analyses. All private and public transactions were classified according to the criteria by simply adding a classification number "SPI" (the product from the three cluster variables) and building the public reference portfolios from companies with the same SPI. For each private deal, one should attempt to identify a control portfolio with the same SPI and attach the respective benchmark (median) multiple to a private transaction multiple. In those cases where it is not possible to match the private companies to the public reference companies according to "SPI", one might release either the industry or the year criteria and compute the median multiples of the transactions involving public targets on "SP", or "SI". This procedure was used for all the multiples and then benchmark multiples for the EV/Sales, EV/EBITDA, EV/EBIT, and P/E multiple were attached.

3.13.5 Cross-Sectional Regression

In order to better interpret the results of the cross-tab analyses, one might use cross-sectional stepwise-regression analyses to encompass more factors which determine observed differences between public and private company multiples. One starts with a pool of potential explanatory variables and the stepwise regression procedure automatically selects variables based on a statistical F-test. The order of inclusion is determined by the significance level of the F-value. The variables with the lowest significance level of their F-value are inserted in the model first. However, variables are only added if their significance level is below 5%. After the inclusion of every variable, it is tested to see whether a previously added variable can be excluded. The criterion is again the significance level of the F-value. If it is above 10%, this variable is excluded. The exclusion of a variable is possible because explanatory variables are correlated with each other. The algorithm of the stepwise regression stops when no variable can be included or excluded with respect to the abovementioned criteria.

The stepwise regression was specified according to Equation 3.3:

$$\text{Ratio}_{m, z, j} = \beta_0 + \sum_{k=1}^{K} \beta_k F_k + \varepsilon \quad \forall\, z = 1 \dots Z \tag{3.3}$$

The number of regression samples z is tailored to the concrete set-up of the studies ($z = 8$ in Section 3.11). The number of cases j depends on the sample and the multiple used, and it can be looked up in Exhibit 3.36. The indicator m is used when discounts on more than one multiple are tested (in Section 3.11 only the EV/EBITDA multiple is used). The use of the vector F_k allows the inclusion of a set of independent variables beyond *Size class*, *Period*, and *Industry group*. The selected regression procedure will test the variables in the vector F_k for inclusion/exclusion given the specified significance level. The variables are shown in in Exhibit 3.33.

Preparation of Regression Analysis – Selection of the Dependent Variable

To reduce the complexity, it makes sense to compute stepwise regressions with only one multiple not with four. Therefore, the multiple(s) are investigated by running some test regressions on discounts with the different multiples. For the German region, regressions for all multiples are computed and the discounts on all private companies are used as dependent variables. It appeared that regressions with the EV/EBITDA, and EV/EBIT multiples led to results which are easier to interpret, and many more factors reveal significant influence. As a next step, the relationships of the computed discounts to each other are computed: Exhibit 3.56 shows

Exhibit 3.56 Correlations between discounts computed on different multiples

		Discount EV/Sales	Discount EV/EBITDA	Discount EV/EBIT
Discount EV/Sales	r2 Pearson	1.00	,497**	,314**
	Significance (2-tailed)	0	0	0
	N	441	206	152
Discount EV/EBITDA	r2 Pearson	,497**	1.00	,742**
	Significance (2-tailed)	0	0	0
	N	206	206	149
Discount EV/EBIT	r2 Pearson	,314**	,742**	1.000
	Significance (2-tailed)	0.000	0.000	0.000
	N	152	149	152
Discount P/E	r2 Pearson	0.181	0.149	0.128
	Significance (2-tailed)	0.366	0.487	0.560
	N	27	24	23

The sample consists of 1,059 completed majority-ownership transactions between January 1997 and June 2011 in Germany, where information for at least one transaction multiple is available as shown in Exhibit 3.35. * denotes significance at a 5% level; ** denotes significance at a 1% level.
Source: Zephyr database, Bureau von Dijk.

the correlation coefficients of the different discounts for Germany. One can see that the relationships between the EV/Sales multiple to the EV/EBITDA and the EV/EBIT multiples are lower than between the EV/EBITDA and EV/EBIT multiple, and that there is no significant relationship to the P/E multiple at all. Discounts computed with P/E multiples are in any case excluded from further analyses due to limited data availability.

Based on this result, regressions on the EV/EBITDA multiple are computed because (a) compared to the EV/Sales multiple, the EV/EBITDA multiple is easier to interpret and widely used in US research, and (b) compared to the EV/EBIT multiple, the regression includes more cases.

Preparation of Regression Analysis – Selection of the Independent Variables

As a preparatory step for all the regression analyses, one might perform multivariate regression models using a method that includes all independent variables as specified. The goal of these regressions is to reduce the number of independent variables already before application of the stepwise regression and increase the robustness of the approach. This procedure is completed for the German and North American regions and based on the results, the same independent variables have been included in the regression analyses for Western Europe and the UK. These regression analyses are not done in order to start interpreting discounts and influence factors, but only for data reduction and simplifying future analyses. Therefore the private companies are not split into independent and dependent here.

The value determining factors F_k as shown in Exhibit 3.57 are included. They can be categorized into three different blocks. The first block includes the factors *Period* and *Industry group* and a variable *Size*, which indicates whether the respective company's target turnover is above the average turnover in its *Size class*. The factor *Industry group* has been split into

Exhibit 3.57 Regression results: private vs. public companies in Germany and North America

Germany: private companies vs. public companies				North America: private companies vs. public companies			
Dependent: discount on EV/EBITDA				Dependent: discount on EV/EBITDA			
Model	Coefficients	Sign	Significance	Model	Coefficients	Sign	Significance
1	(Constant)	+	1%	1	(Constant)	+	1%
	Size	−	1%		Size	−	1%
	Period 1	nm	n		Period 1	nm	n
	Period 2	+	1%		Period 2	+	1%
	Period 3	nm	n		Period 3	nm	n
	Period 4	+	5%		Period 4	+	5%
	Period 5	−	5%		Period 5	nm	n
	Indu 30	nm	n		Indu 30	+	5%
	Indu 40	nm	n		Indu 40	nm	n
	Indu 50	+	5%		Indu 50	+	5%
	Indu 60	−	5%		Indu 60	nm	5%
	Indu 70	−	1%		Indu 70	−	5%
2	(Constant)	+	1%	2	(Constant)	+	1%
	Size	−	1%		Size	−	1%
	Period 1	nm	n		Period 1	nm	n
	Period 2	+	1%		Period 2	+	1%
	Period 3	nm	n		Period 3	nm	n
	Period 4	+	5%		Period 4	+	5%
	Period 5	−	10%		Period 5	nm	n
	Indu 30	nm	n		Indu 30	+	5%
	Indu 40	nm	n		Indu 40	nm	n
	Indu 50	+	5%		Indu 50	+	5%
	Indu 60	−	5%		Indu 60	nm	5%
	Indu 70	−	1%		Indu 70	−	5%
	Cash payment	+	5%		Cash payment	+	5%
	Cross border deal	−	10%		Cross border deal	+	10%
	Listed acquirer	+	10%		Listed acquirer	−	10%
	Private equity investor	+	10%		Private equity investor	nm	n
3	(Constant)	+	1%	3	(Constant)	+	1%
	Size	−	5%		Size	−	1%
	Period 1	nm	n		Period 1	nm	n
	Period 2	+	1%		Period 2	+	1%
	Period 3	nm	n		Period 3	nm	n
	Period 4	+	5%		Period 4	+	5%
	Period 5	nm	n		Period 5	nm	n
	Indu 30	nm	n		Indu 30	+	5%
	Indu 40	nm	n		Indu 40	nm	n
	Indu 50	+	5%		Indu 50	+	5%
	Indu 60	nm	n		Indu 60	nm	5%
	Indu 70	−	10%		Indu 70	−	5%
	Cash payment	+	5%		Cash payment	+	5%
	Cross border deal	−	10%		Cross border deal	+	10%
	Listed acquirer	+	10%		Listed acquirer	nm	m
	Private equity investor	+	10%		Private equity investor	nm	n
	RelSize	−	10%		RelSize	−	10%
	Target D/E	+	10%		Target D/E	+	n
	Target E/A	nm	n		Target E/A	nm	n

(continued)

Exhibit 3.57   *(Continued)*

Germany: private companies vs. public companies				North America: private companies vs. public companies			
Dependent: discount on EV/EBITDA				Dependent: discount on EV/EBITDA			
Model	Coefficients	Sign	Significance	Model	Coefficients	Sign	Significance
Model			R^2	Model			R^2
1			7.4%	1			7.7%
2			7.8%	2			8.3%
3			8.2%	3			8.8%

The samples are based on completed majority-ownership transactions between January 1997 and June 2011, where information for at least one transaction multiple is available as shown in Exhibit 3.35. The table reports the results of linear regressions with the dependent variables computed according to Equation 3.2 in Section 3.13 for the two regions Germany and North America. The dependent variable is the discount on the EV/EBITDA multiple for all private companies vs. the matching public companies. The sample sizes (Germany = 309 and North America = 661) are shown in Exhibit 3.36. For each region, three different models comprising different sets of independent variables are shown. "nm" denotes that the influence of a variable is not meaningful because it shows no significance (denoted "n" in the column "Significance").
Source: Zephyr database, Bureau von Dijk.

several indicator variables. For example, *Indu 40* is an indicator variable. It is "1" if the company's SIC code is between 40XX and 49XX and "0" otherwise. For the remaining four industry variables the indicator variables are similar, so all of the companies are grouped into five industry categories based on the SIC codes (see Exhibit 3.53). The factor *Period* also has been split into several indicator variables, e.g. *Period 1* is an indicator variable. It is "1" if the company was acquired before January 2001 and "0" otherwise. All of the acquisitions are grouped into five categories based on the acquisition date (see Exhibit 3.52).

Size, *Period*, and *Industry group* have been proven to influence company value significantly, as shown in Section 3.6.2, therefore these are included in the first block. The second block includes transaction-related factors like the payment method, the acquirer's origin, the type of acquirer, and his listing. Block three contains characteristics of private firms such as the relative company size (*RelSize*), the Equity/Assets (E/A) ratio[19] of the target (*Target E/A*), or the Debt/Equity[20] (D/E) ratio of the target (*Target D/E*).

One block of variables after the other is added into the regression analysis; consequently, three different models for the two regions Germany and North America were computed. These are shown in Exhibit 3.57, together with the results of the regressions. At this point, the results are only compared across the samples with respect to the sign and significance of coefficients, therefore the absolute size of the coefficients is not given.

Some results can be summarized as follows: the adjusted R^2 of all the models is relatively low, so a substantial part of the variability in the dependent variables is not explained by the models. By adding blocks of variables, the individual variables change their significance levels and some formerly significant variables become insignificant. Adding variables to the

---

[19] The E/A ratio represents the equity ratio and it is defined as the shareholders' equity divided by the total assets (balance sheet amount).

[20] The D/E ratio is defined as the total interest bearing debt divided by the shareholders' equity (share capital + retained earnings - treasury stocks, if applicable) using balance sheet (book) values. It describes the financial leverage of the company. Generally, companies with ratios above 1 are considered high debt, and those with ratios below 0.5 are low debt.

third (full model), the majority of potential influence factors has significant influence, and the adjusted R^2 increases.

For the German sample, the target's size, the time of disposal, as well as the industry group, influence discounts and their significance changes across the samples, and with an increasing number of variables.[21] Whereas the variables *Size* and the service industry (*Indu 70*) decrease discounts, the trade industry (*Indu 50*) increases discounts. All three variables stay significant in all models, whereas the influence of the factor *Period* is different across the models. For example, in the full model, *Period 5* is no longer significant.

Model three shows that discounts increase if the acquirer pays cash. In Germany, the discounts for private companies compared to public companies decrease for transactions involving foreign buyers (*Cross-border deal*). Listed acquirers increase discounts. Private equity investors influence the regression results significantly in the second and in the third (full) model. The relative target size (*RelSize*) influences the discounts in Germany.

The results for North America show a relatively low adjusted R^2 of all the models. Again, by adding blocks of variables, the individual variables change their significance levels and some formerly significant variables become insignificant. In the third (full model), the majority of potential influence factors has significant influence, and the adjusted R^2 is the highest.

As for the German sample, the target's size, the time of disposal, as well as the industry group influence discounts and their significance changes across the samples, and with an increasing number of variables. Whereas the variables *Size* and the service industry (*Indu 70*) decrease discounts, or the trade industry (*Indu 50*) and the manufacturing industry (*Indu 30*) increase discounts and stay significant across all models. The influence of the factor *Period* is different across the models. As in Germany, in the full model, *Period 5* is not significant any more.

Model three shows that discounts increase if the acquirer pays cash. In North America, the discounts for private companies compared to public companies increase for transactions involving foreign buyers (*Cross-border deal*). Listed acquirers and private equity investors do not influence the regression results significantly in the third (full) model. The relative target size (*RelSize*) influences the size of discounts applied.

After computation of the regressions for the two regions, all variables are left in the model for the stepwise regression except for the Target E/A ratio. This variable shows no influence in the third model and its influence on potential discounts is more difficult to interpret than the D/E ratio.

The two-step procedure that firstly benchmarks multiples, and then analyzes the resulting discounts in multivariate regressions (including stepwise regressions) makes the results clearer and more comprehensive. Analyzing discounts that are differentiated across multiples, samples, and influence factors in the cross-tabs analysis shows potential drivers of discounts better than by only computing lump-sum median discounts. The regression explicitly accounts for previously identified influence factors and investigates some findings more deeply.

3.13.6 Databases and Data Collection

Information on private companies is not always as detailed as for public companies. This holds true for some countries more than for others depending on the basic population of available

---

[21] For a detailed description of the independent variables (see Exhibit 3.58 and Exhibit 3.59).

transactions and reporting requirements. The big merger and acquisition databases are, for example, Bloomberg, Mergerstat, Dealogic, SDC Platinum, and S&P Capital IQ. The richest data is available for the US, as some of the databases only include deals with US involvement (e.g. Mergerstat only includes deals with a US parent as either target or acquirer); not all are suited to analyze private transactions (e.g. Bloomberg is more suitable to look for general M&A activity volume and trends) or to systematically analyze and download big lists of transaction data into a format like Excel which is needed to process data further. In research papers, one often finds Thomson Reuter's SDC data and, tailored to private companies, reference to the Pratt's Stats® database that contains information on the sales of privately and closely held businesses for around 22,000 transactions from under USD 1m to USD 15bn since 1990. The sources for the Pratt's Stats® database are US intermediaries and SEC filings and therefore only deals with US involvement are included.

Thomson SDC Platinum is a product of Thomson Financial and provides coverage back to 1979 domestically and 1985 internationally. It includes cross-border deals of all types, therefore those involving a non US target and acquirer. Prior to 1992, only deals of USD 1 million or greater in value or which involved an acquisition of at least 5% interest were included. After 1992, deals of any value are covered. The sources of data include news sources, SEC filings, trade publications, wires, and other proprietary investment bank sources. Unfortunately, the costs of Thomson SDC Platinum are relatively high and charged per session plus data item reporting costs, so downloading a massive list of transaction data can cost several thousands of Euro if not negotiated as a flat fee.

For research outside the US, it is recommended to look for transaction databases that are regionally more diversified and therefore provide a better basis of comparables. For this analysis, the Zephyr database is used. This database is a product of Bureau van Dijk, the leading European electronic publisher of business information. The Zephyr database contains M&A, IPO, and venture capital deals with links to detailed financial company information. Coverage for European targets starts in 1997, North American deals from 2000 and Zephyr has had global coverage since January 2003. As of May 2013, more than 1,000,000 transactions are included in the database.

Most databases have a problem with limited availability of multiples in the data which sometimes reduces samples dramatically and limits the generalizability of study results. For example, Officer (2007) used the SDC databases and concluded that "of the 5,328 acquisitions of subsidiaries reported by SDC, the availability of sensible multiples data for both the unlisted target and comparable public acquisitions limits the number of observed average acquisition discounts to 643 (12% of the original sample)". For use in the study, Zephyr data have been carefully controlled and completed where possible to retain as many transactions as possible, leading to more than 1,000 transactions for Germany with information for at least one multiple shown in Exhibit 3.34.

Another problem of many databases is the noise of the raw acquisition multiples, with extreme outliers in both tails of the distribution. For example, the average/median of the EV/EBITDA multiple reported by Zephyr for acquisitions of independent private targets in Germany is 27.6x/7.9x (based on data from Exhibit 3.34), with a maximum of 220,045.9x and a minimum of −94,329.2x. Similar examples have been found by other researchers using the SDC database, e.g. Officer (2007) finds that the Price/Book multiple reported by SDC for acquisitions in the stand-alone unlisted target category is 774.54, with a maximum of 167,250 and a minimum of 0.23.

3.13.7   Outlier Treatment

To better detect outliers, it can be helpful to use graphical tools. Box plots were computed for the transactions multiples and transactions with multiples more than 1.5 times of the inter-quartile range away from the box were checked. In cases where no additional information on the target financials was available, either the whole transaction or the multiples in question were deleted. In cases where the transactions showed a reasonable EV/Sales multiple (e.g. lower than 10x), but an EV/EBITDA greater than 100, one can conclude that either the EBITDA figure is potentially wrong or the EV/EBITDA multiple cannot be used to value the target. Therefore this EV/EBITDA multiple was excluded from the transaction. Furthermore, transactions where all the multiples are negative were removed, and single negative multiples were classified as "not meaningful" and controlled for double counting. Some upper limits have been set for the multiples: a limit of 10 for the EV/Sales and P/Sales multiples and a limit of 50 for the EV/EBITDA, EV/EBIT and P/E multiples. Given the noise in the data (huge difference between median and average values), it is recommended to use medians anyway. They are more reasonable measures for the discounts because medians are not as affected by outliers.

3.13.8   Measurement of Variables

Search criteria of databases for selection of transactions and the available (meaning available for download) information are somewhat limited. Therefore, some variables need to be added manually. Most importantly, to find independent private firms according to the description in Chapter 1, companies are preselected via the Excel function (a) without a stock quotation and (b) without a seller or (c) with a family or private person as the seller. To find a family or private persons as divestitures, each transaction was checked for terms like "family" or "private shareholder" or "private person" in the divestiture field. In addition, transactions were identified where the name of the seller is included in the target's name indicating that the founders sold the company. After this selection, the transactions without a seller were checked again, using information from other databases and news-runs in order to find the selling shareholders. Furthermore, an additional Excel automatism helps to select transactions focusing on the legal form that might indicate independent private companies: transactions are selected where the legal form includes a private proprietorship or a partnership, meaning transactions where the target's legal form includes "OHG", "KG", "GbR", "EK", or "GmbH". These forms are often used by independent private companies in Germany. To find independent private companies, in other regions like North America, legal forms like "LLP", "LP", or "sole proprietorship" are searched for.

To create the variable *Private equity investor* firstly transactions with the SIC code "6299" ("Investors") were selected. As the SIC codes are often imprecise and sometimes missing, the names of the acquirers were searched for using terms like "private equity", "venture", "capital", or "investment". In addition, the names of the 33 most active private equity houses in the German speaking region (e.g. *3i Group, Afinum, DBAG, EquiVest* etc.[22]) were searched directly. For the analysis involving North America and Western Europe, a list of the top 50 private equity funds provided by PEI (Private Equity International) Media was used.

To create the variable *Cross-border deal*, a country code for the transactions was created in all the data sets using the same notation for all countries. Previously different terms were used

---

[22] See Jowett and Jowett (2011) for a complete overview.

for the same country. For example, "Germany", "GE", or "DE" was used for Germany. After this procedure, the acquirer and target country codes are compared with each other.

To create the variable *Cash Payment*, the method of payment was checked in the data sets defined. The variable is created as a dummy variable indicating all-cash or other (where "other" includes mixed cash and stock and all-stock offers). If only cash was paid, the variable is set to "1". However, if shares are paid or mixed payments with cash, shares, or debt, then the variable is set to "0". Mixed payments are set to "0" because they are only partly cash, so the influence of the desire for liquidity cannot be determined exactly.

When computations lead to a "\#DIV" or "\#NA" in Excel for the multiples and financial ratios, missing values (blanks) are automatically created. The set of variables included in the analyses is shown in Exhibit 3.58 and Exhibit 3.59.

APPENDIX B   THE PCD AND THE RELATIVE VALUATION METHODOLOGY

It has been shown that for a correct application, the DLL/PCD needs to be taken from the appropriate value base. Appropriate in this context means a value base which presupposes liquidity and, in case one is evaluating the sale of a private company, from a control level of value. Theoretically a comprehensive set of methodologies is available to value a private company, in praxis, analysts often solely use relative valuation methodologies, either due to a lack of financial projections or because they need to obtain a first "quick shot" on the value. For the correct application of relative valuation approaches, it is critical to find companies that display similar value characteristics and any differences in characteristics need to be accounted for by a discount or a premium on value. A key problem exists for those analysts who work in markets which are not as deep and rich, such as the North American market with respect to the availability of comparables: there are often not enough comparable public companies in the target's home country.[23] Therefore, investment professionals conduct cross-border research to come to a set of comparables, often including firms from the US and European countries. Exhibit 3.15 showed already that differences in multiples levels between these regions exist. So what should an analyst consider if he needs to apply a PCD to a base value derived with relative valuation approaches and comparables that are not from his home country? He/she needs to think about differences in multiple levels between the subject company's home country and the comparable countries. One way might be to consider level differences by applying a separate country-related discount and then apply a "local" PCD. For example, an analyst valuing a German company with North American comparables would consider the valuation differences between North America and Germany by applying a discount (either on the multiple or the value) derived from differences in multiples as shown in Exhibit 3.15) and the PCD found in Germany. Or he might account for both in one and consider the PCD found when German companies are compared to North American firms, see Exhibit 3.60.

Taking public North American companies as comparables, higher discounts can be found on all multiples. According to Exhibit 3.60, the median PCD for all private companies on the EV/Sales multiple is 33%, on the EV/EBITDA multiple 22%, and on the EV/EBIT multiple 21% (compared to 32%, 20%, and 17% in Exhibit 3.37). The same result holds when looking at the independent and dependent private companies separately: the PCD for independent

---

[23] For example, less than 1% of companies in Germany are listed.

Exhibit 3.58   Data set (part 1)

Number		Scale	Parameters/description
1	Target Private	Nominal	Dummy; 1 if private, 0 otherwise
2	Target independent	Nominal	Dummy; 1 if independent company, 0 otherwise
3	Target name	String	
4	Target country	String	
5	Deal status	String	Withdrawn, announced, pending, completed, rumour
6	Acquirer name	String	
7	Acquirer country	String	
8	Vendor name	String	
9	Vendor country	String	
10	Deal value	Continuous	Consideration paid for shares or equity; EUR '000
11	Target turnover	Continuous	Target turnover; EUR '000; last available figure before transaction
12	Target EBITDA	Continuous	Earnings before interest, taxes, depreciation and amortization; EUR '000; last available figure before transaction
13	Target EBIT	Continuous	Earnings before interest and taxes; EUR '000; last available figure before transaction
14	Target PAT	Continuous	Profit after tax; EUR '000; last available figure before transaction
15	Target total assets	Continuous	in EUR '000; last available figure before transaction
16	Target equity	Continuous	Total shareholders' equity; EUR '000
17	Target debt	Continuous	Total interest bearing debt; EUR '000
18	Target E/A	Continuous	(16)/(15)
19	Target D/E	Continuous	(17)/(16)
20	Acquirer turnover	Continuous	Acquirer turnover; EUR '000; last available figure before transaction
21	Acquirer total assets	Continuous	in EUR '000; last available figure before transaction
22	Stake acquired	Continuous	Acquired stake in transaction in %
23	Equity value	Continuous	Enterprise value - net debt - minority interest; EUR '000., if not stated, computed via deal value (10/22*100); EUR '000.
24	Enterprise value	Continuous	Total firm value

Exhibit 3.58 Data set (part 1) (*Continued*)

Number		Scale	Parameters/description
25	P/Sales	Continuous	(23)/(11)
26	EV/Sales	Continuous	(24)/(11)
27	EV/EBITDA	Continuous	(24)/(12)
28	EV/EBIT	Continuous	(24)/(13)
29	P/E	Continuous	(23)/(14)
30	Majority	Nominal	Dummy, 1 if stake acquired (22) =>51%
31	Target industry code	Ordinal	First two digits of four digit SIC Code
32	Target industry	String	Four digit SIC industry description
33	Target industry group	Ordinal	SIC Group
34	Acquirer industry code	Ordinal	First two digits of four digit SIC Code
35	Acquirer industry	String	Four digit SIC industry description
36	Acquirer industry group	Ordinal	SIC Group
37	Year	Nominal	Year of deal completion
38	Divestitor	Binary	Dummy; 1 if target sold by holding company, 0 otherwise
39	Legal form	String	In Germany e.g.: GmbH, AG, KG, GbR, OHG, EK; in North America, Europe and UK e.g: BV, Corp., Inc., LLC., LLLP. LLP., NV, Oy, Plc., SA, Sole Proprietorship
40	Private equity investor	Nominal	Dummy; 1 if acquired by private equity investor, 0 otherwise
41	Size	Nominal	1 if target turnover (11) > average target tunover in respective size class (50)
42	Payment method	String	Assets, Cash, Convertibles, Debt, Earn Out, Loan Notes, Mixed, Other, Preferred Stock
43	Cash payment	Nominal	Dummy; 1 if (42) is all cash
44	Listed acquirer	Nominal	Dummy; 1 if acquirer is listed on stock exchange (no OTC), 0 otherwise
45	Cross border deal	Nominal	Dummy; 1 if target and acquirer country not identical, if (4)≠(7)
46	Completed deal	Nominal	Dummy; 1 if deal is completed; if (5) = "completed"
47	RelSize (assets)	Continuous	(15)/(21)
48	Region	Ordinal	1 if target region is Germany, 2 if target region is Western Europe (excl. Germany and UK), 3 if target region is North America, 4 if target region is the UK

(*continued*)

Exhibit 3.59 Data set (part 2)

Number	Variable name	Scale	Parameters/description
49	Industry group	Nominal	After recoding the industry groups, values: 30, 40, 50, 60 ,70
50	Size class	Nominal	Ln (target turnover [11]), after recoding, values according size classes
51	Period	Nominal	1 if year (37) < 2001, 2 if year between 01/2001 and 12/2003, 3 if year between 01/2004 and 07/2007, 4 if year between 08/2007 and 03/2009, 5 if year between 04/2009 and 06/2011
52	SPI	Continuous	Cluster variable: (50)*(51)*(49)
53	SP	Continuous	Cluster variable: (50)*(51)
54	SI	Nominal	Cluster variable: (50)*(49)
55	Median P/Sales	Continuous	Median multiple of public companies attached from respective sample, matched according (52), (53) or (54)
56	Median EV/Sales	Continuous	Median multiple of public companies attached from respective sample, matched according (52), (53) or (54)
57	Median EV/EBITDA	Continuous	Median multiple of public companies attached from respective sample, matched according (52), (53) or (54)
58	Median EV/EBIT	Continuous	Median multiple of public companies attached from respective sample, matched according (52), (53) or (54)
59	Median P/E	Nominal	Median multiple of public companies attached from respective sample, matched according (52), (53) or (54)
60	Discount P/Sales	Continuous	1-(25)/(55)
61	Discount EV/Sales	Continuous	1-(26)/(56)
62	Discount EV/EBITDA	Continuous	1-(27)/(57)
63	Discount EV/EBIT	Continuous	1-(28)/(58)
64	Discount P/E	Continuous	1-(29)/(59)
65	Indu 30	Nominal	Dummy; 1 if (49) = 30, 0 otherwise, manufacturing industry group
66	Indu 40	Nominal	Dummy; 1 if (49) = 40, 0 otherwise, transportation inustry group
67	Indu 50	Nominal	Dummy; 1 if (49) = 50, 0 otherwise, trade industry group
68	Indu 60	Nominal	Dummy; 1 if (49) = 60, 0 otherwise, finance, industry group
69	Indu 70	Nominal	Dummy; 1 if (49) = 70, 0 otherwise, services industry group
70	Period 1	Nominal	Dummy; 1 if (51) = 1, 0 otherwise
71	Period 2	Nominal	Dummy; 1 if (51) = 2, 0 otherwise
72	Period 3	Nominal	Dummy; 1 if (51) = 3, 0 otherwise
73	Period 4	Nominal	Dummy; 1 if (51) = 4, 0 otherwise
74	Period 5	Nominal	Dummy; 1 if (51) = 5, 0 otherwise

Exhibit 3.60 Median discounts of German private compared to North American companies

Multiple	Target: Independent private	Dependent private	All private
EV/Sales	45.5%	42.2%	33.3%
EV/EBITDA	30.5%	20.0%	22.0%
EV/EBIT	22.4%	20.2%	20.5%
Average	32.8%	27.5%	25.2%

The sample for the target companies consists of completed majority-ownership transactions between January 1997 and June 2011, where information for at least one transaction multiple is available, of which 145 transactions include acquired independent private companies and 216 transactions include dependent private companies as shown in Exhibit 3.35. The data set used to compute the reference portfolios consists of 2,165 public North American companies. For each transaction multiple, the table reports the ratios computed according to Equation 3.1 (detail in Equation 3.2 in Section 3.13). Different groups of private targets are compared to the reference portfolio of public companies in North America.
Source: Zephyr database, Bureau von Dijk.

private companies amounts to 46%, 31%, and 22% in Exhibit 3.60, vs. 42%, 27%, and 19% in Exhibit 3.37. According to Exhibit 3.60, the PCD for dependent private firms amounts to 42%, 20%, and 20% compared to 31%, 18%, and 16% in Exhibit 3.37. These results show that an analyst should consider that the application of relative valuation methodology makes it necessary to account for the regions of the comparables. Compared to public North American companies, the discounts that need to be applied to private companies seem to be higher than those using only a public German peer group.

APPENDIX C   HOW DIFFERENT IS THE MITTELSTAND COMPARED TO DEPENDENT PRIVATE GERMAN FIRMS?

The previous analysis showed that independent private firms in Germany (the German Mittelstand) seem to have distinctive characteristics that lead to valuation differences compared

Exhibit 3.61 Mittelstand vs. dependent private companies in Germany

Multiple	Target: Reference group:	Mittelstand Dependent private	Dependent: Discount EV/EBITDA	Coefficient	T-Value	Significance
EV/Sales		3.8%	(Constant)	0.163	2.816	1%
EV/EBITDA		17.8%	TargetD/E*Trade industry	0.110	2.437	5%
EV/EBIT		6.9%	Cross-border	−0.040	−1.817	10%
Average		9.5%	Owner-managed	−0.103	−2.152	5%
			R^2	6.1%		

The sample for the target companies consists of completed majority-ownership transactions between January 1997 and June 2011, where information for at least one transaction multiple is available, of which 145 transactions include acquired Mittelstand companies and 216 transactions include other private companies. For each transaction multiple, the left hand side of the table reports the ratios computed according to Equation 3.1 (detail in Equation 3.2 in Section 3.13). The right hand side of the table reports the results of the stepwise linear regression computed according to Equation 3.3 in Section 3.13. As the dependent variable, the ratio computed according to Equation 3.1 (detail in Equation 3.2 in Section 3.13) on the EV/EBITDA multiple is used. The reference group is built using dependent private companies instead of public German companies. The set of independent variables is described in Exhibit 3.33. The variable *Owner managed* is created when the owner/ owners of a Mittelstand companies is/are also in the top management of the firm.
Source: Zephyr database, Bureau von Dijk.

to public but also to dependent private companies. Therefore a closer look at the Mittelstand may give more insights if discounts are computed compared to dependent private companies and analyzed in a cross-sectional regression. Exhibit 3.61 compares the Mittelstand to other private companies in Germany, showing median discounts and the result of the cross-sectional regression. One can see that the Mittelstand is discounted on average at 9.5% compared to dependent private companies. The regression shows the influencing factors which may explain the valuation differences between the Mittelstand and dependent private firms in more detail.

One can see that highly leveraged Mittelstand companies in the trade industry are less valuable.[24] Cross-border transactions are valued more highly. Owner-management increases valuation.

This small analysis shows that the Mittelstand is different to dependent private firms, therefore an analyst should carefully distinguish both groups of companies for valuation purposes.

---

[24] For this analysis, to account for the limited number of cases and given the dependencies between relative size (*RelSize*) and the leverage (*Target D/E*), the variables *RelSize* and *Indu70* were combined as well as the variables *Target D/E* and *Indu 50* for this sample.

References

Acharya, V. and L.H. Pedersen (2005) Asset Pricing with Liquidity Risk. *Journal of Financial Economics*, Vol. 77, pp. 375–410.

Allen, J.W., S.L. Lummer, J.J. McConnell and D.K. Reed (1995) Can Takeover Losses Explain Spin-off Gains? *Journal of Financial and Quantitative Analysis*, Vol. 30, pp. 465–485.

Anderson, R. and D. Reeb (2003) Founding-Family Ownership and Firm Performance: Evidence from the S&P 500. *Journal of Finance*, Vol. 48, pp. 1301–1327.

Andersson, U, J. Johanson and J. E. Vahlne (1997) Organic Acquisition in the Internationalization Process of the Business Firm. *Management International Review*, Special Issue 1997, pp. 67–84.

Ang, J. and N. Kohers (2001) The Take-over Market for Privately Held Companies: The US Experience. *Cambridge Journal of Economics*, Vol. 25, pp. 723–748.

Astrachan, J. and M. Shanker (2003) Family Businesses' Contribution to the U.S. Economy: A Closer Look. *Family Business Review*, Vol. 16, pp. 211–219.

Bajaj, M., D.J. Denis, S.P. Ferris, and A. Sarin (2001) Firm Value and Marketability Discount. *Journal of Corporation Law*, Vol. 27, pp. 89–115.

Beitel, D. and D. Schiereck (2003) Value Creation of Investment Bank Participation in the German M&A Business. Working Paper of the European Business School, Department of Finance, Oestrich-Winkel. No. 03/2004.

Binder, H. (1994) *The Quest for Growth: A Survey of UK Private Companies*. Binder Hamlyn London.

Bradley, M., A. Desai, and E.H. Kim (1988) Synergistic Gains from Corporate Acquisitions and their Division between the Stockholders of Target and Acquiring Firms. *Journal of Financial Economics*, Vol. 21, pp. 3–40.

Burkhart, M., F. and F. Panunzi (2003) Family Firms. *Journal of Finance*, Vol. 58, pp. 2176–2201.

Capron, L. and N. Pistre (2002) When Do Acquirers Earn Abnormal Returns? *Strategic Management Journal*, Vol. 23, pp. 781–794.

Daily, C.M. and M. J. Dollinger (1992) An Empirical Examination of Ownership Structure in Family and Personally Managed Firms. *Family Business Review*, Vol. 5, pp. 117–136.

Das, S., M. Jagannathan, and A. Sarin (2003) Private Equity Returns: An Empirical Examination of the Exit of Venture-Backed Companies. *Journal of Investment Management*, Vol. 1, pp. 1–26.

De Franco, G., I. Gavious, J.Y. Jin, and G.D. Richardson (2007) Do Private Company Targets That Hire Big 4 Auditors Receive Higher Proceeds? *Contemporary Accounting Research*, Vol. 28(1), pp. 215–262.

Deutscher Sparkassen- und Giroverband (2006) *MIND 2006: Aufschwung aus eigener Kraft* [WWW]. Available from, http://www.ifm-bonn.org/assets/documents/Mind-2006.pdf.

Ecker, M. and C. Heckemüller (2005) M&A als Instrument der strategischen Unternehmensführung für den Mittelstand. *M&A Review*, Vol. 10, pp. 421–431.

EMC (2002) Family Businesses: Do they perform better? [WWW] EMC. Available from: http://www.eurofound.europa.eu/ emcc/publications/2003/ef0315en.pdf.

Engelskirchen, C. (2007) *The Role of Family Influence in M&A Transactions*. Reihe: Finanzierung, Kapitalmarkt und Banken, Band 50. Lohmar: Josef Eul Verlag.

Feldman, S.J. (2005) *The Principles of Private Firm Valuation*. 1st edn. New Jersey: Wiley & Sons Finance.

Fishman, M.J. (1989) Preemptive Bidding and the Role of the Medium of Exchange in Acquisitions. *Journal of Finance*, Vol. 44, pp. 41–57.

Flören, R.H. (2002) *Crown Princes in the Clay*. 1st edn. Assen: Van Gorcum.

Gilson, R.J. (1986) *The Law and Finance of Corporate Acquisitions*. 1st edn. New York: The Foundation Press.

Gisser, M.V. and E.E. Gonzales (1993) Family Business: A breed apart in crafting deals. *Merger & Acquisitions*, Vol. 27(5), pp. 39–44.

Hertzel, M. and R. L. Smith (1993) Market Discounts and Shareholder Gains for Placing Equity Privately. *Journal of Finance*, Vol. 48, pp. 459–469.

Jemison, D.B. and S.B. Sitkin (1986) Corporate Acquisitions: A Process Perspective. *Academy of Management Review*, Vol. 11, pp. 145–163.

Johnson, B. (1999) Quantitative Support for Discounts for Lack of Marketability. *Business Valuation Review*, December 1999, pp. 152–155.

Jowett, P. and F. Jowett (2011) *Private Equity: The German Experience*. 1st edn. Basingstoke: Palgrave Macmillan.

Koeplin, J., A. Sarin and A.C. Shapiro (2000) The Private Company Discount. *Journal of Applied Corporate Finance*, Vol. 12(4), pp. 94–101.

Kooli, M., M. Kortas, and J.-F. L'Her (2003) A New Examination of the Private Company Discount: The Acquisition Approach. *The Journal of Private Equity*, Vol. 6, pp. 48–55.

Lang, L., A. Poulsen, and R. Stulz, (1995) Asset Sales, Firm Performance, and the Agency Costs of Managerial Discretion. *Journal of Financial Economics*, Vol. 37, pp. 3–37.

Leenders, M.A.A.M. and E. Waarts (2001) Competitiveness of Family Businesses: Distinguishing family orientation and business orientation. Working Paper of the Erasmus Research Institute of Management No. ERS-2001-50-MKT.

Ljungqvist, A. and M.P. Richardson (2003) *The Cash Flow, Return and Risk Characteristics of Private Equity*. Working Paper No. 3-001, New York University, New York.

Lyman, A.F. (1991) Customer Service: Does family ownership make a difference? *Family Business Review*, Vol. 4(3), pp. 303–324.

McAfee, R.P. and J. McMillan (1999) *Game Theory and Competition*. New York: Oxford University Press.

Mickelson, R.E. and C. Worley (2003) Acquiring a Family Firm: A case study. *Family Business Review*, Vol. 16(4), pp. 251–268.

Misztal, B.A. (1996) *Trust in Modern Societies: The Search for the Bases of Social Order*. 1st edn. Cambridge: Polity Press.

Mulherin, J.H. and A.L. Boone (2000) Comparing Acquisitions and Divestitures. *Journal of Corporate Finance*, Vol. 6, pp. 117–139.

Nilsson, H., A. Isaksson, and T. Martikainen (2002) *Företagsvärdering med fundamental analys*. 1st edn. Lund: Studentlitteratur.

Officer, M.S. (2007) The Price of Corporate Liquidity: Acquisition Discounts for Unlisted Targets. *Journal of Financial Economics*, Vol. 83, pp. 571–598.

Oliver, R.P. and R.H. Meyers, Discounts Seen in Private Placements of Restricted Stock: Management Planning, Inc., Long-term study (1980–1996). In Chapter 5 in R.F. Reilly and R.P. Schweihs (2000) *The Handbook of Advanced Business Valuation*. 1st edn. New York: McGraw-Hill.

Pratt, S.P. and A.V. Niculita (2008) *Valuing a Business – The Analysis and Appraisal of Closely Held Companies*. 5th edn. New York: McGraw Hill.

PricewaterhouseCoopers (2008) Adjusting for Control and Marketability: A global survey of the use of discounts and premia in private company valuation. Available from: PricewaterhouseCoopers LLP, 1 Embankment Place, London WC2N 6RH, United Kingdom, Telephone: [44] (20) 7583 5000 Telecopier: [44] (20) 7822 4652, www.pwc.com.

Reilly, R.F. and R.P. Schweihs (2000) *The Handbook of Advanced Business Valuation*. 2nd edn. New York: McGraw Hill.

Salama, A., W. Holland and G. Vinten (2003) Challenges and Opportunities in Mergers and Acquisitions. Three international case studies, Deutsche Bank-Bankers Trust; British Petroleum-Amoco; Ford-Volvo. *Journal of European Industrial Training*, Vol. 27, pp. 313–321.

SEC (1997) *Discounts Involved in Purchase of Common Stock (1966–1969)*. Institutional Investor Study Report of the Securities and Exchange Commission, H.R. Doc. No. 64, Part 5, 92nd Congress, 1st Session 1997, pp. 2444–2456.

Silber, W.L. (1991) Discounts on Restricted Stock: The Impact of Illiquidity on Stock Prices. *Financial Analyst Journal*, Vol. 47(4), pp. 60–64.

Smit, H.T.J., W.A. Van Den Berg and W. De Maeseneire (2005) Acquisitions as a Real Options Bidding Game. Working Paper of Faculty of Economics and Business Administration. Ghent University, Belgium, No. 05/289.

Tagiuri, R. and J. Davis (1996) Bivalent Attributes of the Family Firm. *Family Business Review*, Vol. 9, pp. 199–208.

Westhead, P. and M. Cowling (1997) Performance Contrasts between Family and Non-family Unquoted Companies in the UK. *International Journal of Entrepreneurial Behaviour and Research*, Vol. 3, pp. 30–52.

Databases

Dealogic is a platform used by global and regional investment banks. For M&A data, M&A Analytics provides a comprehensive view of M&A activity worldwide covering a wide array of transactions including public offers, open market purchases, stock swaps, buy-outs, privatizations, recapitalizations, share buy-backs, and acquisitions. Available from Dealogic (Holdings) plc, Thanet House, 231–232 Strand, London, WC2R 1DA; +44 (0)20-77440-6000; fax: 44 (0)20-7440-6005; www.dealogic.com.

Factset Mergerstat® Review, published annually, tracks mergers and acquisitions involving US companies, including privately held, publicly traded, and foreign companies. Mergerstat Review includes industry analysis, premium, and transaction multiples. It also provides 25 years of summary merger and acquisition statistics, including average premium and price/earnings ratio. Available from Business Valuation Resources, LLC, 1000 SW Broadway, Suite 1200, Portland, OR 9720; (503) 291-7963; fax: (503) 291-7955; www.BVResources.com.

LCD, a unit of Standard & Poor's, is a provider of leveraged finance news and analysis. It provides real-time coverage of the US/European leveraged loan and high-yield bond market: LCD shows loan pricing and trends, provides secondary levels/analysis, credit stats and default analysis. LCD Distressed offers distressed analysis, focusing on recovery scenarios and enterprise valuation for high-profile names as well as key credit fundamentals and financials. Available from Standard & Poor's Financial Services LLC, Canary Wharf 20 Canada Sq. 8th Fl E14 5LH United Kingdom, phone: +44 (0)20-7176-3997; www.lcdcomps.com.

Pratt's Stats® is a database containing information on the sales of privately and closely held businesses for around 22,000 transactions from under USD 1m to USD 15bn since 1990. The sources for the Pratt's Stats® database are US intermediaries and SEC filings, therefore only deals with US involvement are included. The database is updated monthly. Available from Business Valuation Resources, LLC, 1000 SW Broadway, Suite 1200, Portland, OR 9720; (503) 291-7963; fax: (503) 291-7955; www.BVResources.com.

SDC Platinum™ is a product of Thomson Reuters and provides information on new issues, M&A, syndicated loans, private equity, project finance, poison pills, and more. Available from Thomson Reuters, 3 Times Square New York, NY 10036; (646) 223-4000; www.reuters.com.

Standard & Poor's, a Division of McGraw-Hill, provides a wide variety of publications, both print and electronic, on publicly traded companies. These publications are available from Standard & Poor's, 55 Water Street, New York, NY 10041; (800) 523-4534; www.standardandpoors.com, www.compustat.com.

S&P Capital IQ is a business line of The McGraw-Hill Companies and provides multi-asset class data, research, and analytics to institutional investors, investment advisors, and wealth managers through desktop solutions such as S&P Capital IQ, Global Credit Portal, and MarketScope Advisor desktops; enterprise solutions such as Capital IQ Valuations and Compustat; and research offerings, including Leveraged Commentary & Data, Global Market Intelligence, and company and fund research. Available from S & P Capital IQ, McGraw-Hill Financial, 20 Canada Square, London E14 5LH; main: +44 (0)20 7176 1200; sales: +44 (0)20 7176 1233; fax: +44 (0)20 7176 1203; www.capitaliq.com.

Valuation Advisors LLC conducts valuations of privately held businesses for a wide range of financial and tax transactions. They provide the Lack of Marketability Discount Study^{TM} that compares the IPO stock price to pre-IPO common stock, common stock options, and convertible preferred stock prices. The study is web based and includes more than 9,300+ pre-IPO transactions from 1985–present. The database is updated monthly. Available from Business Valuation Resources, LLC, 1000 SW Broadway, Suite 1200, Portland, OR 97205; (503) 291-7963; fax: (503) 291-7955; www.BVResources.com.

Willamette Management Associates conducted a series of empirical pre-IPO studies. For a description of studies see Shannon P. Pratt, Business Valuation Discounts and Premiums (New York: John Wiley and Sons, 2008), pp. 436–438. Studies are available From Willamette Management Associates, 8600 West Bryn Mawr Avenue Suite 950N, Chicago, Illinois 60631; (773) 399-4300; fax: (773) 399-4310; www.willamette.com.

Zephyr M&A database is a product of Bureau van Dijk, the leading European electronic publisher of business information. The Zephyr database contains M&A, IPO, and venture capital deals with links to detailed financial company information. Coverage for European targets starts in 1997 and for North American deals from 2000. Zephyr has had global coverage since January 2003. As of May 2013, more than 1,000,000 transactions are included in the database. Available from Bureau van Dijk, Electronic Publishing GmbH, Hanauer Landstraße 175–179, D-60314 Frankfurt am Main; +49 (69) 96 36 65-65; fax: +49 (69) 96 36 65-50; www.bvdinfo.com.

Glossary

AktG	Aktiengesetz (German Stock Corporation Act)
AMEX	American Stock Exchange
ANOVA	Analyses Of Variance
BR	Business Relationship
CA	Confidentiality Agreement
CEO	Chief Executive Officer
CFO	Chief Financial Officer
DAX	Deutscher Aktienindex
DCF	Discounted Cash Flows
DD	Due Diligence
D/E	Debt/Equity
DLL	Discount for the Lack of Liquidity
DVFA	Deutsche Vereinigung für Finanzanalyse und Asset Management (Society of Investment Professionals in Germany)
E/A	Equity/Assets
EBIT	Earnings before Interest and Tax
EBITDA	Earnings before Interest, Taxes, Depreciation, and Amortization
EMC	European Foundation for the Improvement of Living and Working Conditions
EV	Enterprise Value
EVCA	European Private Equity and Venture Capital Association
EWV	Ertragswertverfahren
FMW	Fair Market Value
IAS	International Accounting Standards
IDW	Institut der Wirtschaftsprüfer (Institute of Public Auditors in Germany)
IFM	Institut für Mittelstandsforschung
IFRS	International Financial Reporting Standards
IM	Information Memorandum
IPO	Initial Public Offering
IRS	Internal Revenue Service
JV	Joint Venture
LBO	Leveraged Buy-Out
LOI	Letter of Intent

M&A	Mergers & Acquisitions
MBO	Management Buy-Out
NAICS	North American Industry Classification System
NASD	National Association of Securities Dealers
NYSE	New York Stock Exchange
OTC	Over-The-Counter
PCD	Private Company Discount
SBA	Small Business Administration
SBA Advocacy	SBA's Office of Advocacy
SEC	Securities and Exchange Commission
SIC	Standard Industrial Classification
SME	Small and Medium-sized Enterprises
SPA	Sales & Purchase Agreement
UMAG	Gesetz zur Unternehmensintegrität und Modernisierung des Anfechtungsrechts (German Code of Corporate Integrity and Modernization of the Right of Avoidance Bill)
USDA	US Department of Agriculture
WpÜG	Wertpapierübernahmegesetz (German Securities Acquisition and Takeover Act)

Index